Analecta Gregoriana

Cura Pontificiae Universitatis Gregorianae edita
Vol. 262, Series Facultatis Theologiae: sectio A, n. 34

WILLIAM A. VAN ROO, S. J.

THE CHRISTIAN SACRAMENT

EDITRICE PONTIFICIA UNIVERSITÀ GREGORIANA

ROMA 1992

IMPRIMI POTEST

Romae, die 27 maii 1992
R. P. GILLES PELLAND, S.J.
Rector Universitatis

IMPRIMATUR

Dal Vicariato di Roma, 1-6-1992

ISBN 88-7652-652-8

EDITRICE PONTIFICIA UNIVERSITÀ GREGORIANA
Piazza della Pilotta, 35 - 00187 Roma

TABLE OF CONTENTS

INTRODUCTION

I present here a work which I began in 1967 and interrupted to consider a number of questions which arose along the way. I dealt with them in a number of books and articles, most of which are listed in the bibliography. To some of them I refer in the course of this work.

Study and reflection through the intervening years occasioned a considerable development of my thought. Consequently what I offer here is far from what I could have intended in 1967. I had done a work in general sacramental theology ten years earlier,[1] and had continued at the Gregorian University to offer courses and seminars on the subject. What I intended in 1967 would have represented what I had been able to develop to that point. It was a theological thought elaborated against the ground of many years of study of philosophy and theology, in great part dedicated to understanding the work of St. Thomas Aquinas, and to developing what seemed to be consistent with the lines of evolution in his thought.

Years of personal study and reflection devoted to the Bible, studies of symbolism and symbol, rethinking of a basic philosophy of the human way of being, elaboration of my own theory of symbolizing and symbol, rethinking the nature of theology and a basic theology of God, and finally in this work developing the analogy of divine-human symbolizing, have contributed to the gradual formation of the thought presented here.

Inevitably a work which results from so many years of study and reflection, and which has been developed in portions through the whole period of my philosophical and theological activity, contains something of the old and of the new. The early chapters, up to the medieval period in the history of the concept of sacrament, represent work done up to roughly 1968, revised for this work. The rest of the historical treatment is recent. My philosophical and theological thought developed beyond its early forms since 1970. What I offer here is my personal theological thought, without critical evaluation of the work of other philosophers and theologians. This is an effort to understand within a life of faith. It

---

[1] *De Sacramentis in Genere*, (Rome: Gregorian University Press, 1957, 1960 [slight revision], 1962 [reprint].

is not a demonstration, much less an attempt to refute any other account of an intelligible structure within the life of faith and religious experience of those who share the same faith. There is, I think, only one kind of "verification" of such thought. It is based on answers to these questions: does it deal with the relevant data, is it coherent, is it open to further questions and the consideration of the relevance of further data, and—most important—does it ring true, does it resonate in those who believe and seek to understand, is it consistent with the "analogy of faith"?

This is not a complete work of general sacramental theology. I have endeavored to develop a conception of the sacrament and a definition, and to trace at the end some implications and agenda: work remaining to be done.

Chapter I

BAPTISM IN THE NEW TESTAMENT:
A TOUCHSTONE

I propose here a summary account of baptism in the New Testament. Presupposing a detailed study of texts which are explicitly or implicitly baptismal, [1] I present here a synthetic treatment, gathering what may be drawn from a reflection on a number of themes which can be discerned in the texts.

Some may wonder at my presentation of a synthesis of biblical teaching on baptism at the outset of a work devoted to the general theology of the Christian sacraments. Baptism is exceptional in the ample biblical teaching concerning it. For many of the rites which we recognize now to be sacraments biblical evidence is scanty. One might suspect, therefore, that I am about to take all that can be found concerning baptism in the New Testament, find an intelligible structure in the data, and set that up arbitrarily as the model for all of the sacraments. That is not my intention. I recognize, as any theologian could, that such a procedure would result in an illusory pseudo-theological fabrication. What, then, do I intend?

First, I suggest that in the very fulness of biblical data concerning baptism, we have a sort of touchstone by which we can test any eventual general theology of the Christian sacraments. Any such general theology which would not account for all of the data in the biblical accounts of baptism would be judged deficient. Thus the rich biblical treatment of baptism serves as a sort of negative norm. Any attempted theology of the Christian sacrament, that is: of what characterizes in varying ways all of the seven Christian sacraments, would founder on any of the aspects of the biblical witness to baptism which it would neglect.

Second, despite the fulness of biblical teaching on baptism, reflection on aspects of this very teaching suggests the need of other factors in the full development of belief and theology regarding the

---

[1] I have done this in two earlier works: *The Mystery* (Rome: Gregorian University Press, 1971), and *Telling About God*, Volume I, *Promise and Fulfillment*, (*Analecta Gregoriana*, 222. Rome: Gregorian University Press, 1986). As occasion requires, I shall cite texts treated in those works.

sacraments in the life of the Church. At the end of this chapter I
shall indicate some of these factors which must be considered in a
general theology of the Christian sacrament.

The Sequence of Actions

In the accounts of how we begin to live in Christ a fairly
constant pattern emerges, indicating the essential actions which are
required. The basic pattern, often to be noted in *Acts*[2] is this:
preaching, *faith* [plus repentance and turning to God], and *baptism*
[with commitment to a way of life]. These actions are indicated in
Jesus' command to baptize, as reported by Matthew (28.18-20) and
Mark (in the longer conclusion, 16.15-16), and they are echoed in
Pauline texts.

To the multitude bewildered by the marvels of Pentecost, Peter
preached Christ, indicating the Old Testament prophecies and
promises, and explaining how God had fulfilled them by raising
Jesus (Acts 2.14-36). With or without preceding signs and wonders,
preaching is the first action. It was commanded by Christ explicitly
in the words recorded by Mark: "Go into the whole world and
preach the gospel to the whole creation...." (16.15); and it is implicit
in Matthew's version of the order to make disciples of all nations
and to teach them (28.19-20). Preaching is Paul's great mission (cf.
Rom 1.1-6,14-17; 1 Cor 1.17). The basic scheme of preaching, faith,
and baptism seems to be echoed in Eph 1.13: "... having *heard the
word of truth*, and having *believed* in him, you were *sealed* [in
baptism] with the promised Holy Spirit."[3]

Faith is the first essential human response to the offer of
salvation and life which God makes through the preaching of the
gospel. Its necessity was indicated by Jesus: "He who believes and is
baptized will be saved; but he who does not believe will be
condemned" (Mk 16.16); and faith is implicit in becoming a disciple
(Mt 28.18-20). In the narrative of Peter's sermon and directives on
Pentecost, the role of faith is implicit in receiving his word (Acts
2.41), and later those who had been baptized and added to the
community of believers are referred to as "all who believed" (2.42).
In other texts of *Acts* faith is clearly the second in the series of three

---

[2] See *Acts*, 2.14-42; 8.4-13; 10.34-48; 16.30-33; 18.8; *The Mystery*, pp. 196-202; and *Telling*, vol. I, pp. 124-129.
[3] For the interpretation of this text and of the apparent parallel in 2 Cor 1.21-22, see *The Mystery*, p. 210, and *Telling*, vol. I, pp. 293-294.

basic acts. The importance of faith in the Pauline texts need not be documented.

The two other principal actions of those who hear the word and respond to the offer of life are *repentance* and *turning* to God. Prominent especially in *Acts* (2.38; 3.19,26; 5.31; 11.18-21) the call to repentance repeats the demand made from the beginning of the preaching of both John the Baptist (Mt 3.2) and Jesus (Mt 4.17; Mk 1.15) and fulfills Jesus' words to the disciples at Emmaus concerning the future preaching of repentance and forgiveness of sins in his name (Lk 24.47).

Baptism differs from the actions by which men and women respond to the divine offer. In faith, repentance, and conversion, though the actions are impossible except by God's gift, those who respond perform the actions. In baptism they are acted upon.

Beyond the acts by which men and women approach Christ and receive baptism, by their very reception of baptism they *commit themselves to a way of life*. This is in accord with Jesus' command to the Apostles, to teach men to observe all that he had commanded them (Mt 28.20). It is implicit in the repentance and turning by which men and women change their way of life. As we shall see more in detail, it is the ground for a whole moral teaching and exhortation based on the baptismal commitment and on the effects of baptism. It is evident in Peter's conception of baptism as an *appeal for*, or a *pledge of*, a *clear conscience* (1 Pt 3.21). [4]

WHO ACTS IN BAPTISM?

Obviously in the perceptible external action a human person is the agent, and it is clear enough from *Acts* that the Church, through authorized members, oversees and directs the action. Yet the preponderant concern of the New Testament writers is the action of God/Father, Christ/Son, and Holy Spirit. I shall deal first with texts which are trinitarian, indicating roles of the Three in baptism; then I shall go on to consider their roles individually as they are revealed in other baptismal texts.

---

[4] For a discussion of this text see *The Mystery*, pp. 227-230. I referred there to thorough studies by W. J. Dalton, S.J.: "Interpretation and Tradition: An Example from 1 Peter," *Gregorianum* 49 (1968) pp. 11-37; and *Christ's Proclamation to the Spirits. A Study of 1 Peter 3.18--4.6 (Analecta Biblica*, 23). Rome: Pontifical Biblical Institute, 1965). I have given a succinct account of this text in *Telling*, Vol. I, pp. 347-348.

(1) *Trinitarian texts.*

The classic text is Mt 28.19: "...baptizing them in the name of the Father and of the Son and of the Holy Spirit." The Greek *eis to onoma* would be translated better by "to/into/unto the name." *Name*, as understood in the Bible, suggests the person, dignity, power, authority of the one who is named: the *name* stands for the person, and somehow is the person. Quite apart from the fact that this text of Matthew most probably reflects the influence of early Christian liturgy, baptism "in/into/to/unto the name" suggests some invocation of the Person or Persons named. Moreover, the expression suggests that the rite is performed by the power and authority of the Father and of the Son and of the Holy Spirit. It suggests too that the meaning and term of the rite are consecration or dedication to them. One further observation seems to be in order: though the text suggests no differentiation of the roles of Father, Son, and Holy Spirit--except for the order in which they are mentioned--still this text must be understood in the light of the whole of New Testament revelation of Father, Son, and Holy Spirit, and of their roles in salvation and in our life in Christ. This is a general hypothesis which is borne out by consideration of other texts. Immediately we must look to other trinitarian baptismal texts or contexts. Then the remaining texts must be considered, in which the roles of one, two, or three are indicated.

The most interesting trinitarian text is in *Titus*:

> ... but when the goodness and loving kindness of God our Savior appeared, he saved us, not because of deeds done by us in righteousness, but in virtue of his own mercy, by the washing of regeneration and renewal in the Holy Spirit, which he poured out upon us richly through Jesus Christ our Savior, so that we might be justified by his grace and become heirs in hope of eternal life (Ti 3.4-7).

The initiative is clearly *God's* [the Father's]: his goodness and loving kindness appeared; he saved us in virtue of his own mercy; he poured out the Holy Spirit. It is *through Jesus Christ* that he poured out the Holy Spirit. Perhaps we are to understand too that it is through the revelation in Jesus Christ our Savior that God's goodness and loving kindness appeared. Finally, we were saved immediately through a washing of regeneration and renewal *of the Holy Spirit*: the genitive is probably subjective, indicating the Holy Spirit as the agent.

One other text may be mentioned here. Immediately it involves the role of the Spirit in baptism, but the context involves Christ and

God. "For just as the body is one and has many members, and all the members of the body, though many, are one body, so it is with Christ. For by one Spirit we were all baptized into one body--Jews or Greeks, slaves or free--and all were made to drink of one Spirit" (1 Cor 12.12-13). "By one Spirit (*en heni pneumati*)" may suggest that the Spirit's role is quasi-instrumental, or may mean "by the power of one Spirit." In either case the action of baptizing is that of the Spirit. On the other hand, "[we] were made to drink of one Spirit" seems to me to suggest another agent, perhaps the Father/God. Christ in this text is the term of the action: we were baptized into one body, the body of Christ (12.27). In the context too, Jesus is honored by a confession inspired by the Spirit: "... no one can say 'Jesus is Lord' except by the Holy Spirit" (12.3). The context also contains a classic trinitarian formula: "Now there are varieties of gifts, but the same Spirit; and there are varieties of service, but the same Lord; and there are varieties of working, but it is the same God who inspires them all in every one" (12.4-6). However the differentiation of roles of the Spirit and of the Lord be understood, one thing is clear: the initiative is God's. The Spirit is the Spirit of God (12.3). Though gifts are given through the Spirit or according to the same Spirit (12.8), by the same Spirit, the one Spirit (12.9), by one and the same Spirit, who apportions to each one individually as he wills (12.11); still it is God who inspires them all in every one, and it is God who has appointed the members of the body of Christ to their functions (12.27-30), as he has arranged the organs of the natural body (12.18,24).

(2) *God/The Father*.

Besides the roles of God/the Father already indicated in the texts which we have considered, we may note others. God has chosen (Col 3.12) and called (Acts 2.39) those who are baptized. Having raised Jesus his Servant, he has sent him first to the sons of the prophets and of the covenant with Abraham, to bless them in turning them from their wickedness (cf. Acts 3.26; 2.39). It is God who has put his seal upon us and given us his Spirit in our hearts as a guarantee (2 Cor 1.21-22). In this text and the parallel in Eph 1.13-14 the sealing and the gift of the Spirit most probably refer to baptism, and from the whole context the agent is God, whose Spirit is given.

Beyond texts which by their context may beconsidered baptismal, the giving of the Spirit is often the action of God, the Father (cf. Acts 5.32; 11.17; 15.18; 1 Cor 5.5; Gal 3.5; 4.4-8). So too the Spirit which is given is often called the Spirit of God (1 Cor 6.11;

Rom 8-9), the Spirit of him who raised Jesus from the dead (Rom 8.11); though he is also the Spirit of Christ (Rom 8.9), the Spirit of his Son (Gal 4.6). The last text cited is remarkable in that it is God "...who sent forth his Son, to redeem those who were under the law, so that we might receive adoption as sons. And because you are sons [or rather: And the fact that you are sons is shown by this, that] God has sent the Spirit of his Son into our hearts, crying, 'Abba! Father!' So through God you are no longer a slave but a son, and if a son then an heir" (Gal 4.4-7). Like Christ, who was raised from the dead by the glory of the Father (Rom 6.4), [5] we have been brought from death to life (Rom 6.13). Buried with Christ in baptism, in him too we have been raised through faith in the working of God, who raised him from the dead: God has made us alive together with him, having forgiven us all our trespasses (Col 2.12-13; cf. Eph 1.18-20; 2.1,4-6). [6] As Christ was raised from the dead by the glory [power] of the Father, we too are to walk in newness of life (cf. Rom 6.4): both the resurrection of Christ and our rising daily to walk in the newness of life are attributable to the glory, the manifest power, of the Father.

(3) *The Son.*

Having commanded his disciples to make disciples of all nations, to baptize, and to teach them to observe all that he had commanded, Jesus promised "... and lo, I am with you always, to the close of the age" (Mt 28.20). He promised that those who believed in him would work signs. "... And they went forth and preached everywhere, while the Lord worked with them and confirmed the message by the signs that attended it" (Mk 15.17,20). The Apostles speak and teach in his name (*epi tōi onomati*: Acts 4.17,18; 5.28,40). Peter commands the crippled man to walk in the name of Jesus Christ (*en tōi onomati*: in/by/by-the-power-of the name: Acts 3.6; cf. 16.18). In both the Jews' question and Peter's answer concerning the case, they speak of the name *by which* (*en* with the dative: in/by/by-the-power-of: Acts 4.7,10). There is no

---

[5] On the shift in meaning of "glory" in Paul, see *Telling*, vol. I, pp. 224-226; 327-338. The shift is from glory as a *symbol* of the presence, power, majesty, sublimity of God to glory as the *symbolized reality*: the divine presence, power, majesty, and sublimity itself. So, in Rom 6.4, Christ was raised, not by the *symbol* (perceptible splendor) of God, but by the *divine power* itself. Thus, from here on, the word "glory" takes on the meaning of the symbolized reality. See Eph 1.16-23, esp. 19-20.

[6] On the interpretation of Col 2.12, see *The Mystery*, pp. 215-221; *Telling*, vol. I, pp. 296-298.

other name in/by which (*en hōi*) we must be saved (4.12). Wonders are performed (4.30) and sins forgiven (10.43) through the name (*dia tou onomatos*). Prior to baptism, the faith demanded for salvation is faith in the Lord Jesus (*epi ton kyrion Iēsoun*: Acts 16.31). According to Paul, it is after having heard the word of truth in him (*en hōi*: in him, or under his influence) and having believed in him (*en hōi*) that we were sealed [in baptism] with the promised Holy Spirit (Eph 1.13).

Consistently with this pattern, with a variety of formulae baptism is said to be given in the name (*epi tōi onomati*) of Jesus Christ (Acts 2.38), to the name (*eis to onoma*) of the Lord Jesus (Acts 8.16; 19.5; cf. 1 Cor 1.13), in the name (*en tōi onomati*) of Jesus Christ (Acts 10.48; cf. 1 Cor 6.11); and it is to be received by Paul calling on his name (*epikalēsamenos to onoma autou*: Acts 22.16). Such formulae do not indicate a liturgical formula of words as an alternative to the trinitarian formula prescribed in Mt 28.19: in neither case can one argue to a liturgical formula. They do indicate that baptism is given in his name: by his authority and power, with some invocation of his name. It is a baptism to/into his name: a rite of consecration or dedication of the baptized to Christ.

John the Baptist designated Jesus as the one who would baptize with the Holy Spirit (Mt 3.11 and par.). Jesus promised to send the promise of his Father upon his disciples (Lk 24.49; cf. Jn 14.16-17,26; 15.26; 16.7), and after his resurrection he connected this promise with John the Baptist's prediction (Acts 1.4-5,8). He gave the Holy Spirit to the Apostles (Jn 20.22-23). On Pentecost Jesus poured out the Spirit (Acts 2.33), and the multitude was directed to be baptized in the name of Jesus Christ for the forgiveness of their sins and the gift of the Holy Spirit (2.38). In baptism, as we have noted in Ti 3.5-6, it is through Jesus Christ our Savior that God pours out upon us the Holy Spirit who performs the washing of regeneration and renewal.

According to Eph 5.25, in a text which is clearly baptismal, it is Christ who acts: sanctifying the Church, cleansing her by the washing of water with the word. By baptism, according to Acts 2.41, souls were *added* [to the community of believers]. The action is attributed to the Lord [Jesus]: "... And the Lord added to their number day by day those who were being saved" (Acts 2.47).

(4) *The Holy Spirit.*

As we have seen, it is by one Spirit that we were all baptized into one body: the Spirit is the agent (cf. 1 Cor 12.13). We were all made to drink of one Spirit : the agent seems to be another, perhaps the Father "... You were washed, you were sanctified [consecrated], you were justified in the name (*en tōi onomati*) of the Lord Jesus Christ and in the Spirit (*en tōi pneumati*) of our God" (1 Cor 6.11). The two phrases are parallel, and seem to indicate the action and the power of the Lord Jesus and of the Spirit of our God. The absolute initiative of the Father/God is indicated by the quali- fication of the Spirit: of our God. We have seen the role of the Holy Spirit in the washing of regeneration and renewal: it is the Holy Spirit, poured out upon us richly by God through Jesus Christ, who acts directly in the washing.

Jesus indicates to Nicodemus roles of water and Spirit: " ... no one can enter the kingdom of God without being begotten of water and Spirit" (Jn 3.5). [7] If one fastens his or her attention on this verse alone, he or she may say that the action of water and Spirit are simply juxtaposed. Few would limit themselves to such a con- sideration. Water and Spirit are not on the same plane. Either water is understood as a symbol of the Spirit, or its action is regarded as subordinate, instrumental. In either case there is question of the real water of baptism. The following verse indicates the primacy of the Spirit both in the action, and in effecting the result of the action: "That which is born [begotten] of the flesh is flesh, and that which is born [begotten] of the Spirit is spirit" (3.6). The action is that of the Spirit, symbolized by the water of baptism. The term of the action is "spirit": a heightening of the powers and operation of the person who is thus begotten from above. [8]

(5) *The Church*.

Little is said explicitly of the role of the Church in baptism; yet enough is said to stimulate reflection, to ground doctrinal affir- mation, and eventually to yield some theological understanding. If one is asked by what authority he or she baptizes, one can only go back to Jesus' command to the Apostles (Mt 28.18-20; Mk 16.15- 16) and to the New Testament evidence of the manner in which that command was carried out in the Christian community. The person who baptizes now does so only with a sense of belonging to that community--or in extreme cases of being at least authorized by it to act--and of exercising a function which Christ committed to his Apostles as qualified members of his Church. The Apostles directed the inquiring believers to be baptized, and they themselves baptized

---

[7] R. Brown's translation: *The Gospel according to John* I-XII (AB, vol. 29. New York: Doubleday, 1966).

[8] For a discussion of this text, see *The Mystery*, pp. 230-238.

or oversaw the performance of baptism. The deacon Philip baptized, but evidently in a role dependent on the supervision of the Apostles (cf. Acts 8.4-25). Paul testifies that he usually did not baptize: one can only conclude that after having preached Christ and brought men and women to believe in Christ, he committed the ministry of baptism to others in the community (cf. 1 Cor 1.14-17).

It is the Church, through her qualified members, who decides policy in the matter of receiving Gentiles (Acts 11.1-18). In general, the Church is the body of Christ, through which alone he is now visibly present and acting among men and women. The diversity of members, and of powers and functions in the body, has been disposed by God (cf. 1 Cor 12 and 14). With the authority given by Christ according to that disposition, the Church knows and indicates who is to baptize and how. In the normal performance of baptism, as in any act of public worship of the Church, the community of believers participates, and in its very action symbolizes the structure of the Church and of the action of the whole body which here and now is concentrated in the act of the minister.

(6) *The baptizer*.

Though little is said in the New Testament concerning the persons who baptize, their role is important, indeed indispensable, and it has occasioned many doctrinal and theological questions in the course of the history of Christian living. We cannot baptize ourselves. Christ himself does not perform the external, visible, audible action. The Church is not an abstraction: its action is concentrated here and now in the action of this qualified member, of any man or woman who is willing to baptize in the manner and with the intention which the Church requires. Especially since so little has been written in Scripture, theologians and the teaching Church have had to consider and answer many questions concerning the baptizer, and in general concerning the human minister of the rites which, like baptism, constitute the major part of the Church's public worship.

WHAT IS DEMANDED OF THE PERSON WHO IS BAPTIZED?

One may answer this question in two stages: actions required as a preparation for baptism, and commitment to a way of life following baptism. In a sense, therefore, it is impossible to give a full answer to our question before treating the meaning and effects of baptism. Since God's saving action comes to term in every person only in a full human response, the full effects of baptism as a saving act are the permanent change in the life of the baptized, and the acts by which the baptized correspond with God's saving grace. I shall treat briefly both sets of acts.

Two things are required of those who approach baptism: faith and repentance. Having dealt with both in the section devoted to the sequence of actions involved in the beginning of Christian life, I shall indicate here only some further data and reflections. Concerning faith, the problem is not to show its necessity, but rather to recognize its full importance, and to acknowledge that Paul's thesis that we are "justified" [or, in terminology which I prefer, "righted" or "made right"] by belief, leaves us with the problem of showing the relevance and necessity of baptism, and to resolve the tension in Paul's gospel between the roles of belief and baptism. [9] In the course of Paul's elaboration of his thesis of being righted by belief in [or *of*] Jesus Christ, he attributes practically all of the blessings of salvation to belief. By belief in, or of, Jesus Christ, one is made right (Gal 2.15; Rom 1.16-17; 3.21-31; 5.1; 10.9-15; see also 2 Tm 3.15). By belief Paul died to the Law, to live to God; he was crucified with Christ, so that it was no longer Paul who lived, but Christ who lived in him (Gal 2.19-20). The Spirit is received by hearing with belief (Gal 3.2,5,14). According to a probable interpretation of 1 Cor 1.21-22 and Eph 1.13, the Spirit anoints with belief prior to baptism. [10] By belief we are sons and daughters of God (Gal 3.26). Sins are forgiven those who believe (Rom 4.5-8). According to the promise to Abraham, those who believe will inherit the world (Rom 4.13-14). In Christ and with Christ we were raised through belief in the working of God, who raised him from the dead; we were made alive, and all of our trespasses were forgiven (Col 2.12-14). [11]

Belief is prominent also in the theology of John. "... To all who received him, who believed in his name, he gave the power to become children of God; who were born, not of blood nor of the

---

[9] I have given ample treatment of Paul's thesis, of belief and rightness, and of baptism in *Telling*, vol. I, pp. 252-299; see also "In Hearing and Believing," *Telling*, vol. II, pp. 173-200. The problem of the relationship of belief and baptism arises from reflection not only on Paul's teaching, but on other portions of the New Testament too. See, regarding the gospel of John, the brief exposition of the roles of belief and baptism in *Telling*, vol. I, pp. 188-189.

[10] See *The Mystery*, pp. 209-210, and *Telling*, vol. I, pp. 293-294, where I have given a brief exposition of the exegesis proposed by I. de la Potterie, S.J., "L'onction du chrétien par la foi," *Biblica* 40 (1959) 12-69, also published in S. Lyonnet and I. de la Potterie, *La vie selon l'Esprit* (Paris: Les Éditions du Cerf, 1965), pp. 107-167.

[11] With regard to Col 2.12-14, see above, note 6.

will of the flesh nor of the will of man, but of God" (Jn 1.12-13).
Everyone who sees the Son and believes in him has eternal life (Jn
6.40,47; cf. 3.15-21; 5.24-25,28-29). One who comes to Jesus will not
be cast out (Jn 6.37). Everyone who see the Son of man and believes
in him will be raised up by him at the last day (Jn 6.40; cf. vv. 39,44;
1 Jn 5.1,4,13).

Repentance figures prominently in the Synoptics, especially in
Luke (3.3,8; 5.32; 10.13; 11.32; 13.3,5; 15.7; 16.30; 14.47), and *Acts*
(2.38; 3.19; 5.31; 8.22; 11.18; 13.14; 17.30; 19.4; 20.21; 16.20). It is
rarely mentioned by Paul in his letters: once in connection with
what may be regarded as a person's first conversion (Rom 2.4; cf. 1
Tm 2.25), and twice with reference to sins committed by Christians
(2 Cor 7.9-10; 12.21). It is never mentioned by John. Grouping *Luke*
and *Acts* on one side, and *Paul* and *John* on the other, one finds the
importance of belief and repentance in inverse proportion. Beyond
the common meanings of change of mind, remorse, regret, or
sorrow for shortcomings and errors, both the verb *metanoeō* and the
noun *metanoia* in the New Testament and in Christian writings
signify religious and moral conversion, a turning to God, a complete change of one's way of life. Such repentance and conversion is
the act of a man or woman who repents, but radically it is a gift of
God: cf. Acts 5.31; 11.18; 1 Tm 2.25.

Commitment to a new way of life, consequently, is implicit in
repentance and conversion, for repentance is not a matter of a
momentary feeling or of a single act. John the Baptist, having
preached repentance and a baptism which was a sign of repentance,
demanded sincerity and bearing fruits that befit repentance. When
the crowds asked what they were to do, John indicated the moral
norms for their life (Lk 3.8-14). Sending his disciples to make
disciples of all nations, Jesus ordered them not only to baptize, but
to teach them to observe all that he had commanded (Mt 28.20).
The results are shown in the description of the life of the first
Christian community: "... they devoted themselves to the apostles'
teaching...." (Acts 2.42). Most of all, commitment to a new way of
life is implicit in the meaning and effects of baptism, as we shall see.

THE MEANING AND EFFECTS OF BAPTISM

I combine here the account of meanings and effects because
they are correlative: baptism is a symbolic saving act whose effects
are indicated in the very symbolism of the act as it is interpreted in
New Testament documents and understood in the Church. Sys-

tematic order here is hardly possible, since we are gathering the data concerning a multiple intuitive symbolism, and the many symbols themselves have a rich but manifold, obscure meaning: they are not sharply defined conceptual symbols. [12] In such intuitive biblical symbolism inevitably there is a considerable overlapping, and an order of intelligibility can hardly be established as long as one holds to the symbolism of the Bible itself. In this introduction I intend to hold to biblical symbolism, biblical concepts and language. Later, in dealing with the development of a conceptual theology regarding the meaning and effects of the sacraments, we shall treat them as they are formulated in conceptual symbols which have been developed in the continual effort to reach a further understanding, and a teaching which, in response to further questions, seeks a sharper conceptualization.

One more general note may be in order here. In dealing with agents involved in baptism, I did not include the person who is baptized, since baptism is not something which he or she does, but something done to them. However, as I indicated in dealing with the demands made of the person who is baptized, baptism involves a commitment to a personal response and a new way of life. Its full effects are realized, then, in the full personal response of the baptized, and in the whole of a continuing way of life. We shall complete our treatment of this aspect of the demands by showing more in detail to what baptism by its meaning and effects commits a man or woman.

(1) *Saving*.

Beginning with the most general indication of baptism's effects, we may say simply that baptism *saves* a man or woman. This is the promise of Jesus: "He who believes and is baptized will be saved..." (Mk 16.16) Having told the multitude that they were to repent and be baptized, Peter exhorted them, saying, "'Save yourselves from this crooked generation.' So those who received his word were baptized...." (Acts 22.40). The baptismal text in *Titus* adds indications of how God saves us through baptism: "... he saved us ... by the washing of regeneration and renewal in the Holy Spirit, which he poured out upon us richly through Jesus Christ our Savior, so that we might be made right [justified] by his grace and become heirs in hope of eternal life" (Ti 3.5-7).

---

[12] On my distinction between conceptual and intuitive symbols, see *Man the Symbolizer* (*Analecta Gregoriana*, vol. 222. Rome: Gregorian University Press, 1981) pp. 186-194.

(2) *Union with Christ.*

We are baptized *into Christ* (cf. Gal 3.27; Rom 6.3). Though *baptize* etymologically means *dip, immerse, plunge into* [water in this case], "to be baptized" into Christ probably retains little of the original meaning, as if it were to be plunged into Christ as into some mystic reality. "Baptize" in the Pauline texts seems to have a technical sense: baptism is a ritual consecration, in this case terminating in Christ, in union with Christ, or in belonging to Christ. Immediately, then, the result of baptism is union with Christ. One must recognize, however, that the intuitive symbol "baptized" retains the muted overtones of the primitive sense of being plunged into Christ.

(3) *Union with all who have been baptized.*

Having "put on" Christ, being one with Christ, the baptized is intimately united with all who have been baptized into Christ. All merely human differences, between Jew and Greek, slave and free, male and female, are now relatively insignificant: all are one in Christ (cf. Gal 3.27-28); all are members of the body of Christ (cf. 1 Cor 12.12-13,27). In the Pauline conception, then, those who become disciples (cf. Mt 28.19) and who by baptism are "added" to the community of believers (cf. Acts 2.41) are most intimately united with one another by virtue of their personal union with Christ. They are members of one body, with a diversity of dignity and function disposed by God for the good of the whole (cf. 1 Cor 12 and 14). Being in Christ, they are the offspring of Abraham and heirs to the promise.

(4) *Deliverance from sin.*

The symbolism of immersion into water is multiple, and two aspects of that symbolism indicate that element of salvation which consists in deliverance from evil. In our case the evil is sin. Deliverance is expressed by the symbolism of dying in union with the death by which Christ destroyed sin, and by the symbolism of bathing, washing, cleansing, to signify the forgiveness of sin. Immersion into water symbolizes, among other effects, death; and in Christian baptism a universal, primitive symbolism is given a uniquely Christian meaning. To be baptized into Christ, as the symbol is understood in the context of the whole of the Christian world which has been revealed, is to be baptized into, plunged into, his death: into Christ in the very mystery of his dying. Our baptism, then, as a symbolic imitation of the death of Christ, terminates in a

symbolic, spiritual death. By his death Christ destroyed sin, died
to sin. United with him in the mystery of his death, buried with
him (Rom 6.4), we die to sin, break irrevocably with sin (Rom
6.3-14). The symbolism of death is reinforced by that of burial
(Rom 6.6), of the crucifixion of our old self to destroy the sinful
body (Rom 6.6), and of a spiritual circumcision which consists in
putting off the body of the flesh (Col 2.11). Dead to sin, the
baptized has also died to the Law through the body of Christ
(Rom 7.4-6). He or she has been delivered from sin and from the
captivity of the Law.

By a second symbolism, baptism in water signifies and effects
our deliverance from sin. It is a washing, cleansing, which expresses God's forgiveness of our sins (cf. Acts 2.38; 5.31; 10.43;
Col 2.13 for the theme of forgiveness of sins, and Acts 22.16; 1 Cor
6.11; Eph 5.26; Heb 10.22 for the symbolism of baptism).

In connection with these texts which express deliverance from
sin, we may note one text in which again a very general statement
is made concerning the effect of baptism. Having reminded the
Corinthians that the unrighteous (*adikoi*) will not inherit the
kingdom, having enumerated some of the kinds of unrighteous,
and having reminded the Corinthians that some of them had been
such, Paul adds: "But you were washed, you were sanctified, you
were *made right* [*justified*] in the name of the Lord Jesus Christ and
in the Spirit of our God" (1 Cor 6.11). I have italicized *made right*
[*justified*], since it is a highly significant element in the text. It is
one of the many indications of the tension in Paul's theology
between the effects of belief and of baptism. There is no question
here of claiming a rightness or justice based on one's own works.
As Paul has affirmed at the beginning of the letter, God is the
source of our life in Christ Jesus, "... whom God made our
wisdom, our rightness and sanctification and redemption; therefore, as it is written, 'let him who boasts, boast of the Lord'" (1
Cor 1.30-31). According to this text, clearly baptismal, those who
had been unrighteous have been washed, sanctified [consecrated,
dedicated], made right [justified] by a gift of God through Jesus
Christ and the Spirit. It is a text in which the parallelism between
the effects of belief and of baptism is remarkable. Because of
belief, not works of the Law, God does not reckon sins, but
reckons rightness (Rom 4.1-8): God makes right [justifies] those
who believe in Jesus (Rom 3.25-26). By *baptism*, through Jesus and
the Spirit, God washes them clean of their sins, consecrates them,
makes them right [justifies] them (cf. 1 Cor 6.11).

(5) *Raising from death to life.*

One with Christ in the mystery of his death, we remain united with him, and together with him we have been raised from the death of sin, made alive (cf. Col 2.13; Eph 2.1,5-6), and, in anticipation of our future glory, made to sit with him in heavenly places (cf. Eph 2.6). Having been buried with Christ in baptism, we have been raised with him through belief in the working of God, who raised him from the dead (Col 2.12).

There is a subtle difference of interpretation of Paul's thought concerning the symbolism of baptism. It regards two possible interpretations of the classic text Col 2.11-13. I have referred to this text above, and to my interpretation of it in earlier writings. Yet I can hardly expect my readers to consult other works, without giving here briefly the pivotal phrase whose interpretation is crucial. The phrase is *en hōi kai*, which is usually taken to mean "in *which* [baptism] ... also" [thus the RSV]. I take it as meaning "in *whom* [Christ] ... also." It may seem to be a slight matter of syntax: whether the Greek relative pronoun expressing the object of the preposition refers to the nearer "baptism" or the more distant "Christ" (at the end of verse 11).

Why do I make an issue of what may seem to be a trivial matter? I do so because the difference of interpretation affects our understanding of the symbolism of baptism in the letters of Paul. If the version of the RSV and perhaps most others were maintained, this would be the only text in the Pauline writings in which the symbolism of the rite itself would be double, as it is in the later interpretations of some of the Fathers. In that interpretation, the *immersion* symbolizes death or burial, and *emersion* symbolizes rising to new life in and with Christ. I maintain that the whole structure of the text, from 2.2 "Christ" to the whole of the symmetrical passage 2.6-15, favors the second interpretation of verse 12. The key phrases are these:

> [1]in him
> [7]in him
> [8]according to ...
>   according to ...
>   and not according to Christ
> [9]in him
> [10]in him
> [11]in whom too
>   with him in baptism
> in *whom* too [or in *which* too]
>   with him
> [15]in him

How does this affect our conception of Pauline symbolism of baptism? The explicit meaning of the symbolic act of baptism is death or burial with Christ. By our symbolic ritual immersion we are united with Christ in the very mystery of his death and burial. How, then, is being raised from death to life somehow an effect of baptism? We are raised to life because we undergo this symbolic death and burial *believing* in the working of God who raised him from the dead. In this complex interpretation, we see once more the tension in Paul's thought between the effects of belief and of baptism. [13]

The fundamental pattern here is that of the saving action of the God who, for those who believe, gives life to the dead (Rom 4.16-25). Biblical types indicated in the New Testament are the Exodus (cf. 1 Cor 10.1-2) and the deluge (cf. 1 Pt 3.20-21). As in much intuitive symbolism, the suggestive power of the symbol is manifold. We were dead in our sins. In baptism, believing in the power of God to raise us to life, we underwent a symbolic dying and burial as we were united with Christ in the very mystery of the dying by which he destroyed sin and death. As God raised Jesus from the dead, he has raised us, united with Christ in his death and burial.

(6) *Gift of the Spirit.*

It seems reasonable to affirm the gift of the Spirit through baptism, though there is considerable obscurity in the variety of accounts of the gift of the Spirit.

In *Acts* the gift of the Spirit occurs in four different patterns. (a) On Pentecost the disciples received the Holy Spirit, and there is no mention of their ever having been baptized. (b) Those to whom Peter preached seem to have received the Holy Spirit as a result of their having been baptized. Peter directed them: "... be baptized ... *and* you shall receive the gift of the Holy Spirit" (2.38). The most reasonable interpretation of the text is that the conjunction of being baptized and receiving the Spirit means that the gift of the Spirit is the effect of baptism. Moreover, no other event is recorded besides their baptism, and the description of their subsequent life implicitly indicates the effects of the reception of Holy Spirit (2.42-47). Similarly in the case of Paul's baptism the text suggests that it is through baptism that he is to be filled with the Spirit (9.17-19). (c) In Samaria those baptized by Philip did not receive the Holy Spirit until Peter and John laid hands on them (8.12-17). Similarly

---

[13] Once again I refer to my more ample exposition of Col 2.11-15 in *The Mystery*, pp. 215-220, and *Telling*, vol. I, pp. 296-298.

at Ephesus, those who had received only the baptism of John were baptized in the name of the Lord Jesus, and then, when Paul laid his hands on them, the Holy Spirit came upon them (19.1-6). (d) At Caesarea Peter preached Jesus to the Gentiles, and as he was speaking the Holy Spirit fell on all who heard the word and they spoke in tongues; then they were baptized (10.44-48). Later Peter affirms that God cleansed their hearts by belief (15.9): apparently their sins were forgiven when they believed and received the Spirit, before their baptism. [14]

Pauline texts leave the matter obscure. "By one Spirit we were all baptized into one body--Jews or Greeks, slaves or free--and all were made to drink of one Spirit" (1 Cor 12.13). Though exegetes differ, there is some probability that being made to drink of one Spirit refers to baptism, and to a gift of the Spirit made by the Father in baptism.

Two parallel texts may indicate a gift of the Spirit in baptism: "... it is God who strengthens us together with you as Christ's, and who anointed us, and sealed us, and gave us his Spirit in our hearts as a pledge" (2 Cor 1.21-22); "... having heard ... and believed, you were sealed with the promised Holy Spirit, which is the pledge of our inheritance" (Eph 1.13). [15] Four actions are indicated in 2 Cor, and probably they are to be understood in this way: (1) God now strengthens both Paul and the Corinthians in their consecration to Christ, as belonging to Christ; (2) before baptism God anointed them (figuratively, spiritually) with faith: a gift which is the effect of an operation of the Spirit; (3) he sealed them with baptism: as in the Old Testament circumcision was a sign or seal of faith, so baptism as the Christian circumcision (cf. Col 2.11; Phil 3.3) is a seal: in baptism God sealed their faith; (4) in baptism too God gave his Spirit in their hearts as a pledge. [16]

Titus 3.5 leaves the matter obscure. Through Jesus God pours out upon us the Holy Spirit, who performs the washing of regeneration and renewal. At most the text would indicate explicitly an outpouring of the Spirit which must be understood as prior to its operation in baptism. In what sense this would constitute a gift of the Spirit, and whether there is any permanent gift of the Spirit, a

---

[14] For the interpretation of these texts, and for the general problem of the relationship between baptism and the gift of the Spirit in *Acts*, see *The Mystery*, pp. 200-202, and *Telling*, vol. I, p. 125.

[15] I give my own translation of 2 Cor 1.21-22, and take as probable the interpretation of the two texts given by De la Potterie, indicated above in note 10.

[16] See *The Mystery*, pp. 209-210, and *Telling*, vol. I, pp. 293-294.

reverberation in the person who is regenerated and renewed, are questions which one cannot answer from this text.

Finally, the relationships between the Spirit and baptism and a gift of the Spirit is indicated in Jesus' words to Nicodemus. One must be begotten *from above* [or: *anew*] of water and Spirit. What is begotten of the flesh is flesh; what is begotten of the Spirit is spirit (cf. Jn 3.3,5-6).

Jesus' whole conversation with Nicodemus, as given by John in the gospel as it stands, is complicated and very rich, and fits into the total development of John's gospel. I can neither glide over it without mentioning that it bristles with difficulties which have called for serious reflection, subtle distinctions, and varied interpretations by exegetes, nor attempt here to set forth anything like an adequate summary. I have treated the matter fairly fully, [17] and I quote here only my conclusions:

> From verse five it is clear that water and Spirit are the principles of the begetting or birth. What is the term of their action? The next verse indicates the immediate effect: in Brown's translation, which I have given, it is rendered, "Flesh begets flesh, and Spirit begets *spirit*." More closely to the Greek construction, the verse means: "What is begotten [or: born] of the flesh is flesh, and what is begotten [or:born] of the Spirit is *spirit*." I have italicized the answer to my question concerning the term of the action of water and Spirit: it is *spirit*. The term is not the Spirit of God, or the Holy Spirit, but a person transformed by this begetting or rebirth. He or she is now *spirit*. The effect of the begetting by water and Spirit is a heightening of one's life and power and manner of acting. Without leaving the level of strict exegesis, one must acknowledge this element in Jesus' teaching as reported by John....
>
> Concluding briefly we may say this about Jesus' words in the conversation with Nicodemus: (1) Jn 3.5 as it stands is clearly baptismal. (2) The Spirit is active in baptism, and the coupling of water and Spirit may be simply a matter of joining Spirit and its symbol, water; the Spirit is both the agent and somehow gift; this action of the Spirit must be inserted into the whole pattern of operations before baptism, in baptism, and in subsequent Christian life. (3) The latter part of Jesus discourse suggests that begetting by water and Spirit is part of that gift of the Spirit which depends on

---

[17] See *The Mystery*, pp. 230-238, drawing heavily from the work of R. E. Brown, S.S., *The Gospel according to John* (Anchor Bible, volumes 29, 29a. New York: Doubleday & Co., 1966, 1970) and I. de la Potterie, S.J., "Naître de l'eau et naître de l'Esprit," in *Sciences Ecclésiastiques* 14 (1962) pp. 417-443; also published in Stanislas Lyonnet and Ignace De la Potterie, S.J., *La vie selon l'Esprit* (Paris: Les Éditions du Cerf, 1965), pp. 107-167.

Jesus' glorification. Other Johannine texts subtly suggest the connection between Jesus' death-glorification and the gift of the Spirit.
(4) Faith is of supreme importance, as is evident in this text and in
the whole of John's gospel and first letter (pp. 237-238).

(7) *Summary*.

Since some of the texts cited mention two or more effects, and
there is a considerable overlapping, I simply enumerate distinct
effects as they are expressed in biblical symbolism. This is a list
which, I believe, is complete: saving or salvation, union with Christ,
union with one another in Christ, deliverance from sin / death to sin
/ washing from sin, resurrection with Christ, gift of the Spirit,
justification / being made right, sanctification, second begetting /
birth / regeneration as sons and daughters of God.

REFLECTIONS

(1) *A field of relationships*.

Having considered the sequence of actions in which baptism
occurs, and a number of factors involved in baptism itself, we may
reflect on some of the relationships which result: relationships of
both baptism as an action/event and of the baptized who is affected
by the action.

I set this section apart from the rest because what I am doing
here goes beyond what I have been presenting to this point. The
previous sections are part of what may be called biblical theology: a
synthetic account of themes running through baptismal texts which
I have interpreted individually in earlier works. Here I am not doing
biblical theology, but the beginning of a theological reflection. A
"field of relationships" surely is not the sort of theme which could
be regarded as pertaining to biblical theology. It is an initial attempt
to determine some order in the data gathered from the texts, or
rather in the factors which we have noted in the total phenomenon
of baptism.

In turn, this reflection on relationships will serve to suggest
further initial theological reflections on questions which arise as we
begin to seek an intelligible structure, to come to some deeper
understanding. That understanding must be not only of baptism
itself, but of all of the seven principal ceremonies of Christian
worship which the Church has come to call sacraments, and of
which theologians have sought some general concept, a definition of

the Christian sacrament which fits all seven, and which is in harmony with broader notions of sacramentality which especially in modern times have extended the use of the term "sacrament" to Christ himself as *prime sacrament*, and to the Church, which *in Christ* is in the whole of its perceptible reality a great sacrament. That definition, in turn, will set the task for the further elaboration of all of the elements involved.

(a) Baptism. First, baptism is relative to all of the agents who are involved, divine and human: God/Father, Son/Christ, and Holy Spirit; the Church; the baptizer.

Baptism has a special relation to the Paschal Mystery, to salvation history culminating in the death and resurrection/ glorification of Jesus. This is brought out most strikingly in Paul's thought. Christian life begins in a re-living of the principal mysteries of Christ, the great events in which our salvation was accomplished in him. To be baptized is to participate in the death and resurrection of Christ. It is the power and salvific value of Christ's death and resurrection which make baptism both meaningful and effective. By virtue of Christ's death, which destroyed sin and death, in our symbolic imitation of Christ's death in baptism we die with him, die to sin, break with it irrevocably. Believing in the power of the God who raised Jesus from the dead, we are raised with him and in him.

Baptism is related also to the future life of the baptized, and to the consummation of our life in a share in Christ's glory. Consequently, it cannot be understood in isolation, simply as a moment in a person's life, without a bearing on all that is to follow. Nor can baptism be understood by concentrating solely on strictly baptismal texts. These texts involve many factors of Christian life, and their full implications can be understood only when the data of baptismal texts, concerning, for example, the roles of the Holy Spirit in our lives, are considered as opening on the whole of New Testament revelation, concerning not just the beginnings, but also the fulfillment of Christian life. It is only in the ever-inadequate grasp of what has been revealed of this fulness of life, that we can appreciate what it is that begins with baptism. Thus, in the context of St. Paul's treatment of our death to sin and to the Law, he continues with the great eighth chapter of *Romans*, a capital text on the fulness of Christian life. To cite just one more example, from the great baptismal text of Col 2.9-15, Paul passes first to the irrelevance of worthless worldly wisdom and norms of action (vv. 16-23), and then to the beautiful code of Christian life which is a consequence of our having been raised with Christ (3.1--4.6).

God's saving action comes to its relative term in the life of every man or woman in the full human response to the divine offer of a fulness of life beyond human conception or imagination. Baptism is a continuation of that saving action, reaching individual men and women, to bring them salvation and life in Christ. It is a divine action which terminates in the full human response, not only in the moment of believing and of receiving baptism, but in a continuing response to the offer of richer graces. New Testament texts, even if we look beyond strictly baptismal passages, do not suffice to give a full account of the response and the fulness of life to which baptism is directed. There are, however, many indications. The repentance demanded for the full efficacy of baptism is not a matter of a single act, a momentary performance of a prerequisite to baptism: it is the beginning of a complete change of one's way of life, a deep religious and moral conversion, a new way of life.[18]

(b) The baptized. There is no need to do more here than to suggest that baptism resonates in the life of the baptized. Its meaning and effects ground, in the person who has been baptized, correlative relationships which correspond to those of baptism itself. As a result of his or her reception of baptism, the baptized person stands in new relationships to all of the agents whom we have noted in baptism as it is portrayed in the New Testament. He or she enters upon a new way of life, with a commitment to a full response which ideally will lead to a relative fulness of life, a share in the divine life, in union with Father, Jesus, and Holy Spirit, in this mortal life and forever. Surely the effects in the baptized are far more important than the baptism which in a mysterious way mediates those effects. Yet our concern in the theological inquiry which we are beginning is the mystery of baptism itself, and of the other "sacraments" which gradually have been conceptualized, and which are an important part of the whole Mystery which we seek to understand.

Admittedly, then, in what we shall call a general theology of the Christian sacrament, we are concerned with elements of the Mystery which in themselves are of a lesser importance: the sacraments have been given for the sake of human persons in the total Mystery, and their importance is relative to what they mediate

---

[18] I need not spell out further what I have treated rather fully in *The Mystery*, pp. 243 to the end, in all of the sections of *Telling*, vol. I, which set forth the fulfillment of the promise in us, and in the whole of *Telling*, vol. II, designed to foster a deeper and richer experience of God. These volumes are the real introduction to the present work, and they set baptism and all of the Christian sacraments in the context of the whole Christian Mystery.

in human persons. Yet they are mysterious, a challenge to understanding, to the theologian who seeks an intelligible structure of
the whole of revealed truth: all that pertains to the Mystery.

(2) *Factors in the development of belief and theology of the
sacrament.*

(a) Tradition. Initial theological reflection on biblical teaching
of baptism, and on the contrast between baptism and other
sacraments which do not have a comparable biblical foundation,
highlights what is characteristic of sacramental theology to a far
greater degree than most other areas of theological reflection, but
which characterizes all Roman Catholic theology.

What do I mean? The theology of the Christian sacrament
illustrates strikingly the degree to which Church teaching and
theological understanding must reckon with the witness of the living
tradition of the Christian community through the centuries. We
cannot erect a theology of the Christian sacraments--or "sacrament"--upon the basis of New Testament witness alone. This is true
of baptism. It is true far more of the other rites of Christian worship
which the Church recognizes as sacraments instituted by Christ and
constituting the principle part of the Church's public worship. It is
true of all theology. Any Christian theology which is elaborated at
any stage in the life of the Church must take account of many
non-biblical questions which call for answers. The questioners will
not simply cease to question, or go away. Even if they did, other
thinking men and women would come forward to repeat and
further develop the same persistent questions and demands for
understanding. "Blind faith" is not the Christian ideal. Much less is
it theology. Nor is the slogan "Scripture alone!" which ironically is
accompanied by dogmatic concentration on a few texts of Scripture
and a refusal to face the challenges of the rest of biblical revelation
and its inexorable demands.

(b) Continuing doctrinal and theological development. Through
the centuries The Holy Spirit has illumined the Church, and that
illumination continues. Through the centuries theologians who have
done their work have paid attention to that continuing illumination.
Through the centuries thinking men and women have questioned,
seeking either to challenge a belief and a theology which they do not
share, or to penetrate to a deeper understanding of Christian tradition and belief which they treasure. And Christians, theologians
themselves and others, will continue to question to the end of time,
for the inquiring mind is a precious endowment of men and women

who *are* in the distinctively human way of being. The Holy Spirit will continue to illumine until the end of time, when questions will cease and illumination of believers will yield to vision.

Beyond biblical teaching regarding the rites which we now believe to be sacraments, principal ceremonies of Christian public worship, we need continuing reflection, and doctrinal and theological development, for a deeper understanding of baptism and the other individual rites, and of what characterizes all of them. This last is the goal of a general theology of the Christian sacrament.

With regard to baptism itself, I have said that the insufficiency of biblical witness for theological understanding is true even of baptism. How so? Consider the themes which I have traced through the biblical texts regarding baptism. What forces us to go beyond biblical resources to come to rest in some understanding of baptism? These are some of the questions which cannot be answered by mere recourse to the New Testament texts--or to the whole Bible.

(i) The tension between belief and baptism. This is striking in both John and Paul, and it calls for reflection and the elaboration of sharper conceptualization and distinction than we can find in the Bible. To be true to Paul or John in rendering their thought in a biblical theology, we must allow the tensions to stand as they are in the texts: unresolved. To be true to ourselves as honestly inquiring men and women, living in the Spirit and guided by the Spirit in our effort to understand, we must recognize the limits of Pauline and Johannine understanding--or at least written elaboration of a further understanding. In going beyond them, we are not doing a work of biblical exegesis or theology. We are simply attempting to satisfy another exigency of the Christian life of inquiring men and women.

(ii) The uncertainty of the relationship between baptism and the gift of the Spirit.

(iii) The obscurity of the relationships between the many agents and their actions.

(iv) Questions concerning the roles of the Church and of recipients.

(v) Questions concerning sharper conceptualization of the effects of baptism, and their relationships.

As for other sacraments individually, if biblical teaching does not suffice for an understanding of baptism, much less could it suffice for the understanding of the other rites which in the Roman Catholic Church are believed to be sacraments instituted by Christ. I need not elaborate: it is enough to recognize that biblical witness is so scanty that most of our seven sacraments are not even recognized by some Christians to be sacraments instituted by Christ.

Finally, the concept of the Christian sacrament, the recognition that there are indeed seven and only seven sacraments, and understanding of what is common to all analogously have developed only slowly in the life of the Church. Classic theologies were elaborated only as the fruit of reflection upon insights gradually reached and shared through the centuries. Much remains to be done. In the course of this work, I shall attempt to note stages in developing teaching and theology, and to make some personal contribution to a deeper understanding.

Chapter II

MYSTĒRION AND *SACRAMENTUM*:
FROM THE BIBLE TO ISIDORE OF SEVILLE

Working as a theologian within the Christian tradition, and within the Roman Catholic Church, I shall seek to set forth the pertinent biblical data, to trace some important stages of the development of both Church teaching and theology, and then as far as possible to make some personal contribution.

Dealing with the doctrine and theology of the Christian sacrament, one faces a special difficulty in tracing its history. Whereas it is relatively easy or difficult to work out the history of baptism or of the Eucharist, or even of anointing and laying on of hands in Christian life and worship, it is impossible to trace from the beginnings of Christian life a history of the "sacrament." Nowhere in Scripture does the word *mystērion*, and the Latin *sacramentum* which generally translates it, have the technical meaning which they have taken on in Christian teaching and theology since the twelfth century. Consequently, before the twelfth century it was impossible to enumerate seven sacraments, or to give a systematic sacramental theology.

Certainly John Chrysostom wrote much of *mystēria*, and treated both baptism and the Eucharist among the *mystēria*. Augustine and Ambrose used *sacramentum* in writing of baptism and of the Eucharist. But both the Greek and the Latin Fathers used the *mystērion/sacramentum* terminology in a much broader sense than it has been given in later theology, and a theology of *sacramentum* in Augustine would deal with a multitude of things which are not sacraments as we understand the word now, as referring to the seven principal rites of Christian worship.

Yet there is a historical preparation for the classic definitions of the sacrament, and for the theologies which have been elaborated since the twelfth century. One can trace the principal lines of the development of notions which eventually contributed to the formation of the classic definitions and of classic sacramental teaching and theology. Though the order of exposition in such a history is chronological, it is commanded by the movement of an investigation which is retrogressive, analytic, seeking in Scripture and in Christian tradition and theology the sources of medieval and later sacramental doctrine and theology. Such a historical account must be selective, or it will never come to term. Dealing with various senses of *mystērion* or *sacramentum*, we cannot be drawn into complete treatment of all persons, things, and actions which have ever been called by these words, for example: the pagan cult mysteries. [1] We are interested in those elements which as a matter of fact have contributed to the development of the concept of sacrament as we now know it.

One more methodological note is important. Often, in the long history of human thought, what has been achieved by one great thinker has not been fully understood and retained by later generations. In tracing significant contributions, for example in Augustine, we must strive to retain elements which were overlooked or simplified and impoverished by medieval thinkers. So too, going farther back, not all of the dimensions which we have noted in New Testament teaching on baptism have been retained as guidelines for the development of theologies of the sacrament.

Historical investigation, however, is not my only concern. It is necessary, for without it one cannot trace the evolution of dogma and of classic theological definitions of sacrament and elaborations of sacramental theologies. It is not sufficient, however, for one who seeks to gather and hold all the data which are pertinent to a present-day definition and theology of the Christian sacrament. Consequently, after having traced the evolution of classic formulae, and the emergence of more recent concepts, I shall go beyond them, seeking to define the sacrament in terms of the whole field of relationships in which alone it can be understood. That field, in broad terms, is the whole of the Mystery: God's eternal decree and its realization in the history of salvation, the Mystery of Christ. Important as they are, defined dogmas and classic formulae grasp only parts of the truth concerning the Christian sacrament. I am concerned with presenting the whole truth, as far as I can grasp it, and with locating dogmatic propositions and classic formulae within the whole field of relationships.

I shall begin this treatment of the approach to a definition of the sacrament by considering some stages in the meaning of the words *mystērion* and *sacramentum*.

---

[1] Our method cannot, therefore, be that of the lexicon-concordance approach to the study of biblical words. Such a study is concerned with words, and with all instances of the use of those words, and all of the realities which have been called by the words. It may be useful as one starting point, but eventually one must concentrate on those instances of the use of the words in which they name the full realities, and only the full realities, in which we may be interested.

MYSTĒRION

(1) *In the Old Testament and in apocalyptic books.* [2]

The word *mystērion* occurs only twenty times in the Septuagint, in later books of the Hellenistic period. Often it means simply "secret" or "secret plan" (as in Jdt 2.2). In the sapiential books it signifies a divine secret, God's plan for salvation of men and women, concerning blessings to be given in the last days (Wis 2.22-23), or divine wisdom itself which is not hidden but is revealed (Wis 6.22).

The most important text is in *Daniel*, concerning Nebuchadnezzar's dream. Here *mystērion* is used of both God's plan concerning the latter days (Dn 2.28,44-45) and the dream, which is an obscure revelation of the divine secret (vv. 18-19). To God alone belongs wisdom (v. 20). He gives wisdom to the wise, and reveals deep and hidden things (vv. 21-22), mysteries (vv. 29-30). This twofold sense of mystery, the divine plan concerning final salvation, and its obscure revelation, is developed in the Jewish apocalyptic writings, especially in *Enoch* and the fourth book of *Esdras*. In these writings *mystērion* is applied to the symbolic revelation of final salvation, the divine interpretation of such revelation, and the perfect manifestation to be made at the end of time.

(2) *In the New Testament.* [3]

Jesus told his disciples: "To you has been given the secret (*mysterion*) of the kingdom of God, but for those outside everything is in parables; ...."(Mk 4.11; cf. Mt 13.11; Lk 8.10). From the context the mystery seems to be that the messianic kingdom has come in Christ. Some vague, general knowledge of this secret can be had from the parables, but they cannot be understood without further revelation, which Jesus gives only to his disciples in private.

---

[2] See G. Bornkamm, "*mysteriōn*," in G. Kittel, *Theologisches Wörterbuch zum Neuen Testament* (Stuttgart, vol IV, 1942) pp. 820-823; D. Deden, "Le 'mystère' paulinien,"*Ephemerides Theologicae Lovanienses* 13 (1936) 427-435.

[3] See Bornkamm, *op. cit.*, 405-442; S. Lyonnet, S.J., "Hellénisme et Christianisme. A propos du Theologisches Wörterbuch," Biblica 26 (l945) 115-132; R. E. Brown, S.S., "Mystery (in the Bible)," in *The New Catholic Encyclopedia* (New York: McGraw-Hill, 1967) vol. X, pp. 148-151.

The Mystery is an important Pauline theme, and his statements concerning it provide the elements for a synthesis of salvation history. [4]

(a) There is question of the secret (*en mysteriō*), hidden wisdom of God (1 Cor 2.7), his eternal purpose (Eph 3.11), which he decreed before the ages for our glorification (1 Cor 2.7), concerning what he has prepared for those who love him (1 Cor 2.9-10).

(b) It is the mystery of his will, according to the purpose which he set forth in Christ, as a plan for the fulness of time, to unite all things in him, things in heaven and things on earth (Eph 1.9-10). The mystery is Christ (Col 2.2; 4.3), Christ in whom all the treasures of wisdom and knowledge are hidden (Col 2.3), Christ in you (Col 1.27); the mystery of how the Gentiles are fellow heirs, members of the same body, and partakers of the promise in Christ Jesus through the gospel (Eph 3.6).

(c) The divine plan was kept secret for long ages (Rom 16.25; cf. Col 1.26; Eph 3.5,9). None of the rulers of this age understood it (1 Cor 2.8).

(d) Now it is disclosed and through the prophetic writings is made known to all nations, to bring about the obedience of faith (Rom 16.26). God has revealed it to us through the Spirit (1 Cor 2.10). The mystery is now made manifest to his saints (Col 1.26), to his holy apostles and prophets (Eph 3.5), and to Paul (Eph 3.3).

(e) Through Christ the manifold wisdom of God is to be made known to the principalities and powers in the heavenly places (Eph 3.10).

(f) Paul imparts this in words not taught by human wisdom, but taught by the Spirit, interpreting spiritual truths to those who possess the Spirit. The unspiritual do not receive the gifts of the Spirit of God, for they are folly to them and they are not able to

---

[4] I base this synthesis on elements taken from these texts of Paul: 1 Cor 2.7-10; Rom 16.25-25; Col 1.26-27; 2.3; 4.3; Eph 1.9-10; 3.3-12; plus 1 Tm 3.16 (without claiming that this letter was written by Paul). The elements are Paul's. The rest is mine: the thematizing, the intelligible order found in the texts, and the organization and presentation according to that order. I make no claim, therefore, that this is Paul's synthesis, or that this is the unity which these elements have in Paul's explicit thought. Nor do I claim that this is purely and simply biblical theology--if such theology be understood as limited severely to both the concepts and the explicit elaborated thought of the individual biblical writer. What is offered here is a stage in the total work of theology, concerned with understanding within a life of belief. It may be situated between pure biblical theology and further theological insight and elaboration. This synthesis is helpful, I believe, for further consideration of patristic texts, and for understanding later theological and dogmatic development.

understand them because they are spiritually discerned (1 Cor 2.13-14).

(g) God has realized his eternal purpose in Christ Jesus our Lord (Eph 3.11). This is the great mystery of our religion: "He was manifested in the flesh, vindicated in the Spirit, seen by angels, preached among the nations, believed in the world, taken up in glory" (1 Tm 3.16). In Christ we have boldness and confidence of access through our faith in him (Eph 3.12). The mystery, Christ in us, is the hope of glory (Col 1.27).

In Pauline usage *mystērion* means *hidden*, as opposed to revealed or manifested. The divine plan, the mystery, was hidden, kept secret for long ages. Even now that it has been revealed and realized in Christ, it is a mystery, because it has been revealed only by the Spirit, and it is communicated only in words taught by the Spirit to those who possess the Spirit: to the unspiritual it remains hidden. Hence in general *mystērion* indicates directly a relationship to knowledge, principally human knowledge.

The doctrinal context of the Pauline mystery is clear: it is intimately connected with the notion of mystery which we have indicated in late Old Testament texts and in Jewish apocalyptic writings. No link with pagan cult mysteries can be demonstrated.

The word *mystērion* is not used by Paul to designate baptism or the Eucharist or any other Christian rite. When he calls matrimony a mystery (Eph 5.32), he is hardly calling it a mystery/sacrament in our modern sense. Rather he means that matrimony from the beginning was a mystery, a type, foreshadowing the union of Christ and his Church, a reality whose hidden meaning has now been revealed.

(3) *In the Greco-oriental mystery religions.* [5]

Without entering into details of a vast and complicated subject, we must note some of the typical terminology of the mystery religions which was a matter of common knowledge in the early Christian centuries, and which explains some of the terminology adapted by some of the Fathers of the Church.

Many cults which flourished especially between the seventh century B.C. and the fourth century A.D. were called *mystēria*. Though the etymology of the word is uncertain, it seems to have

---

[5] See K. Prümm, "Mystery Religions, Greco-Oriental," in *The New Catholic Encyclopedia* (New York: McGraw-Hill, 1967) vol. X, pp. 153-164; Bornkamm, *op. cit.*, pp. 810-820.

been derived from the verb *myein*, to close, to be shut (said of the eyes or mouth). *myein* means to initiate into the mysteries. The *mystē-ria* were sacred rites of worship in which the lot of some god was represented before the initiate by means of sacred actions, in order that the initiate might share the lot of the god. Technical words for the performance of the *mystēria* were *epitelein, hieropoiein, lei-tourgein, poiein*. The ceremonies were also called *telē, teletē, orgia*.

Only the initiate (*myētheis, mystēs*) could take part in the mysteries. Knowledge of the mysteries and access to them was forbidden to the non-initiated. In the whole mystic rite some ceremonies were preparatory, pertaining properly to the initiation, but in many cases it is not clear where the line was drawn between initiation and the subsequent ceremonies. Thus *myēsis* sometimes signifies initiation; sometimes, the whole sacred action. The initiate constituted a sacred society, bound to secrecy, and they were distinguished from others by symbolic signs.

The mystery cults offered salvation (*sotēria*) through the communication of cosmic life. The gods of the mysteries belonged to the cycle of life-death-life in vegetative and human nature. Their sufferings (*pathē*), which the initiate imitate and participate through symbolic rites, express in the manner of mythic personification the elements of the cycle. The sacred secret of these ceremonies is the union between the suffering god and the initiate, a union which is effected in various ways in various mysteries through symbolic actions: sacred meals, marriages, fertility and generative rites, immersions, rites of death and of a kind of rebirth. Three genera of rites occur: sacred actions, sacred drama, and the vision of sacred objects (*epopteia*).

Cult mystery terminology was applied to two other kinds of "mystery": philosophic and gnostic. Plato applied mystic terminology to the contemplation of the supreme truth, of true being. In this sense, the *mystēria* are no longer rites of worship, but an obscure and secret doctrine, from which the uninitiated are excluded. By analogy with the cult mysteries, here too a preparation and purification was demanded: in this case the discipline which prepares the intellect for contemplation. Through contemplation of the divine, of the idea of the good, one is assimilated to the divine and acquires a certain immortality. [6] This mystical conception was retained by Philo, [7] the Pseudo-Dionysius, and the neoplatonic tradition.

---

[6] See A. J. Festugière, O.P., *L'idéal religieux des Grecs et l'Évangile* (Paris, 1932), pp. 43-53; 116-142.

[7] *Ibid.*, p. 129, note 1: mystery terminology which is found in the works of Philo.

Like the mystery religions and philosophy, various gnostic religions promised salvation to the initiate, and applied mystery terminology to the *gnōsis*, the knowledge of a revealed secret doctrine. The doctrine in this case was not philosophical, but mythological, dealing with god and man, the formation of the world, the original fall of man, the divine element in him, and the way of salvation revealed by the saving god. Though gnostics also had rites of worship, their mysteries consisted chiefly in the communication of sacred mythological doctrine. [8]

(4) *In patristic writings.*

The first extensive adaptation of mystery terminology by Christians is found in the works of the Alexandians, who applied gnostic-neoplatonic terminology to the truths of the Christian religion. Clement of Alexandria distinguished minor mysteries, which are to be revealed to all, from major mysteries, which are to be communicated only to "gnostics." As he uses the word *mystē-rion*, it refers to allegorical exegesis, and implies a divine knowledge which is concealed under the external form in which the truth is presented, and is revealed only to a few. He does not apply the word *mystērion* to the rites of baptism and the Eucharist, but he does use the related adjective and adverb, *mysticos* and *mysticōs*, concerning the Eucharistic "symbols," of the bread and of the holy blood. [9]

The notion of mystery is fundamental in Origen's Christian gnosticism. [10] The word *mystērion* is part of a fluid terminology, in which it is associated with *symbolon, ainigma, skia* (shadow), *semeion* (sign), *typos* (type), *eikōn* (image, likeness), and Latin translations, *species, forma, sacramentum, argumentum*. [11] One can distinguish in Origen's doctrine between the Mystery and mysteries. The great Mystery is the threefold manifestation of the Word: in the Incarnation, in the Church, and in Scripture. Baptism and the Eucharist, rites of the Christian religion, are certain derived mysteries, somehow participating the great ge-

---

[8] See L. Cerfaux, "Gnose," *Dictionnaire de la Bible, Supplément*, III (Paris, 1938) col. 659-701.

[9] See H. G. Marsh, "The Use of *mysteriōn* in the Writings of Clement of Alexandria with Special Reference to his Sacramental Doctrine," *Journal of Theological Studies* 37 (1936) 64-80, esp. 75-80.

[10] See H. von Balthasar, "Le mystère d'Origène," *Recherches de science religieuse* 26 (1936) 513-562; 27 (1937) 38-64.

[11] *Ibid.*, 515.

neric-concrete Mystery, according to Origen's neoplatonic conception. [12]

Later too the cult mystery terminology was applied to Christian rites. Even Clement, condemning the cruder mysteries, acknowledged a likeness between the higher forms of mystery and Christian rites. [13] In the fourth and fifth centuries, perhaps because the danger of contamination by mystery religions was considered remote, the Fathers adapted a full mystery terminology to Christian worship. The outstanding example is John Chrysostom. [14]

These are the significant features of his notion of mystery and of his use of the term *mystērion*:

(a) The meaning of *mystērion* is the unknown, the secret; after revelation the *mystērion* is paradoxical, marvelous, venerable, awesome. Basically the word *mystērion* indicates a relationship to knowledge: from eternity God alone knows the mystery; it has been revealed to his saints, but not to all men; it has been known by angels and heavenly powers only since the Incarnation; even those to whom it has been revealed know it only imperfectly.

(b) The following especially are called mysteries: God's plan for salvation in Christ; Christ himself and all that he did and suffered; the Church; Christian dogmas; Christ in his faithful; the Christian rites of baptism and the Eucharist.

(c) God's plan itself, as it is in him eternally, is simply unknown to others. In any other mystery, any manifestation of the divine saving plan and action, there are two elements: the *aisthēton* (sensibly perceptible) and the *noēton* (intelligible). [15] This is not a philosophical distinction between what can be known by sense powers and what can be known only by intellect. It is rather a theological distinction: only the Holy Spirit gives the power by which the believer believes, sees with spiritual eyes.

(d) Of the 200 texts in which the plural *mystēria* is used, 160 deal with cult mysteries: baptism and especially the Eucharist. Here

---

[12] *Ibid.*, 38-42, esp. p. 54 and note 2, on participation and on the terminology *signum-signaculum*.

[13] See his *Protrepticus* (Exhortation to the Gentiles) xii (PG 8.240b-241a).

[14] See G. Fittkau, *Der Begriff des Mysteriums bei Johannes Chysostomus* (Bonn, 1953). Typical texts of Chrysostom are these: Homily 19 on Rom 11.25 (PG 60.591c); Homily 42 on 1 Cor 15.51 (PG 61.364b); Homily 5 on Col 1.26-28 (PG 62.331-334); Homily 7 on 1 Cor 2.6-7 (PG 61.55-56); Homily 85 on Jn 19.31-37 (PG.59.463bc); Homily 82 on Mt 26.26-28 (PG.743ab); Epistle 2 to Olympias (PG.557ab).

[15] See Fittkau, *op. cit.*, pp.101-118.

the basic meaning remains: unknown, secret. [16] In these texts one finds a full cult mystery terminology. [17]

(e) These elements pertain to the doctrinal context of Chrysostom's *mystērion*: the efficacy of the Christian cult mysteries; and moral demands on the part of the participants: the necessity of faith and of a worthy response: "Let us live in a manner worthy of this mystery .... let us strive to be faithful in keeping this mystery...." [18]

Such a conception of *mystērion* is both rich and obscure. It is rich, for it retains the sense of mystery which is characteristic of both the Old Testament and Paul's letters, and it adapts suitable elements of philosophic, gnostic, and cult mystery terminology.

Its application ranges from the divine plan for man's salvation in Christ, through every stage of its manifestation and realization, to the final consummation. Though both the hidden sacred reality and its manifestation are called mystery, still formally *mystērion* almost always means *hidden*. Manifestations of the hidden sacred reality are called mysteries, not because they are manifestations, but because even the obscure revelation remains a mystery.

Granted the evident defects of conceptualization and terminology, one must recognize the contributions made in the elaboration of this notion of the Christian mystery. It suggests the unity of God's plan for salvation: the Christian cult mysteries pertain to the whole plan of the Incarnation, of the manifestation and accomplishment of our salvation in Christ. In the very polarity of hidden-revealed, the notion of *mystērion* suggests aspects of that sacramentality which is a constant dimension of the divine saving action. God saves by word and action: by a symbolic perceptible action, and by the word of revelation and of preaching which illumines the mysterious action and calls for a human response; in a manner proportioned to human nature, God employs sensibly perceptible symbolic realities; all sacramentality, involving sensibly perceptible symbols, remains imperfect as a manifestation of the reality of the divine saving action and of its effects in men and women: all of the manifestations themselves remain mysteries.

---

[16] *Ibid.*, pp. 88-89.

[17] *Ibid.*, p. 100.

[18] Homily 11 on 1 Tm 3.8 ff. (PG 62.555ac); see Fittkau, pp. 118-144.

SACRAMENTUM

I shall treat briefly three early influences on Latin Christian terminology: the ancient Latin translations of the Bible, the pagan Roman *sacramentum*, and the meanings of the word in Tertullian; then I shall indicate Augustine's contribution; and finally note an element contributed by Isidore of Seville.

(1) *Ancient Latin translations.*

How the biblical *mystērion* came to be translated generally in Latin as *sacramentum* is itself something of a mystery. Though much has been done to explain the etymology and classic meaning of *sacramentum*, [19] it has little bearing on the question of why the early Christian translators chose it. [20] The fact is simply that they did. The reason probably is that they wished to avoid words such as *mysteria, sacra, arcana, initia*, which were in use in the pagan mystery cults, and which might have prejudiced the meaning of Christian texts. Since *sacramentum* is the common translation for *mystērion*, it has all the meanings of the biblical *mystērion*. Consequently, the first significant terminological influence on later Latin doctrine and theology in this matter is this biblical use of *sacramentum*.

(2) *The pagan Roman "sacramentum".*

Sacramentum in classic Roman usage is important for our study because Tertullian applied it to the mysteries of Christian initiation. Etymologically, *sacramentum* is taken from *sacrare*: to constitute [a thing or person] of divine right. This was an action which could be performed only by public authority. Anyone could constitute a thing religious, but to make it sacred pertained to public authority. The suffix *-mentum* could designate the agent, or the action, or the object which was made sacred, or the means by which it was made sacred. [21] Two classic usages appear.

The military *sacramentum* was an oath by which soldiers, invoking the gods, bound themselves to loyalty and obedience. The

---

[19] See A. Kolping, *Sacramentum Tertullianum* (Regensburg-Münster, 1948) pp. 21-43, with abundant citation of the literature.
[20] See C. Mohrmann, "Sacramentum dans les plus anciens textes chrétiens," *Harvard Theological Review* 47 (1954) 141-152.
[21] See Kolping, *op. cit.*, pp. 22-25; Mohrmann, *op.cit.*, pp. 145-147.

man who swore truly thus implored the divine favor and aid. One who would knowingly take the oath falsely would consign his life and his home to the wrath of the gods. Thus *sacramentum* had the force of a religious initiation or consecration.

In a civil process according to Roman law, the *sacramentum* was the money to be deposited in a sacred place by the litigants. The winner in the process received his money back. The loser left it for sacred uses. This usage too seems to have implied a religious invocation of the gods to witness to the truth of what was said in the trial, and a certain consecration of the one who swore.

(3) *Tertullian's usage.*

Tertullian used *sacramentum* very often, with a variety of meanings, and applied it to very many things. Often, though what is called *sacramentum* is clear, the meaning of the word is not easy to determine. Consequently opinions differ among interpreters of Tertullian. Without entering into controversies which have no important bearing on the development of sacramental theology, I shall simply indicate the range of meanings of the word in Tertullian's texts. [22]

First of all, evidently, Tertullian uses *sacramentum* with the meanings which it has in Scripture, since he retains the common translation of *mystērion* by *sacramentum*. Secondly, the word appears with a closely related meaning in Tertullian's statements concerning the order of Persons in God; the plan of salvation in the Incarnation, life, death, and resurrection of Christ; and the obscure prediction and prefiguration of Christ in the Old Testament. Moreover, *sacramentum* means religion, religious truth or teaching, the rule of faith, and the rites of Christian initiation.

The proper element in Tertullian's use of the word is his comparison of Christian initiation with the Roman military oath. Considering the fact that the use of *sacramentum* in biblical translations antedates Tertullian, one can hardly accept as convincing the opinion of De Backer that the sacrament as oath is the fundamental sense of the word in Tertullian's texts, from which all other meanings are derived. [23]

---

[22] Besides the studies of Kolping and Mohrmann already cited, see E. de Backer, "Tertullien," in J. de Ghellinck, S.J., *Pour l'histoire du mot "sacramentum"* (Louvain, 1924).

[23] See De Backer, *Op.. cit.*, pp. 143-152.

(4) *Augustine's use of "sacramentum"*.

Though a vast amount of research has been done on *sacramentum* in the works of Augustine, [24] there is no full synthetic account of his thought. I shall indicate the elements which seem to me to bear most directly on our study of the development of Latin sacramental doctrine and theology, especially now in what concerns the very notion of sacrament.

A fundamental distinction in the teaching of St. Augustine is that between *things* and *signs*: "All teaching is of things or signs, but things are learned through signs." [25] Some things are not used to signify anything, for example wood, a stone, a sheep. Other things are also signs. What, then is a sign? It is a thing which, besides the appearance which it brings to the senses, causes something else to come to thought. [26]

Signs which pertain to divine things are called sacraments. [27] A visible sacrifice is the sacrament, that is to say: sacred sign, of the invisible sacrifice. [28] These two statements are the source of the formula later attributed to Augustine as his definition of the sacrament: *sacrae rei signum*, sign of a sacred thing. The authentic Augustinian formula is simply *sacrum signum*, sacred sign. Augustine indicates one more specific factor in the sacrament: it is not any sort of arbitrary sign of a sacred or divine thing, but one which has some likeness to the thing signified. "... For if sacraments did not have a certain likeness to the things of which they are sacraments, they would not be sacraments at all...." [29]

---

[24] See C. Couturier, *"Sacramentum" et "Mysterium" dans l'oeuvre de saint Augustin*, in H. Rondet ..., *Études augustiniennes* (Paris, 1953), 163-332; N.-M. Féret, O.P., *"Sacramentum, Res, dans la langue théologique de S. Augustin,"* RSPT 29 (1940) 218-243; P.-Th. Camelot, O.P.,"Réalisme et Symbolisme dans la doctrine eucharistique de S. Augustin," *RSPT.*, 31 (1947) 394-410; *Id.*, *"Sacramentum fidei"*, in *Augustinus Magister* (Congrès International Augustinien, Paris, 1954) vol. II, pp. 891-896; A. Michel, "Sacrements," *DTC* 14/1, col. 519-525;P. Pourrat, *La théologie sacramentaire*³ (Paris, 1908) pp. 21-31. E. Hocedez, S.J., "La conception augustinienne de sacrement dans le *Tractatus 80 in Ioannem*," *RechScRel* 9 (1919) 1-29; F. Van der Meer, *"Sacramentum chez saint Augustin," La Maison-Dieu* 13 (1948) 50-64.

[25] Omnis doctrina vel rerum est vel signorum, sed res per signa discuntur (*De Doctrina Christiana*, Bk. I.2.2 (PL 34,19).

[26] Signum est enim res, praeter speciem quam ingerit sensibus, aliud aliquid ex se faciens in cogitationem venire ...(*ibid.*, Bk. II.1.1; PL 34, 35).

[27] Nimis longum est convenienter disputare de varietate signorum, *quae cum ad res divinas pertinent, sacramenta appellantur* (*Epistola* 138.7; CSEL 44, 131; PL 33, 527).

[28] Sacrificium ergo visibile invisibilis sacrificii *sacramentum*, id est *sacrum signum* est.... (*De Civitate Dei*, Bk. X.5 (CSEL 40. 452.18-19; PL 41, 282).

[29] ... Si enim sacramenta quandam similitudinem rerum earum, quarum sa-

This notion of sacred sign is perhaps the greatest factor in the development of medieval and classic scholastic definitions of the Christian sacrament. In the works of Augustine, however, *sacramentum* is by no means a sharply defined term. The distinction of meaning between *sacramentum* and *mysterium* is not clear. [30] Moreover, *sacramentum* is closely related to *figura*, *allegoria*, *prophetia*, *velamen*, and *symbolum*. Thus, in a remarkable text in which Augustine is probing the meaning of Jacob's struggle with the angel, he says: "... What comparison can there be of the power of an angel and that of a man? Therefore it is a mystery; therefore it is a sacrament; therefore it is a prophecy; therefore it is a figure; therefore *let us understand*." [31] Whereas in the Greek patristic *mystērion* there is a play of *hidden* and *manifest*, but the emphasis is clearly on the *hidden*, in the Augustinian *sacramentum*, *mysterium*, *figura*, and related words there is an *obscure meaning*, and the emphasis is not on the obscurity but on the meaning: sacraments are signs, causing something else to come to thought: therefore let us understand.

Though it is difficult to differentiate kinds of *sacramentum* and the corresponding classes of things which are called sacraments, three general classes can be indicated: (1) rites or ceremonies of the Old Testament or of the New, or of any religion; (2) symbols or figures; (3) mysteries in the sense of revealed dogmas of the Christian religion.

The first class is very broad. In the Old Testament it includes the sabbath, circumcision, sacrifices, victims, ceremonies, the temple, altars, feasts, priesthood, anointing, and observations concerning food. *Sacramenta* in the New Testament include baptism, the Eucharist, Easter, ordination, anointing, the sign of Christ, the laying on of hands, religious profession, the symbol of faith, Scripture, the Lord's prayer, feasts, Amen, and Alleluia. [32]

The second class, *sacramentum-figura-symbolum*, extends to practically the whole of Scripture. By allegorical exegesis Augustine finds a symbolism in practically all persons, things, and events. [33]

---

cramenta sunt, non haberent, omnino sacramenta non essent.... (*Epistola* 98.9 (CSEL 34, 530.10--531.18; PL33, 363-364).

[30] See Couturier, *op. cit.*, pp. 164-165; 263-274.

[31] Quae virtus comparari potest angeli et hominis? Ergo mysterium est, ergo sacramentum est, ergo prophetia est, ergo figura est; ergo intelligamus....(*Sermo* 122.3.3 (PL 38, 682a).

[32] See Couturier, *op. cit.*, pp. 181,183.

[33] *Ibid.*, pp. 189-155. See also M. Pontet, *L'exégèse de S. Augustin prédicateur* (Paris, 1944) pp. 255-383.

The symbolism in large part refers to the mystery of Christ and his Church.

In the third class are the "mysteries" of the Trinity and the Incarnation, and in general the mystery of Christ, about whom the whole Scripture speaks. [34]

It is clear from this attempt to classify sacraments according to types that the notion of sacrament in Augustine's works is vague and fluid. The divisions really do not separate. Rites, especially the rites of the Old Testament, are figures, types, symbols of the rites of the New Testament and of Christian life. All sacraments pertain somehow to the great sacrament-mystery: Christ and his Church.

A few more observations seem relevant here, concerning (1) the relationship of *sacramentum* to *celebratio*; (2) the relationships of *sacramentum* to *res*; (3) sacraments of the Old Testament in comparison with those of the New; (4) the general context of the history of salvation.

With regard to *sacramentum-celebratio*, I wish simply to note a classic text which at times has been passed on in mutilated form (for example in the text of Isidore, which I shall consider later), and at times I think has been misinterpreted. The portion of the text usually cited is this:"...*Sacramentum est autem in aliqua celebratione, cum rei gestae commemoratio ita fit, ut aliquid etiam significare intelligatur, quod sancte accipiendum est....*" [35] This text should not be cited to indicate that for Augustine liturgical celebration is a dimension of *sacramentum*. What Augustine is saying here is this: not every celebration is sacramental; there *is* a sacrament in a celebration when the commemoration of a past event is made in such a way that it [the commemoration] is understood also to signify something which is to be taken in a holy way. In the context he contrasts the celebrations of the Lord's nativity and of his passion. The birthday of the Lord is not celebrated *in sacramento*, but is simply recalled to memory. The Pasch, on the contrary, is celebrated *in sacramento*: there is a *sacramentum* in its celebration. Why? Because by a multiple symbolism we not only recall Christ's passage from death to life, but also signify our own passage from death to life. Our passage is effected now *by faith*, for the remission of sins, *in hope* of eternal life, of future resurrection and glory. In the subsequent portion of the text Augustine enumerates and

---

[34] See Couturier, *op. cit.*, pp. 256-262.
[35] The text from which this sentence is excerpted is found in *Epistola* 55.1.2--2.3 (CSEL 34, 170-173; PL 33, 204-206).

explains the many symbols involved in the Paschal celebration: the Passage itself, the new month, the third day, the lunar number seven, the turning of the moon, the sabbath, and the Lord's day.

As we have seen, the basic distinction underlying Augustine's notion of sign is that of *thing* and *sign*. Some things are not used to signify anything; others are. In the latter case, the sign makes something else come to thought, and that *something else* is the *res* which technically is correlative with the sign: it is the thing made known, the thing learned through the sign. In various ways Augustine indicates the distinction between sign and thing. In the case of baptism and the Eucharist, which interest us especially, the distinction runs thus:

(1a) what you see on the altar
(1b) what it is; what it means; what great thing it signifies (quam magnae rei sacramentum contineret)

(2a) what you see: bread and cup
(2b) what your faith demands to be taught: the body of Christ, the blood of Christ

(3a) one thing is seen: it has a bodily appearance
(3b) another is understood: it has a spiritual fruit. If you wish to understand the Body of Christ, you are the body of Christ and members. Your mystery was placed on the Lord's table: you receive your mystery (or: the mystery which is you)[36]

(4a) the water of the Sacrament
(4b) what happens in the soul[37]

(5a) the sacrament
(5b) faith, conversion, burial with Christ[38]

(6a) the Paschal celebration: commemoration of the Lord's passage from death to life
(6b) our passage from death to life now through faith, for the remission of sins, in hope of life eternal, resurrection, and glory[39]

(7a) the sacrament of grace
(7b) grace

(8a) baptism
(8b) remission of sins[40]

---

[36] *Sermo* 272 (PL 38, 1246bc--1247a).
[37] *In Epistolam Joannis ad Parthos*, tractatus 6.3.11 (PL 35, 2026c).
[38] *Epistola* 98.9 (CSEL 34, 530.10--531.18; PL 33, 363-364).
[39] *Epistola* 55.1.2 (CSEL 34, 170-173; PL 33, 204-206).
[40] *De baptismo contra Donatistas* 5.21.29 (PL 43, 191ab).

(9a) baptism
(9b) new life, future resurrection[41]

(10a) water showing outwardly the sacrament of grace
(10b) spirit producing inwardly the gift of grace, loosing the bond of sin, reconciling, regenerating[42]

(11a) bath
(11b) regeneration, grace[43]

St. Augustine often compares the sacraments of the two Testaments. There is the same faith, and the same salvation through Christ in both; but the sacraments, the signs, differ in accordance with the different relationships in time. The signs and sacraments of the Old Testament prophesied the Christ to come; ours announce him present.[44] In the desert there was the same spiritual food and drink in mystery, in meaning, but not in appearance: the same Christ who was shown to them figuratively in the rock has been manifested to us in the flesh.[45] Christ fulfilled the first sacraments, which signified his future coming: when by his coming Christ had fulfilled them, they were taken away precisely because they had been fulfilled.[46] The sacraments of the New Law are few in number, easy to perform, most august in meaning, most pure in the manner of their observation.[47] In comparison with the old, they are more powerful,[48] more beneficial, more blessed. The sacraments of the New Testament give salvation; those of the Old promised a Savior.[49]

Finally I should like to note explicitly what is implicit in the data concerning the *res* and the comparison with the sacraments of the Old Testament: how for St. Augustine the Christian sacraments, especially in the texts which we have considered regarding baptism and the Eucharist, are set in the full context of the history of salvation. They announce Christ present as the fulfillment of the signs of the Old Testament. They are in continuity with the faith and salvation of the Old Testament, which was also through Christ.

---

[41] *Contra Faustum* 19.9 CSEL 25, 507; PL 42, 353).
[42] *Epistola* 98.1-2 (CSEL 34, 520-522; PL 33, 359-360).
[43] *Enarratio in Pss.* 77.2 (PL 36, 983d--984a).
[44] *Epistola* 102, 1.12 (CSEL 34, 554; PL 33, 374).
[45] *Enarratio in Pss.*, 77.2 (PL 36, 983d--984a).
[46] *Contra Faustum* 19.13 (CSEL 25, 510-511; PL 42, 355).
[47] *De Doctrina Christiana.* 9.13 (PL 34, 70d--71a).
[48] *Contra Faustum* 19.13 (CSEL 25, 510-511); PL 42, 355).
[49] *Enarratio in Pss.*, 73.2 (PL 36, 930-931).

They commemorate the death and resurrection of Christ, and signify our salvation both present and future.

(5) *Isidore of Seville.*

Without pretending to do justice to the whole of St. Isidore of Seville's theology of the sacrament, I wish to indicate certain elements in his writings which were destined to re-echo through theological works for four centuries. His influence was exerted chiefly through the brief quotable texts which were often repeated without any indication of their context. In context, Isidore retained elements of both the Greek patristic *mystērion* and the Augustinian *sacramentum.* Thus, for example, in his treatment of the Paschal cycle he paraphrased Augustine's text (*Epistola* 55, to which I have referred above), and he spoke of both *recalling to memory* the death and resurrection of Christ, and *considering the meaning of the "sacraments"* (the multiple symbolism). Yet in one of his formulae which was destined to survive from the same context, he gives a definition which does not contain the notion of sign, which gives a bewildering example of a sacrament, and which shifts the emphasis to the hidden. Here is Isidore's text:

> There is a sacrament in some celebration when an event occurs in such way that it is understood to signify something which is to be taken in a holy way. [Examples of] sacraments are *baptism and chrism, body and blood.* These are called sacraments *because under the cover of bodily things divine power more secretly effects their salvation, whence they are so called from secret power or from holy [things]. They happen fruitfully in the Church, because the Holy Spirit remaining in it produces the effect of these sacraments.... whence in Greek [that] is called mystery which has a secret and hidden disposition.* [50]

First, there is a significant change in the formula of Augustine's *Epistola* 55, which I have quoted above, p. 16: *rei gestae commemoratio* (the commemoration of an event) is changed to *res gesta* (an event). One suspects that the *res gesta* is not the past event, but

---

[50] Sacramentum est in aliqua celebratione, cum *res gesta* ita fit ut aliquid significare intelligatur, quod sancte accipiendum est. Sunt autem sacramenta *baptismus* et *chrisma, corpus et sanguis.* Quae ob id *sacramenta* dicuntur, *quia sub tegumento corporalium rerum virtus divina secretius salutem eorumdem operatur unde et a secretis virtutis vel a sacris dicuntur.* Quae ideo fructuose penes Ecclesiam fiunt, quia sanctus in ea manens Spiritus eumdem sacramentorum operatur effectum.... *unde et Graece mysterium dicitur quod secretam et reconditam habeat dispositionem.* (*Etymologiae,* bk. VI, ch. 19, nn. 39-42 (PL 82, 255cd).

the action of the liturgical celebration. In any case, the explicit mention of commemoration is gone.

Then, in the enumeration of sacraments, along with baptism and chrism Isidore mentions the body and blood [of Christ in the Eucharist]. For Augustine, the perceptible sacraments are the bread and the cup of wine: the body and blood are the first great *thing* signified. Isidore's including the body and blood as sacraments was to have its own important consequences in the course of later efforts to define *sacramentum*.

The following proposition gives what is to be regarded as a definition of the sacrament: sacraments are so called because under the cover of bodily things divine power more secretly effects their salvation: whence they are named from secret power [literally: the secrets of power] or from the holy [things]. The definition makes no mention of sign, though the notion may be implicit in the expression "their salvation": that is, the salvation which the sacraments signify. The whole emphasis is on secret power: the Holy Spirit working under the cover of perceptible bodily things. These perceptible things are not signs so much as covers which hide. Understandably then Isidore concludes with the reference to the Greek *mystērion*, stressing the hidden, the secret.

I leave the treatment of Isidore for now, having set forth what I consider the most important fragments of his works which had a role in later development of definitions of the sacrament. In the next chapter I shall indicate the role which these texts played.

CHAPTER III

DEVELOPMENT OF SCHOLASTIC DEFINITIONS OF THE SACRAMENT [1]

Evidently it is impossible to undertake within this work a complete history of scholastic definitions. I shall review here the principal formulae proposed during the period from the eleventh to the thirteenth century, concluding with St. Thomas' definitions. I shall add a few representative definitions of later scholastics.

The early classic formulae have more than merely historical interest, for, together with the early patristic and theological *auctoritates*, they provide the background for the terminology of many Church documents. In the last section of this chapter I shall indicate some of the echoes of scholastic formulae in these Church documents. I do not include here Vatican Council II, since its teaching and terminology reflect some later theological developments.

THE OCCASION: BERENGARIUS' USE OF AUGUSTINIAN FORMULAE

Though I am not interested in treating here Berengarius' Eucharistic doctrine and the question of his errors concerning the real presence, I wish to note his use of Augustinian sign formulae, which were extremely important as a catalyst in the development of classic medieval definitions or descriptions of the sacrament.

During the four centuries which had passed from the time of Isidore of Seville, the Isidorean conception prevailed. Its influence is witnessed in the writings of Paschasius Radbertus, Ratramnus of Corbie, and Fulbert of Chartres. On the contrary, the Augustinian notion of the sacrament as sign is not conspicuous.

Berengarius of Tours changed the situation by his use of Augustinian formulae in support of his opinions on the Eucharist. His technique is shown especially well in his letter against Adel-

---

[1] For the history of this development see the excellent study of D. Van Den Eynde, O.F.M., *Les définitions des sacrements pendant la première période de la théologie scolastique* (1050-1240) (Rome-Louvain, 1950).

mannus [Almannus], in which he cites the following definitions or principles, either taken directly from Augustine's works, or adapted according to Augustine's mind: sacrament, that is sacred sign; a sacrament is a visible form of invisible grace; a sacrament is a visible sign of an invisible divine thing; all bodily sacraments are nothing but certain quasi visible words, sacrosanct indeed, yet changeable and temporal; visible sacrifices are signs of invisible [sacrifices]; a sign is a thing which besides the appearance which it brings to the senses causes something else to come to *knowledge, cognitionem* [cf. Augustine's *thought, cogitationem*]. [2] Elsewhere he cites Augustine's statement that a sacrament must have a likeness to the thing of which it is a sacrament. [3]

In the controversies over Berengarius' opinion, and in subsequent elaboration of definitions of the sacrament, the authority of Augustine prevailed, and his formulae figured prominently. Through the writings especially of Lanfranc of Bec, Ivo of Chartres, and Peter Abelard, they passed into common use among theologians. Before noting some of the stages of the elaboration of definitions, it may be good to reflect on some of the factors which increased the difficulty of defining the sacrament.

COMPLICATING FACTORS

A number of factors confused the issue of the definition of the sacrament and made the whole process seem painfully slow and the final products rather unsatisfactory.

(1) *What was to be defined.*

To begin with, it was not clear *what* was to be defined: what persons, things, or actions were involved. I have noted some of the things which were called *sacramenta* of the Old Testament or of the New in the writings of St. Augustine. Besides the many examples which belong to the class of ritual sacraments, one must recall that Christ and the Church were sacraments, and all the persons, things, and actions which in any way signified Christ and his Church. Even if one limited the field to ritual or ceremonial sacraments, there re-

---

[2] See Beringerius, "*Purgatoria epistola contra Almannum,*" in E. Martène and U. Durand, *Thesaurus Novus Anecdotorum*, tomus IV (Lutetiae Parisiorum, 1717) 112-113.

[3] Beringarius, *De sacra Coena adversus Lanfrancum*, 44, edited by W. H. Beekenkamp (La Haye, 1941) p. 150: text quoted by Van den Eynde, *op. cit.*, p.6.

mained questions concerning which were to be included: sacraments of the Old Law and the New, or only those of the New; if only those of the New, both "major" and "minor" rites, or only the major? A lot of sifting had to be done before theologians could fix on what they were trying to define.

(2) The number of major rites.

Even when theologians restricted their consideration to baptism, the Eucharist, and other major rites, at the beginning of the process of definition the number of these major rites was not yet a matter of consensus. It was hardly possible to treat the sacrament universally from the outset.

(3) Factors to be included.

In particular, when theologians considered baptism or the Eucharist, they had to reckon with many elements which enter into the whole baptismal or Eucharistic rite. In both cases a full consideration of the factors would include the roles of Father, Son, and Holy Spirit; of the human nature and operation of Christ, and especially of his passion, death, and resurrection; of the whole Church somehow present and acting, and of the particular minister in whom all of the other agents' action is concentrated and manifested in the actual performance of the rite. Concerning the minister, there are questions about the bearing of his special power, his own holiness and devotion, and his intention.

At the level of the perceptible external action, there is the whole complex of things, actions, and words making up the full ceremony, and at their core those elements which are considered essential and indispensable in any case. In baptism there is question of the recipient, of his or her role in baptism; of the permanent effect which gradually is called the character, and which in Augustinian terminology was called the permanent baptism, or permanent sacrament; and of the other effects of the rite, since the saving action comes to term only in the full human response. In the case of the Eucharist there is question of the visible elements of bread and wine, the words of consecration, the invisible Body and Blood of Christ, the whole Body comprised of the members of Christ and signified also by the external sacrament, and finally the effects of sanctification in the participant in the sacrifice and the recipient of the sacrament.

All of these elements are involved in what could be called the encounter of men and women with Christ, and through Christ with the Father in baptism or the Eucharist. In this whole complex what precisely is to be called the sacrament, and how can it be defined? The relevancy of this question, and the reality of the problem, may be indicated briefly by two examples: (a) in the course of the twelfth century baptism was identified with these three different factors: water, dipping or washing, and the character; [4] (b) Stephen Langton held that these elements are of the *substance* of baptism: the formula of words, water, the intention, and the person of the baptizer and of the one to be baptized. [5]

(4) *Elements of both Isidorean and Augustinian sacramental teaching.*

Isidore's definition of the sacrament, emphasizing the hidden divine power at work under the cover of bodily things, and his listing of the Body and Blood of Christ as sacraments, were bound to cause difficulty for any theologian attempting to work out a definition on the lines of the Augustinian perceptible sign. Even Augustine contributed to the difficulty of applying his own notion of sign: in his writings against the Donatists he insisted that baptism remains, is permanent, that the Christian sacraments cling even to those who do not have the Holy Spirit and charity. [6] Such a conception gravitates toward the invisible permanent effect, rather than toward the perceptible sacramental rite. Understandably a theologian would be inclined to insist on the element of greater dignity: on the Body and Blood of Christ as more properly sacrament than the visible appearances and the words of consecration; and on the permanent consecration, the character, as more important than the passing rite.

Reviewing the history of the development of classic definitions of the sacrament, one must keep in mind that the "tradition" of calling the Body and Blood of Christ sacraments was a school tradition going back to the period of the prevalence of the Isidorean definition. In the Isidorean sense of sacrament, such predication is perfectly intelligible. What is to be said of later theological usage,

---

[4] See N. Haring, S.A.C., "Berengar's Definitions of *Sacramentum* and Their Influence on Medieval Sacramentology," *Medieval Studies* 10 (1948) 109-106; and A. Landgraf, "Die Definition der Taufe," in *Dogmengeschichte der Frühscholastik*, vol. III/2 (Regensburg, 1955) 7-46, also published in *Gregorianum* 27 (1946) 200-219; 353-383.

[5] Stephen Langton, *Quaestiones* (Cambridge, St. John's College, 57, f. 308c) as cited by D. Van den Eynde, O.F.M. "The Theory of the Composition of the Sacraments in Early Scholasticism (1125-1240)" *Franciscan Studies* 11 (1951) 125.

[6] For a summary of Augustinian formulae of this type, see N. Haring, *p. cit.*, p. 121.

after the triumph of the Augustinian type of definition, remains to be seen.

(5) *Sacraments of the Old and New Testaments.*

In the fluctuation between definitions common to sacraments of both the Old and the New Testaments and definitions restricted to the sacraments of the New, the matter was complicated by differences of opinion concerning the efficacy of the sacraments of the Old Testament. Some theologians held that efficacy is essential to a sacrament in the strict sense; that the sacraments of the Old Law were not efficacious, and hence not sacraments strictly speaking. Others admitted that efficacy is essential, but held that the sacraments of the Old Law too were efficacious, and hence they defined sacrament in a way to include both the Old and the New.

(6) *Method.*

Beyond these difficulties arising from the subject matter, there was another arising from a defect in method. It was the reliance on, and insistence upon, the method of citation of *auctoritates*. In a technical sense in medieval theology, the *auctoritates* were not "authorities": the Saints or Doctors or Fathers who by their authority were to be revered and followed. Rather they were the texts themselves, quotable fragments separated from their context, and retained with veneration, if not with equal care for exact quotation and for the sense in context. Too much of the medieval theological effort was hampered by the incubus of these *auctoritates*, principally Augustinian formulae which, though they expressed precious insights, still belonged to a stage of inchoate theological conceptualization, and were retained and manipulated in a variety of ways. Too much attention was paid to these *auctoritates*, and too little to the full reality of Christian life and worship, and to the full biblical doctrine concerning baptism especially. As a consequence, few theologians broke out of the narrow range of possible manipulation--and adulteration--of revered formulae. [7]

---

[7] For a good treatment of the method and use of the *auctoritates* see M.-D. Chenu, O.P., *Introduction a l'étude de Saint Thomas d'Aquin* (Montréal: Institut d'Études Médiévales--Paris: Vrin, 1950) pp. 106-131; *Toward Understanding Saint Thomas*. Translated ... by A.-M. Landry, O.P. and D. Hughes, O.P. (Chicago: Regnery, c. 1964) pp. 126-155.

(7) *The notion of definition.*

Finally I should like to note what is a more serious defect in method: it regards the very notion of definition and of the manner in which a reasonably satisfactory definition may be reached. In a sense the definitions which are the result of the long dialectical process of the eleventh and twelfth centuries are adequate: they pertain to all and only the sacraments of the New Law, where this is the intention of the definer. They are sufficient to tag all of the Christian sacraments, and only these, and thus to set them off from all other rites.

In another sense, measured by the rather ingenuous aspirations of theologians of the high middle ages, these definitions are woefully inadequate. The fault lies in ancient and medieval notions of definition as expressing a full knowledge of the thing defined. Thus "rational animal" is regarded as a definition by genus and specific difference, expressing a full knowledge of man's essence. Yet who among men or women has ever really grasped the essence of human being?

What is the "essence" of the Christian sacrament, and what sort of definition could ever express the full knowledge of the "essence"? What is the full reality whose knowledge and definition is sought? Even if the sacrament is taken to be the external symbolic complex of word and action, its full reality, its full meaning and value, can be grasped and expressed with some relative adequacy only by one who has come to an understanding of the sacrament in the full field of relationships which alone can somehow define it. Even then, such a definition would be a delimitation in terms of correlations, and of a relatively full field of relationships. It would point to the reality which grounds the relationships, but would never express a full grasp of that reality. In this case the reality involved is the whole of the divine saving action as it bears on this man or women here and now, and as it is directing him or her to fulfillment in eternal life. This reality is beyond human grasp, just as the meaning of Scripture is beyond it.

In part, then, the medieval definers aspired too highly: they sought to grasp and express fully the essences of things, sacraments included. In part they failed because of a defective method, relying on the sifting of texts and *auctoritates* rather than on a patient study of the data, of the field of relationships to be established by a thorough study of revealed truth, a deep reflection on the reality of Christian life and worship, and a continuing effort to answer the ever-rising further questions.

The Principal Early Definitions and Formulae

(1) *Sacrum signum* and *sacrae rei signum* (sacred sign, and sign of a sacred thing). [8]

The first is an authentic Augustinian formula, proposed by Berengarius as the principal definition, and recognized as a definition by Lanfranc, Ivo, Alger of Liège, and Abelard. The second formula, a modification of the first, appears in the early twelfth century. Master Simon, adversary of Berengarius, changed the definition to *sacrum signatum* (the sacred signified), because he held that the Body of Christ must be called sign and signified. In general the formula *sacrae rei signum*, adopted even by Berengarius' adversaries, was applied to the Body and Blood of Christ, with evident difficulty in explaining how they were signs. Retained by most theologians, it was not regarded as a strict definition, since it was too broad.

(2) *Invisibilis gratiae visibilis forma* (the visible form of invisible grace). [9]

Proposed by Berengarius, consistent with Augustine's thought, but not a direct quotation, the formula was kept by the *Summa Sententiarum* and by Peter Lombard and his school. Later it was criticized as not fitting all the sacraments, or what is most important in them. This was the position of those who affirmed against Berengarius that the Body of Christ is a sacrament, and who developed the new terminology to fit it: *sacramentum et res*: (sacrament and thing). Asked how it could be visible, they replied with a variety of weak explanations: to the angels, to God, to the blessed with glorified eyes. Failing to explain, they attacked the definition. A similar position, consistent with the Isidorean notion of sacrament, was maintained with regard to baptism, confirmation, and orders, and was extended even to the anointing of the sick and to matrimony. By the thirteenth century this formula was regarded as a good generic definition.

(3) *Hugh of St. Victor's description and definition.*[10]

Explaining the definition *sacrae rei signum* (sign of a sacred thing), Hugh indicates the difference between an ordinary sign and a

---

[8] See Van den Eynde, *Les définitions des sacrements....*, pp. 18-26; 41; 63-68; 69-76.

[9] *Ibid.*, pp. 27-31; 37-38; 40; 77-91; 105-106; 117-127.

[10] *Ibid.*, pp. 32-37; 52-56; 113-114. See also H. Weisweiler, S.J., *Die Wirk-*

sacrament: a sign only signifies by reason of its institution (i.e. its having been constituted a sign); a sacrament also *represents* by reason of its likeness to the thing signified. Moreover, a sign can signify a thing, but not confer it; but in a sacrament there is not only signification but also *efficacy*. Summing up, Hugh describes the sacrament thus: by institution it signifies, by likeness it represents, by sanctification it confers [the thing signified and represented]. [11] Thus Hugo gathers in one description most of the elements traditionally associated with the sacrament. Most noteworthy is his inclusion of efficacy.

In his treatise *De Sacramentis* Hugh proposes a fuller and more perfect definition than *sacrae rei signum*: a sacrament is a bodily or material element externally proposed to the senses, by likeness representing, and by institution signifying, and by sanctification containing some invisible spiritual grace. Though in this definition he says *containing* rather than *conferring*, Hugh goes on to explain. A sacrament must have *sanctification*, through which it *contains* the thing signified and is *efficacious in conferring* it to those who are to be sanctified. [12] Though the *bodily or material element* might suggest that Hugh regarded the sacrament as something stable and permanent, a sort of consecrated material element, this impression is corrected in the context, where he says that the matter of the sacrament is either things or deeds (gesture, movement, act) or words. Without the explanation supplied in the context, Hugh's definition is imperfect, and it was rarely cited in the twelfth century except by canonists and theologians of the school of Bologna. In the thirteenth century, slightly enlarged, it was regarded as the equivalent of the definition given by Peter Lombard.

(4) *The definition in the Summa Sententiarum.*

A sacrament is the visible form of the invisible grace conferred in it, that is: of the grace which the sacrament itself confers. For it is not only the sign of a sacred thing, but also

---

samkeit der Sakramente nach Hugo von St. Viktor (Freiburg Br., 1932); *Id.*, "Hugos von St. Viktor 'Dialogus de sacramentis legis naturalis et scriptae' als frühscholastisches Quellenwerk," in *Miscellanea G. Mercati* (Vatican City, 1946) vol. II, pp. 179-219.

[11] In sacramento autem non sola significatio est, sed etiam efficacia;ut videlicet simul et ex institutione significet, et ex similitudine repraesentet, et conferat ex sanctificatione (*De Sacramentis Legis Naturalis et Scriptae Dialogus* (PL 176, 34d--35a).

[12] *De Sacramentis Christianae Fidei* 9.2 (PL 176, 317c--318b).

efficacy.[13] After enjoying a rapid success, this definition was replaced by Lombard's.

(5) *Peter Lombard's definition.*

After giving the common definitions, Augustine's division of signs into natural and given (*data*), and his axiom on the need of likeness, Lombard proposes his own proper definition: a sacrament properly so called is the sign of God's grace and the form of invisible grace in such a way that it bears its image and is its cause.[14] In his discussion of the definitions current in his time, Lombard excludes both *sacrum secretum* and *sacrum signatum* from consideration, since here there is question of the sacrament in so far as it is a sign. Lombard's definition stands out for its emphasis on grace and on causality. He proposes it as a proper definition of the sacrament of the New Law. Its defects are pleonasm and exaggeration of the notion of natural likeness of the sign to grace. In Peter's own theology, two elements make it difficult to apply his definition to the sacraments of the New Law: according to him, matrimony is a sacrament, but does not confer grace; moreover, among the sacraments of the Old Law, circumcision conferred the same remedy for sin which baptism now gives.

Lombard's definition dominated subsequent theology of the sacraments, though it was often cited rather freely, and ultimately passed on in the form given it by William of Auxerre: *invisibilis gratiae visibilis forma ita ut eius similitudinem gerat et causa existat* (the visible form of invisible grace such that it bears its likeness and is its cause).

(6) *A common axiom.*

Finally we may note a formula which appeared in the twelfth century and became the most common axiom concerning the sacraments: *id efficit quod figurat* (it produces what it signifies [or: that of which it is a figure or likeness]).

---

[13] *Summa Sententiarum*, tractatus 4.1 (PL 176, 117b). See Van den Eynde, *op. cit.*, pp. 37-40; 48-56.

[14] Sacramentum enim proprie dicitur quod ita signum est gratiae et invisibilis gratiae forma, ut ipsius imaginem gerat et causa existat (*Liber Sententiarum* 4.1 (PL176, 117b). See Van den Eynde, *op. cit.*, 40-46; 49-52; 103-110.

REFLECTION

Three things seem particularly noteworthy about the results of this process of formation of definitions of the sacrament.

First, in spite of the prejudice caused by Berengarius' abuse, the "Augustinian" definitions, stressing the sign, prevailed over the Isidorean definition. After long controversy the notion of the sacrament as sensibly perceptible withstood the efforts of Berengarius' adversaries to direct sacramental theology to the *sacrum secretum signatum*, the hidden sacred thing which was signified.

Second, to provide a proper definition of the sacrament of the New Law, theologians added to the notion of sign that of efficacy. In the stage of theological development reflected by Peter Lombard's *Sentences*, four elements characterized a sacramental theology which was not yet completely coherent: sign, efficacy, the number seven for the sacraments of the New Law, and the doctrine then common concerning matrimony: it was a sacrament of the New Law, but did not confer grace.

Third, we may note the role played by these three elements: the Isidorean notion of the sacrament, his listing of the Body and Blood of Christ among the sacraments, and the Augustinian notion of the permanent sacrament. Though for a time they confused the work of definition of the sacrament, yet eventually they contributed to the elaboration of an important concept: that of the *sacramentum et res* ([both] sacrament [sign] and thing [signified]). This terminology was applied in different ways to the Body and Blood of Christ under the appearances of bread and wine, to the permanent consecration or character produced by baptism, confirmation, and orders, and then to analogous effects of other sacraments. With variations, the terminology provided for the *sacramentum tantum* (the external, perceptible sign, which is *only* a sacrament), the *sacramentum et res* (the invisible effect: which is the first thing, *res*, signified by the external sign, and is itself somehow the sign of a further effect), and the *res tantum* (the thing only: signified and effected finally, and not signifying).

With a great dialectical effort, theologians gave various explanations of how the invisible sacrament and thing could be a sign. The real explanation is not to be found in such dialectical play, but in the simple historical fact that before the prevalence of the Augustinian sign formulae there were school traditions which called the Body and Blood of Christ and the permanent sacrament or character sacraments. The nomenclature becomes an anomaly after the adoption of the sacrament-sign conception.

St. Thomas' Definitions [15]

Having traced the development of the principal definitions and axioms during the formative period of early scholasticism, I shall treat separately the principal definition proposed by St. Thomas, in the *Summa Theologiae*. It represents a later, more fully developed stage of sacramental theology, and it was destined to influence a long school tradition. Moreover, its setting in the whole of St. Thomas' conception of the theology of redemption and of worship is significant.

In his commentary on Peter Lombard's *Books of Sentences*, St. Thomas regarded Lombard's definition as the most complete. [16] As for the difference between the sacraments of the Old Law and of the New, they are not species of the same genus, but rather analogous. Strictly speaking, a sacrament is what *causes* sanctity. What merely signifies it is only a sacrament in a limited sense, *secundum quid*. [17]

In two minor works St. Thomas offers no personal definition of the sacrament. He repeats in his work *On the Articles of Faith and the Sacraments of the Church* (1261-1268) some classic formulae, and in this work and in his *On the Form of Absolution in Sacramental Penance* (1269-1272) he insists especially on the efficacy of the sacraments of the New Law, which differ in this respect from those of the Old. The sacraments of the Old Law only signified the grace of Christ: they did not cause it. Hence the Apostle in Gal 4.9 calls them *needy and weak elements*. The sacraments of the New Law contain and confer grace. [18] They effect what they signify, and they signify by both the matter and the formula of words. They are not like the sacraments of the Old Law, which only signified, but did nothing. If the priest merely discerned and pronounced the sinner's absolution, he would do nothing, but only signify. He does something by applying his ministry of absolution: the sacramental words effect what they signify. [19]

---

[15] See H.-F. Dondaine, O.P., "La définition des sacrements dans la *Somme théologique*," RSPT 31 (1947) 214-228; E. Frutsaert, S.J., "La définition du sacrement dans saint Thomas," NRT 55 (1928) 401-409; H. Schillebeeckx, O.P., *De sacramentele heilseconomie* (Antwerpen 'T Groeit, 1951) pp. 125-183.

[16] In IV Sent. d. 1, q. 1, a. 1, qc. 3 resp.

[17] Ibid. qc. 3 ad 5.

[18] *De Articulis Fidei et Ecclesiae Sacramentis*, in S. Thomas Aquinatis *Opuscula Theologica*, ed. R. Verardo, O.P. (Romae: Marietti, 1954) vol. I, pp. 139-151, n. 612.

[19] *De Forma Absolutionis Poenitentiae Sacramentalis*, in the edition cited in the preceding note, pp. 169-180, nn. 678, 693, 699.

There is a definite shift in Thomas' treatment of the definition of the sacrament in the *Summa Theologiae*. *Sacramentum* can be said analogously of anything which has a relationship to holiness. If it has some hidden holiness in itself, it is called *sacramentum* in the sense of *sacrum secretum*. But a thing can be called *sacramentum* if it has the relationship of cause or sign, or any other kind of relationship, to such holiness. In the case of the sacraments of the New Law we are speaking of sacraments especially as they involve the relationship of sign. Consequently this kind of sacrament is put in the genus of sign. [20] This is the first step in the definition of the sacrament. Whereas in the commentary on the *Sentences* Thomas had emphasized causality as the principal element in the sacrament, here he shifts to the relationship of sign. [21]

Not every sign of a sacred thing is properly called a sacrament. Properly speaking a sacrament is a sign of a sacred thing considered precisely as it is sanctifying men:

> ... Signs are given to men, who reach the unknown through what is known. Accordingly that is properly called sacrament which is the sign of a sacred thing which pertains to men, so that a sacrament properly so called, in the sense in which we are now speaking of sacraments, is the *sign of a sacred thing in so far as it is sanctifying men (signum rei sacrae inquantum est sanctificans homines)*.

> ... Sensibly perceptible creatures signify something sacred, namely the divine wisdom and goodness, in so far as they [the divine wisdom and goodness] are sacred in themselves: but not in so far as we are sanctified through them. Therefore they cannot be called sacraments in the sense in which we are now speaking of sacraments.

> ... Some things pertaining to the Old Testament signified Christ's holiness in so far as he is holy in himself. Some things on the contrary signified his holiness in so far as through it we are sanctified: such as the immolation of the paschal lamb signified the immolation of Christ, by which we have been sanctified. Such things are called properly sacraments of the Old Law. [22]

That which is signified, the *sacred thing sanctifying men*, is threefold, but with a unity of order. The sacraments signify the *cause of our sanctification, which is Christ's passion; the form* of our

---

[20] S.T. III, 60, a. 1 resp. and ad 3.
[21] He proposes his own former conception now in the form of an argument opposed to his present position, and answers it in a purely dialectical fashion: *ibid.*, arg. 1 and ad 1.
[22] *Ibid.* 60, 2, resp., ad 1, and ad 2.

sanctification, which consists in grace and the virtues; and the *ultimate end* of our sanctification, which is eternal life. Hence the sacrament is a sign commemorative of what preceded, the passion of Christ; demonstrative of what is effected in us through the passion of Christ, grace; and prognostic, that is predictive, of future glory. Though it thus signifies many things, the sacrament is not an ambiguous sign, apt to deceive. It signifies many things in so far as they have a certain unity of order. [23]

It seems that St. Thomas has completed his definition of the sacrament with these three steps, in the first three articles of question 60. Clearly this definition differs from that given in the commentary on the *Sentences*. Here he stresses the sign and says nothing of efficacy. Consequently his definition can be applied to the sacraments of the Old Law and to others, and as a matter of fact St. Thomas proceeds to make a comparison of diverse sacraments. [24] The threefold sacred thing signified is the same in the Old Testament and in the New, though the sacraments of the Old were merely prognostic, and did not signify a holiness conferred through the sacraments themselves. [25] He considers too the aptness of sacraments universally, and then according to the diverse historical conditions of mankind. [26]

Though Thomas' definition emphasizes sign rather than cause, there remains a sign-cause tension in his theology, which appears when he treats the question of the causality of the sacraments. It is necessary to say that the sacraments of the New Law cause grace instrumentally. [27] Nor is there any obstacle in the fact that the sacrament is a sign, and that the character of sign belongs to the effect rather than to the cause. Here, as in the commentary on the *Sentences* the explanation is subtle:

> ... A principal cause cannot be said properly to be a sign of its effect, though the effect be hidden and the cause be manifest to the senses. But an instrumental cause, if it is manifest, can be called a sign of a hidden effect. The reason is that it is not only a cause, but also somehow an effect, in so far as it is moved by the principal agent. According to this the sacraments of the New Law are at once causes and signs. Hence, as it is commonly said, they *effect what they signify* (*efficiunt quod figurant*). From this it is clear that they have perfectly the nature of sacrament (*habent perfecte rationem sacramenti*), in that

---

[23] Cf. *Ibid.* 60, 3 resp. and ad 1.
[24] 60, 5 ad 3.
[25] 60, 4 resp. and ad 2,3.
[26] 61, 1-4.
[27] 62, 1 resp.

they are related to something sacred not only as sign but also as cause. [28]

The explanation is ingenious, but it is not the most important element in this text. More interesting is Thomas' conclusion, that the sacraments of the New Law have the nature of sacrament *perfectly* because they are not only signs of the sacred, but also causes. His definition stressed sign, and is applicable to sacraments not only of the New Law, but also of the Old, and of the state of man before the Old Law was given. Still, only the sacraments of the New Law have the full nature of sacrament. I should say that in this dialectical play his definition is analogous, not generic. Sacraments in all states of human nature have analogous relationships to the sacred. Causality is not the final, specific difference in the sacraments of the New Law, within the *genus* of sign. If it were, then the tension between two *genera*, one as the specific difference of the other, would be beyond resolution. Rather, the twofold relationship of sign and cause is characteristic of the sacraments of the New Law: the most perfect *mode* within the analogy of sacrament.

The sacraments of the New Law contain grace in two ways, as in signs and in a cause. [29] They have power [30] from the passion of Christ. [31] Thus they differ from the sacraments of the Old Law, which could not confer grace by their own power nor by the power of the passion of Christ, but only signified a faith by which men were being justified. [32] Obviously Thomas distinguishes as clearly here as in his earlier writings between the sacraments of the New and Old Laws. Here in the *Summa Theologiae* too only the sacraments of the New Law have perfectly the nature of sacrament.

Beyond what pertains directly to the definition of the sacrament in the *Summa*, two things are notable regarding the doctrinal context of Thomas' consideration of the sacraments. First, he clearly relates the sacraments to the whole mystery of the plan of the incarnation and redemption, as his teaching on the threefold meaning of the sacraments shows. Secondly, the sacraments are intimately related to his general theology of worship. This relationship is suggested only in passing allusions in the questions which

---

[28] 62, 1 ad 1. See also In IV Sent. d. 1, q. 1, a. 1, qc 4 ad 1.
[29] 62, 3 resp.
[30] 62, 4.
[31] 62, 5.
[32] 62, 6.

deal directly with the sacraments. It is clear in his treatment of worship,[33] and of the ceremonial precepts of the Old Law.[34]

SOME OTHER DEFINITIONS OR DESCRIPTIONS

Without attempting to give a complete history of scholastic definitions of the sacrament, I should like to give a few representative formulae, and note the elements stressed in them.

Understandably many theologians have retained the definition given by St. Thomas in the *Summa Theologiae*. Among them are John of St. Thomas, Billuart, Hugon, Daffara, and Doronzo.[35] The definition is usually regarded as generic and univocal, fitting all sacraments of the Old and New Laws.

Suarez, intending to interpret St. Thomas' definition, defines thus: "A sacrament is a sensibly perceptible sign instituted to give some sanctification and to signify true holiness of soul. Or (if we wish to define in the Aristotelian manner) we can say: a sacrament is a sacred, sensibly perceptible ceremony, somehow sanctifying men, by its institution signifying true holiness of soul."[36] By his distinction between conferring *some* sanctification and signifying *true* holiness of soul, Suarez allows for the difference between the sacraments of the Old and New Laws: those of the Old signified true interior holiness, but conferred only ritual sanctification; those of the New both signify and confer true interior holiness.

De Lugo defines the sacrament as a sensibly perceptible ceremony which, sanctifying the recipient by its use, signifies internal grace, of which it is a cause.[37]

Among the modern manualists, Lennerz defined thus: "a sensibly perceptible rite, instituted by Christ, which signifies interior grace and confers it by the very act performed."[38]

For my present purposes, this sketch of stages in the conceptualization of "sacrament" will suffice. In the following section

---

[33] S.T. II-II, 81-91.

[34] S.T. I-II, 101-103.

[35] See the full treatment of the matter in E. Doronzo, *De Sacramentis in Genere* (Milwaukee: Bruce, 1946) pp. 33-79.

[36] Franciscus Suarez, *In Tertiam Partem D. Thomae...*, disputatio I, sect. 4 (*Opera Omnia*, vol. XX. Parisiis, 1860) p. 23.

[37] Ioannis De Lugo, *Disputationes Scholasticae...*, t. III (Parisiis, 1869) *Tractatus de Sacramentis in Genere*, disp. I, sect. II, n. 23, p. 203.

[38] H. Lennerz, S.I., *De Sacramento Baptismi*³ (Romae, 1955) n. 90.

I shall note some of the uses of common terminology in some documents of the Church.

"Sacramentum" in Church Documents

I am concerned here only with elements in Church documents touching questions of definition or description of "sacrament," containing elements of formulae elaborated by theologians in the process of conceptualization.

I note first three texts which, in a sense, do not concern the definition of *sacrament* as it is generally considered; yet I should say that they pertain to any relatively adequate definition which may be given ultimately. They concern the agent or principal cause of the sacraments. Thus, the sinfulness of a human minister does not block the effects of a baptism duly performed, since it is *Christ* who baptizes. [39]

A second text, in the Council of Florence's decree for the Armenians, comes in the reply to questions concerning the form of baptism, and the Council states an important truth as the basis of its decision: "...the principal cause, from which baptism has power, is the Holy Trinity; the minister is [an] instrumental [cause]." [40]

Finally, concerning justification, the Council of Trent teaches that the principal cause is the merciful God who freely washes and sanctifies.... the instrumental [cause] is the sacrament of baptism. [41]

In my judgment, the first document which clearly echoes theological formulae is that of Innocent III distinguishing three [elements] which are discerned in the sacrament of the Eucharist: the

---

[39] Cf. Nicolaus I, in his reply to the Bulgarians, Nov. 13, 866: DS 644. Nicolaus is not anticipating here later documents, but echoing the teaching of St. Augustine. Against the Donatists Augustine holds that the sinfulness of the minister does not impede baptism's effects, because "Our God is a living God, and it is he who baptizes" (*Contra Epistulam Parmeniani*, lib. 2, c. 4 [CSEL 51. 71]). In his commentary on *John*, regarding the text "though he himself did not baptize, but his disciples," Augustine wrote: "He himself, and not he himself; he himself by power, they by ministry. Their role as servants moved them to baptize, [but] the power of baptizing remained in Christ. Those therefore whom Judas baptized are not to be baptized again. Are those whom John [the Baptist] baptized to be baptized again? Certainly, but not by a repetition of [the same] baptism. For those whom John baptized, John baptized. Those whom Judas baptized, *Christ baptized*. Thus those whom a drunkard or a murderer or an adulterer baptized, if it was Christ's baptism, Christ baptized" (*In Joannem*, tractatus 5, 18 [PL 35. 1424]).

[40] Council of Florence, "Decree for the Armenians," Nov. 22, 1439: DS 1314.

[41] Council of Trent, "Decree on Justification," Jan. 13, 1547: DS 1529.

visible form, the reality of the body, and the spiritual power. The form is that of bread and wine, the reality is that of the flesh and blood, the power is that of unity and love. The first is "a sacrament and not a thing (*sacramentum et non res*)." The second is "a sacrament and a thing (*sacramentum et res*)." The third is "a thing and not a sacrament (*res et non sacramentum*)." But the first is the sacrament of a twofold thing. The second is the sacrament of one thing and the thing of another [sacrament]. The third is the thing of a twofold sacrament. [42]

There is an interesting development in the texts which enumerate the Christian sacraments. In an early partial enumeration: the sacrament of the body and blood of our Lord Jesus Christ, baptism, confession of sins, matrimony, or other church sacraments; [43] and in the full mention of the seven sacraments by the Council of Lyons II [44] no definition of *sacrament* is given. On the contrary, the Council of Florence, in its "Decree for the Armenians," not only gives the full enumeration of the seven sacraments, but, taking over much of St. Thomas' teaching in his short early work on the articles of faith and the sacraments of the Church, gives a fairly ample treatment of what can be said to pertain to the definition of the sacrament. The seven sacraments of the New Law differ greatly from those of the Old Law. Those [of the Old Law] did not cause grace, but only bore a likeness to (*figurabant*) the grace to be given through the passion of Christ; ours both contain grace and confer it upon those who receive them worthily. There are three elements by which they are performed: things as matter, words as form, and the person of the minister conferring the sacrament with the intention of doing what the Church does. Three sacraments imprint an indelible character. This last element of the teaching, I should say, suggests implicitly that "sacrament" refers to the external, visible sign: the character imprinted is its effect. As I have pointed out, the council distinguishes between the principal cause, the Holy Trinity, and instrumental cause: the minister who gives the sacrament externally. [45]

The same council, in its decree for the Jacobites, further distinguishes the sacraments of the Old and New Laws. Those of the

---

[42] Innocent III, Letter "Cum Marthae circa," Nov. 29, 1202: DS 783.

[43] Council of Verona, Oct.-Nov., 1184: DS 761. Cf. DS 794, 802.

[44] "Profession of faith imposed on Michael Paleologus," July 6, 1274: DS 860.

[45] DS 1310-1314.

Old Law were fitting for the worship of that age, but when Jesus Christ, signified by them, had come, their efficacy ceased; and, after the promulgation of the Gospel, hoping in their efficacy or having recourse to them is gravely sinful. [46]

The next principal Church documents bearing on our present matter are those of the Council of Trent. I cite here only some of the salient features of its teaching and terminology, both of which are related to earlier conceptions of the sacrament and to later theological teaching. Trent both echoes earlier formulae and defines elements of belief which will figure in later definitions. I shall indicate first the principal truths defined by Trent. Then I shall note some of the terminology.

All of the sacraments of the New Law were instituted by Christ. They are seven in number, no more, no less, and every one is truly and properly a sacrament. [47] The difference between the sacraments of the New and Old Laws is not simply that of different external rites. [48] The sacraments of the New Law contain the grace which they signify, and confer it upon those [recipients] who do not place an obstacle [to the reception of grace]. They are not merely external signs of grace or rightness received by faith, or certain marks of Christian belief [profession], by which believers are distinguished from unbelievers. [49] In three sacraments, baptism, confirmation, and orders, a character is impressed on the soul: hence they cannot be repeated. [50]

Implicitly baptism involves matter, [51] form, and the minister's intention of doing what the Church does. [52]

---

[46] DS 1348.

[47] Council of Trent, Session VII, "Decree on the Sacraments," March 3, 1547, canon 1 on the sacraments in general: DS 1601. In this exposition of Trent's teaching, I am not translating, but paraphrasing or summarizing.

[48] *Ibid.*, canon 2: DS 1602. The meaning seems to be that they are not just varying rites of the same general nature or dignity. The Council does not settle the scholastic dispute about the number and efficacy of the sacraments of the Old Law. The minimum meaning of the difference to be affirmed may be understood to be implicitly that of the Council of Florence.

[49] Canon 6: DS 1606. The defined truth is in the first sentence. The erroneous notions are rejected in their exclusive sense, as the word "merely" (*tantum*) indicates. One could affirm that the sacraments are also such signs or marks. In defining the efficacy of the sacraments (they *confer* grace), the Council rejects the errors which it is condemning. It does not settle the scholastic controversy concerning the kinds of causality which the sacraments exercise.

[50] Canon 9: DS 1609.

[51] Cf. "Canons on Baptism," 2: DS 1615.

[52] Cf. *id* canon 4: DS 1617.

The Eucharist is a *symbol* of the unity and love by which our Savior wished all Christians to be joined and linked.[53] After the consecration of bread and wine, our Lord Jesus Christ, true God and true man, is contained really and substantially under the appearances of those sensibly perceptible things.[54] Our Savior wished this sacrament to be the pledge of our future glory and perpetual happiness, and thus a *symbol* of that one *Body* of which he himself is the head, and to which he wished us as members to be bound together by the closest union of faith, hope, and love....[55] The most holy Eucharist has this in common with other sacraments: "to be the *symbol* of a sacred thing and the visible form of invisible grace."[56] The Eucharist is a "...*sign* of unity, ...bond of love,... *symbol* of harmony...."[57] The body and blood together with the soul and divinity of our Savior Jesus Christ is contained truly, really, and substantially in the sacrament of the most holy Eucharist.[58]

In the distinction between the sacraments of penance and of baptism, the first difference is that the matter and form, by which the essence of the sacrament is completed, differ extremely.[59]

In its teaching on the Mass, the Council employs as parallel expressions "under the *appearances* of bread and wine," "under the *symbols* of the same things," and "under *visible signs*."[60]

In his encyclicals on the Mystical Body of Christ and on the Mediator between God and men, Pius XII echoes some familiar formulae concerning the sacraments, and develops other elements which pertain to a more adequate conception of the sacraments, understood in their full field of relationships.

In "The Mystical Body of Christ" Pius stresses Christ's acting in his Church, and mentions elements which bear on the whole

---

[53] Cf. "Decree on the most holy Eucharist," *Preface*: DS 1635.

[54] *Ibid.*, chapter 1: DS 1635; cf. ch. 3: DS 1640.

[55] *Ibid.*, chapter 2: DS 1638.

[56] *Ibid.*, ch. 3: DS 1639.

[57] *Ibid.*, ch. 8: DS 1649.

[58] *Ibid.*, "Canons on the most holy Eucharist," canon 1: DS 1651; cf. canons 2, 3: DS 1652, 1653. In these texts on the Eucharist I have italicized *symbol*, to show that in the terminology of the Council it is synonymous with *sign*.

[59] Session XIV, "On penance and extreme anointing," ch. 2 DS 1671. I have italicized "essence" to note how clearly the Augustinian notion of the sacrament as a sign prevails. The sacrament is constituted essentially by its matter and form: it is not, for example, the permanent sacrament, or character, which according to Trent is imprinted by three sacraments (cf. canon 9 on the sacraments in general, DS 1609.

[60] Session XXII, "Decree on the Mass," ch. 1: DS 1740, 1741.

analogy of the instrumental roles of Christ's human nature, the Church, the minister, and the sacraments.

First, without using the technical term "analogy," the pontiff stresses the similarity between the roles of Christ's human nature and the Church. Jesus Christ could have given grace directly by himself to the whole human race, but willed to give it through a visible Church, so that through it all might somehow play an associate role in imparting the divine fruits of redemption. As he wished to use our nature, to redeem men by his pains and tortures, so in somewhat the same way he uses his Church to perpetuate the work which he began. [61] "...Therefore, as in the first instant of the incarnation the Son of the Eternal Father adorned with the fullness of the Holy Spirit the human nature substantially united with himself, so that it might be an apt instrument in the work of the redemption through his blood, so in the hour of his precious death he willed that his Church be endowed with the gifts of the Paraclete, so that in imparting the divine fruits of the redemption it might be the instrument of the incarnate Word, never to fail...." [62]

What seems to this point to be a powerful statement of the instrumentality of the Church is broadened--and, in what regards the sacrifice and sacraments, I should say weakened--by what follows immediately: attributing this instrumental role to what is called a "juridical mission" of *teaching, governing*, and a "power" *of administering the sacraments*. By linking a so-called juridical mission of teaching and governing and a power of administering the sacraments, Pius seems to level or equate two distinct modes of empowerment, and consequently to level or equate the three functions of the Church, and so by a stroke to weaken the concept of the unique type of instrumentality of the sacraments, which the Church recognizes and many theologians have sought to understand. The Eucharistic sacrifice and the sacraments involve an instrumentality which is grounded in a power conferred sacramentally, not by any "juridical mission."

Anticipating an objection, I recognize that the line of instrumentality which is to be acknowledged in the case of baptism evidently does not call for a power conferred on the minister by a sacrament: anyone, baptized or unbaptized, can baptize validly by performing the necessary rite with the intention of doing what the Church does.

---

[61] Cf. "Mystici Corporis Christi" AAS 35 (1943) 199.
[62] *Ibid.*, 206-207.

Beyond the exception regarding baptism, I wish to note a very subtle question involved here, which can be posed and answered only later. It regards the diverse manners of empowerment of the Church and of its ministers. Evidently the Church herself was not "ordained" sacramentally. But Christ gifted his Church with diverse powers, exercised diversely. The "Church" does not exercise any of her powers except through her qualified members. And her members are empowered diversely, on the one hand to teach and to govern, and on the other to administer the sacraments.

At another point in the encyclical Pius refers similarly to the broad notion of a "juridical mission." "... Through what is called a juridical mission, by which the Divine Redeemer sent the Apostles into the world as he had been sent by the Father, it is he who through the Church baptizes, teaches, rules, absolves, binds, offers, sacrifices...." [63] Here, it seems to me, the classic concept of Christ's acting through the Church in sacrifice and sacraments, of his baptizing when his minister baptizes, is weakened by being linked with the diverse manners in which he acts in the teaching and governing functions of the Church.

One more level of the analogy is mentioned: that of the instrumentality of the sacraments. As the human body is fitted out with its proper *instruments*, by which it cares for the life, health, and growth of its individual members, so the Savior of the human race ... provided wonderfully for his Mystical Body, endowing it with *sacraments*, by which [the needs of its members] are most abundantly cared for. [64]

One step in the total analogy is left unmentioned: the instrumental role of the human minister of the sacrifice and sacraments.

In his encyclical "The Mediator between God and the Human Race" [65] Pius develops an ample teaching on the liturgy. In it he stresses many elements which are important for a sacramental theology.

First, he treats the ways in which Christ is present in his Church. "... Therefore in every liturgical action, together with the Church its divine founder is present. Christ is present [*praesens adest*] in the august Sacrifice of the altar, both in the person of his minister and most of all under the Eucharistic appearances [*speciebus*]. He is present in the Sacraments by his power, which he

---

[63] *Ibid.*, 218.
[64] *Ibid.*, 201 (my italics).
[65] Pius XII, "Mediator Dei et hominum," AAS 39 (1947) 521-595.

pours into them as *instruments of holiness to be effected*. Finally he is present in praises and supplications addressed to God, according to the word: 'For where two or three are gathered in my name, I am in their midst.'" [66]

Second, he develops the concept of the public worship of the Church. "... The sacred liturgy constitutes the public worship which our Redeemer, the Head of the Church, offers to his heavenly Father; and which the society of Christian believers offers to its Founder and through him to the eternal Father. In short, it constitutes the whole public worship of the mystical Body of Jesus Christ, that is, of the Head and of his members." [67] In the course of the encyclical he clarifies the relationships of public and private or personal worship, and of the complementary roles of all forms of worship of God in the Church.

Third, to make abundantly clear the difference of roles of various members of the Body of Christ, Pius marks the unique role of ordained priests. "Only to the Apostles, and then to those who from them and their successors duly received the imposition of hands, is the priestly power given. By [this power], just as in the presence of the people entrusted to them they bear the person of Jesus Christ, so in the presence of God they bear the person of the people. This kind of priesthood is not transmitted by heredity or blood relationship; nor does it arise from the community of Christians, nor is it given by the people's delegation.... The power committed to him [the priest] by its very nature is in no way human, since it is absolutely from above, and comes from God...." [68] "...The sacrament of Orders distinguishes priests from all other Christian believers not endowed with this charism, for they [priests] alone... are made as it were divine instruments, by which the heavenly life is shared with the Mystical Body of Jesus Christ.... They alone are marked with that indelible character by which they are made like Christ the priest...." [69]

Finally, the sacraments are special instruments by which the higher life is shared by men. [70] They are the seven principal sources of salvation. [71] The efficacy of the Eucharistic sacrifice and of the sacraments is from the very operation performed [by the minister] (*ex opere operato*); whereas that of the prayers and ceremonies with

---

[66] *Ibid.*, 528 (my italics).
[67] *Ibid.*, 528-529.
[68] *Ibid.*, 538.
[69] *Ibid.*, 539.
[70] Cf. *Ibid.*, 522.
[71] Cf. *Ibid.*, 529.

which the Church adorns the Sacrifice and Sacraments, and of "sacramentals" and other rites instituted by the ecclesiastical hierarchy, is from the operation of the Church which is operating (*ex opere operantis Ecclesiae*), since it is holy and operates in most intimate union with its Head. [72] The Sacraments and the Sacrifice of the altar have power [*virtutem*] in themselves, since they are Christ's actions which transmit and spread grace to the members of the Mystical Body.... Yet, for them to have their due efficacy, it is absolutely necessary that the right dispositions of our spirit be present. [73]

For the present I reserve my reflections on the whole process of conceptualization of *sacrament* which I have sketched. I turn now to other developments in theological thought and to the adoption of further theological terminology by the Second Vatican Council.

---

[72] Cf. *Ibid.*, 532.
[73] Cf. *Ibid.*, 533.

CHAPTER IV

RETURN TO THE BROAD SENSE OF *SACRAMENT*

One striking feature of the documents of the Second Vatican Council is the use of *sacramentum* in the broad sense, concerning Christ and the Church. To those familiar with the use of the word *sacrament* exclusively of the seven sacraments of Christian worship this terminology sounded strange. Yet it was not new. Its origins in Christian usage can be recognized in the broad application of *mystērion/sacramentum* to the eternal hidden divine plan and to all of its obscure realizations and manifestations. It is found in the teachings of Origen and Augustine. [1] Moreover, in the century and a half preceding the Council several theologians returned to the ancient broad sense of *sacrament* as designating Christ and the Church. In this section I give examples of such thought. In the following, I shall synthesize the teaching of the Second Vatican Council.

SIX THEOLOGIANS

(1) *Johann Adam Möhler* [2]

I shall present elements of Möhler's theology found chiefly in his early work, *Die Einheit in der Kirche*. Surprisingly, perhaps, some significant formulations of the same elements are found in his classic work, *Symbolik*. [3]

---

[1] See chapter II.

[2] See my article, "Möhler's Earlier Symbolism," *Gregorianum* 72 (1991) 129-138. For a helpful introduction to Möhler's life and theology, see Hervé Savon, *Johann Adam Möhler* (Paris: Fleurus, 1965). For a study of Möhler's theology the following works are of help: Harald Wagner, *Die eine Kirche und die vielen Kirchen*. Ekklesiologie und Symbolik beim jungen Möhler (München: Schöningh, 1977); Rupert Josef Geiselmann, *Die katholische Tübinger Schule*, ihre theologische Eigenart (Freiburg-Basel-Wien: Herder, 1964); ----, *Die theologische Anthropologie Johann Adam Möhlers*. Ihr geschichtlicher Wandel (Freiburg: Herder, 1955).

[3] Möhler, Johann Adam, *Die Einheit in der Kirche*, oder Das Prinzip des Katholizismus... (Mainz: Grünewald, 1925); *Symbolik* (Regensburg: Manz, 1871).

Möhler's fundamental principle is that body is the image or expression of spirit. This principle he applies analogously to the Church. "... Man's body is a revelation of the spirit, which makes known in him and develops his being...." Therefore [analogously in the case of the spirit and the body of Christ] "... with the entrance of a divine spirit into mankind, with the placing of this new power, there must have been given a new external manifestation corresponding to it, hitherto not even suspected...." [4] "... [It] is through the arrangement, the organs, and the functions of the body that the human spirit works and creates. Just so does the spirit ruling in the Church beget the organs of its activity.... [5]

The Church mediates the reception of the Spirit/spirit. The Apostles received it immediately. Those remote in time received the life through the mediation of those who had received it from the Apostles, so that all intermediate generations formed steps in a propagation. ... This self-propagating, ongoing hereditary life power in the Church is Tradition, the inner, mysterious, completely invisible aspect of the Church...." [6]

The same principle explains analogously the origin of the Church's teaching. The inner spiritual life of the Christian, the work of the divine Spirit giving life to the believers, must, as soon as it is present, seek an expression. It must press outward and express itself.... The inner however was to be present first, partly because inner belief is the root of outward, partly since the inner, rightly understood, is given prior to the outer, prior to teaching. Christ bore his teaching in his consciousness before he expressed himself. Peter, by divine influence, was convinced of Christ's dignity before he answered Jesus' question.... We must say of ourselves ... that we do not understand the teaching, the intelligible expression of the new life imparted by the Holy Spirit, before we have received the new life principle itself.... Teaching is the expression of inner religious life. [7]

---

   [4] *Einheit*, 49, p. 130.
   [5] *Ibid.*, p. 132. There is an obscurity in what Möhler has written here concerning spirit and body. Except where he writes explicitly of the *Holy* Spirit, I have translated *Geist* here as *spirit*, not *Spirit*. It is not altogether clear whether he is thinking of the Holy Spirit or a divine spirit given to believers. The context seems to settle the question in favor of the participated spirit given by the Holy Spirit. First, he writes of the divine Spirit, through whose communication the Christian [spirit] is given to believers. Second, he could hardly have written about the Holy Spirit as "... wandering about in dubious, unsure manifestations...." If, then, he is thinking of a participated, divinely given spirit, one must note the extreme dualism of his anthropology. On his analogy of human spirit and body, the spirit given here forms a body for itself.
   [6] *Ibid.*, 3, pp. 10-11.
   [7] *Ibid.*, 8, pp. 19-21.

So also "... Christian morals are to be considered as the representation and unfolding of the inner holy principle in life...." [8] Though Möhler does not use the word "symbol" here, his concept of the origin of morals parallels that of the origin of teaching: the manifestation and representation of the Church's inner life in doctrinal symbols.

"Worship (cult), as it is considered here, is the representation of religious ideas, movements [*Bewegungen*: emotions?], and realities through forms in space, through bodily symbols and symbolic actions, alternating with words, or accompanied by them... As teaching is the inner faith of the Church grasped in concepts, so worship, in a significant part, is the same faith reflecting itself in meaningful [significant] signs.... From this inner identity of worship and teaching one can make clear why already in the second century Christians insisted on the unity of both teaching and worship...." [9]

Möhler asks: "... is it lawful for Christianity, a spiritual religion, to employ bodily symbols? ...It is based upon a drive of nature. We are constrained, presupposing that we have a powerful religious spirit, to bring forth such reflexes, until our whole proper religious character is revealed in them, as in teaching. We believe that it is not really alive in us if we do not find it fully reflected externally." [10]

"The Christian religion is necessarily communal. We do not know any immediate contact of finite spirits. Symbols mediate inner feelings as words do. Thus they become not only points of unification of all, but also the organ through which what is interior to one streams out to the totality, and flows back from this to the one. This holy symbolism [*Symbolik*] is therefore an expression of ineffable experiences. What the word cannot do, [that is:] to signify the overflowing, that the meaningful action often accomplishes...." [11]

Having given illustrations of Christ's use of symbols, Möhler gives his norms for use of symbols in the Church. "It is fitting, however, that what he [Christ] left behind for the continual use of his believers be distinctive: symbol and content, sign and thing coincide: it is a sacrament. Bread not only signifies him, but is he himself. ... Baptism not only signifies purification: true baptism is purification itself. If now however the symbols which the Church still brings forth from inner drive do not have this power, yet they

---

[8] *Ibid.*, 43, p. 104.
[9] *Ibid.*, 47, p. 117.
[10] *Ibid*, p. 118.
[11] *Ibid.*, p. 118.

gather the believers about her, and they are altogether an organ and
an expression of love, and where two or three are gathered in
Christ's name, he is among them...." [12]

Möhler insists on the free evolution of the symbols employed
in the Church's worship. "... What the series of symbols and
symbolic actions should be, and their connection with or change
from the words and poetry which might be joined with those
ordered by Jesus, is left to his Church and its individual parts....
little was prescribed by Apostles.... All was to be a free external
representation of the religious [spirit], which in the course of the
centuries must develop spontaneously [*von selbst*] according to
needs, and only that which is not imposed from without, but is
produced outwardly from within, is to be viewed as fitting
according to the end." [13]

The basic principle is applied too to the formation of the body
of the Church, to its organs. The divine principle imparted to
believers is one in itself, begets unity of faith, and unites in love.
Moreover, this unity must be visible, according to the type
pervading all orders of being and life. [14] As the life of the Church
progresses, there is a need for a visible expression of unity first in
the bishop, then in the metropolitan, in the unity of all bishops, and
finally in the primacy of the successor of Peter.

Möhler begins his mature work, *Symbolik*, with a definition of
the term with which he entitles the work: "... the scientific
exposition of the doctrinal differences among the various religious
parties opposed to each other, in consequence of the ecclesiastical
revolution of the sixteenth century, as these doctrinal differences are
evidenced by the public confessions or symbolical books of these
parties...." [15] That definition would seem to exclude from his
present consideration the sense of symbolism which is prominent in
his *Einheit*. Yet in at least one place he writes of Christ and of the
Church in a manner which recalls what we have considered in his
earlier work. Against the Protestant conception of an invisible
church, Möhler holds that a visible Church alone is consistent with

---

[12] *Ibid.*, p. 119. Some questions rise here, concerning (1) the accuracy of
Möhler's formula: symbol and content, sign and thing coincide: it is a sacrament;
(2) the application to the Eucharist: not the bread, but what seems to be bread, is
he himself; (3) the identification of baptism and the purification which is its effect;
(4) the sense of his view of the decreased power of the symbols of the Church.

[13] *Ibid.*, 48, p. 120.

[14] *Ibid.*, 49, pp. 129-130.

[15] *Symbolik* p. 1; *Symbolism*. Translated ... by James Burton Robertson, ed.
3. p. 1.

the incarnation itself. "...Christ wrought miracles... nay his whole life was a miracle, not merely to establish the credibility of *his words*, but also *immediately to represent and symbolize* the most exalted truths...." [16] Divine truth was embodied, bodied forth in Christ. [17]

Often in *Symbolik* Möhler writes of the Church in a manner which recalls and further elaborates the thought which characterizes *Einheit*. The Church is the external manifestation of Christ and his continuing work, and of the Christian religion. "The Church, considered from one point of view, is the living figure of Christ, manifesting himself and working through all ages, whose atoning and redeeming acts, it, in consequence, eternally repeats, and uninterruptedly continues...." [18] It is "...the visible community of believers, founded by Christ, in which, by means of an enduring apostleship, established by him, and appointed to conduct all nations, in the course of ages, back to God, the works wrought by him during his earthly life, for the redemption and sanctification of mankind, are, under the guidance of his spirit, continued to the end of the world." [19] "...The Church is the body of the Lord; it is, in its universality, His visible form--His permanent, ever-renovated, humanity--His eternal revelation...." [20]

"... The ultimate reason of the visibility of the Church is to be found in the *incarnation* of the Divine Word.... Since the Word became *flesh*, it expressed itself in an outward, perceptible, and human manner.... This decided the nature of those means, whereby the Son of God, even after He had withdrawn himself from the eyes of the world, wished still to work in the world, and for the world.... Thus the visible Church, from the point of view taken here, is the Son of God himself, everlastingly manifesting himself among men in a human form, perpetually renovated, and eternally young--the permanent incarnation of the same...." [21] As in Christ divinity and humanity are distinguished but united, so in the Church are the divine and the human.

---

[16] Thus Robertson translates, *Symbolism*, p. 260. Möhler's expression is *darzustellen und zuversinnlichen* (*Symbolik*, p. 341) literally, "represent [or exhibit] and make sensibly perceptible." Though Möhler does not use the term *symbolisieren*, Robertson's translation seems reasonable. Surely there is question of external manifestation of inner reality, and that is the basic principle which commands Möhler's thought in *Einheit*.

[17] *Symbolism*, p. 259.

[18] *Ibid.*, p. 231 in Robertson's translation, which I shall be citing.

[19] *Ibid.*, p. 253.

[20] *Ibid.*, p. 273.

[21] *Ibid.*, p. 253.

Reflection and evaluation. Positively, Möhler hit on an important truth regarding the life of the Church and its symbolizing activity. Fleeting as his thought may be, he goes far beyond the notion of sacrament-sign. The external manifestations of Christian life are symbols, not "signs, *things* which when they are known cause something else to come to thought." As Christ did in word and act, in the whole of his sensibly perceptible being, so the Church, in the whole of its continuation of the action of Christ, symbolizes. Möhler does not work out the nature of the process of symbolizing or of its products. He does, however, call attention to an aspect of the whole truth concerning Christ and Church and their symbolizing operation. Möhler's thought is *there*. It is a stimulating bit of personal speculation. Further insight and elaboration of an adequate theory of symbolizing and symbol, and of how Christ and the Church are symbols, remain important agenda for theologians.

Having said this, one must recognize shortcomings in Möhler's *Einheit*. In general, Möhler pays little heed to any normative role of the New Testament in the elaboration of his theology of the Church, of the development of Christian teaching, and in particular of the sacraments. His thought is characterized by a free development of his basic principle: the Church, its form, its teaching, and its worship are the product of the spirit or life given to believers by the Holy Spirit. Development of the Church and of all aspects of its external life is a function of the developing consciousness of the whole body of believers. How this consciousness itself evolves, what is the object of believers' contemplation, remains obscure. When, in a particular instance, Möhler indicates one line of thought regarding the primacy, his reference to the biblical Peter and the will of Christ is no more than an undocumented affirmation, with no serious effort to ground his affirmation in biblical evidence. His conception of the free development of symbols of Christian worship flows simply from his general hypothesis of free development from the inner life of the Church. What biblical data demand, and what is the role of a teaching authority in the Church, are not mentioned. In brief, Möhler has worked out a free-ranging elaboration of what I have called his fundamental principle.

Perhaps Möhler's "fundamental principle" should be called more properly a vaguely formulated hypothesis regarding inner life and external manifestation. It is a good hunch, a recurring flash, rather than a clear insight and well elaborated principle.

(2) *Matthias Joseph Scheeben.*[22]

Scheeben defines *mystery* thus: "...Christian mystery is a truth communicated to us by Christian revelation, a truth to which we cannot attain by our unaided reason, and which, even after we have attained it by faith, we cannot adequately represent with our rational concepts." [23]

Within the general notion of mystery, he determines the nature of what he calls sacramental mystery. The idea of sacramental mystery runs through the whole of Christianity. In its original meaning *sacrament* can be synonymous with *mystery*. "But in the course of time *sacramentum* came to mean, for the most part, visible things which in some way or other involve a mystery in the narrower sense, and which therefore are mysterious despite their visibility. In such things the mystery, the hidden element, was linked with the visible element, and the whole composed of both elements shared in the character of its two parts: it could appropriately be called a sacramental mystery....

"With regard to the sacramental mystery, two factors evidently must be considered: first the mystery concealed in the sacrament; secondly the connection between this mystery as such and the sacrament, the visible thing. Only when both factors are present in a fully developed sense can we speak of a sacramental mystery in the complete sense.

"As concerns the first factor, there can be question only of a mystery in the strict theological sense, something truly supernatural....

"With respect to the second factor, the connection of the supernatural mystery with the visible object, such connection may be either real or logical. The latter is the case when a visible thing houses some mystery within itself, and is the symbol and likeness of the mystery. The symbol or likeness enables me to make the mystery known to my understanding, or at any rate makes it possible for some other intelligence to acquaint me with the mystery. In this sense the Fathers sometimes speak of the sacrament of the Trinity in creatures. But this purely logical connection does not really cause the visible element to combine with the invisible element to form a whole. If the sacramental mystery is to have objective reality, there must be a real connection, as, for example, the connection between the divine person of Christ and His human nature, between the

---

[22] Matthias Joseph Scheeben, *The Mysteries of Christianity*. Translated by Cyril Vollert, S.J. (St. Louis: B. Herder, c. 1946).
[23] P. 13.

spiritualized body of Christ and the sacramental species, or between grace and the man endowed with grace. In the case of the logical connection the sacrament is indeed a sacrament, but a *sacramentum vacuum*, which does not really contain the mystery; in the case of the real connection it is a *sacramentum plenum*, that is, it is really filled with the mystery, it is full of mystery. Since in the latter case the mystery is actually present in the visible object, it is also actually present to him who sees the visible object, not indeed in the sense that he thereby perceives the mystery as it is in itself, but in the sense that when by faith he is apprised of the union of the two elements, he knows upon seeing the visible object that he actually has the mystery before him.

"It pertains to the essence of the sacramental mystery that the mystery remains a mystery even in the sacrament.... This does not exclude the possibility that the sacrament may make known the inner nature and meaning of the mystery.... It is only the essence of the supernatural mystery that may not become visible in the sacrament. This essence must ever remain the object of faith....

"Most of the mysteries of Christianity are sacramental mysteries in the sense that there is a real connection between the hidden element and the visible element. The Trinity is not one of these, at least directly in itself; it becomes such only indirectly in the God-man. But the first man, as he came forth from the hand of God, was a sacramental mystery, inasmuch as supernatural, invisible grace was joined to his visible nature. Still more the God-man was such; He is the great sacrament, the 'evidently great *sacramentum* of godliness,' as the Vulgate here significantly renders the Greek *mystērion*, 'which was manifested in the flesh.'" [Cf. 1 Tm 3.16] [24]

Scheeben indicates three principal sacramental mysteries: the God-man, the Eucharist, and the Church. [25] He distinguishes two degrees of sacramental mystery. In the first, the supernatural mystery merely enters into the visible object. In the second, the mystery makes its way to us in and through the visible object, and operates and communicates itself in it and through it as a vehicle or instrument. [26] The God-man, the Eucharist, and the Church are sacramental mysteries in the second sense.

Sacraments in the narrower sense are those external signs by which the grace of Christ is conferred on us and is signified to us. [27]

---

[24] Pp. 558-560.
[25] Pp. 560-561.
[26] P. 562.
[27] P. 567.

In Scheeben's conception, the theological explanation of moral causality does not suffice to express the efficacy of the sacraments. They are not merely pledges assuring us of efficacy, but true vehicles of the power flowing into the members from Christ. Their causality should becalled physical, or rather hyperphysical. [28]

Reflection. One feature of Scheeben's conception deserves notice: his notion of the full sacrament, really filled with the mystery. Along with other variations on Isidore's conception, which we considered in Chapter II, this notion grasps an element of the full truth which should be recognized and retained. In any eventual theory of the Christian sacrament as symbol, the inner mystery, the hidden sacred reality, is part of the imaged reality, part of the mystery of the prime Symbolizer and of the human symbolizers who are taken up into the whole process. The inner mystery is *what* the perceptible symbol represents.

(3) *Henri de Lubac.*

Two of De Lubac's works are of particular interest, *Corpus Mysticum* and *Méditation sur l'Église.*[29] In his preface to *Corpus Mysticum* De Lubac makes clear his purpose. It is not to write the history of the Eucharist, but to trace the history of one or two words. [30] As the subtitle of the book indicates, the words concern both Eucharist and Church. I shall not attempt a summary of the argument, which is dense and erudite, with a wealth of details of the thought of Fathers and early medieval theologians. The exposition moves from the Eucharist as mystical body through the relationship of the sacramental body to the body of the Church, to the terminology fixing the Church as Mystical Body.

For our present purpose, it is interesting to note De Lubac's theological preference, which emerges as he works out his history of words. Having traced the development of variations on the classic threefold terminology for the sacraments, *sacramentum tantum, res et sacramentum, res tantum* (sacrament only, thing and sacrament, and thing only), De Lubac notes that in this set of concepts the

---

[28] Pp. 570-571.

[29] Henri de Lubac, *Corpus Mysticum.* L'Eucharistie et l'Église au moyen age. Étude historique. Ed. 2. ([Théologie, 3] Paris: Aubier, 1949); *Méditation sur l'Église*³ ([*Théologie*, 27] Paris: Desclée de Brouwer, 1985); *The Splendour of the Church.* Translated by Michael Mason (New York: Sheed and Ward, c. 1956 [based on second French edition, 1953]). I have worked from the French original, and translations are my own.

[30] *Corpus Mysticum*, p. [5].

Church is only a "thing," not a sacrament. In this view, the Church is considered in its "natural place," in the sacramental frame, in relation to the Eucharist. Later, theologians came to treat the Church outside the sacramental context. [31] I simply point out that as long as the theology of the Church would be confined to the sacramental context, there could be no question of conceiving it as a sacrament.

Méditation sur l'Église is not a scientific theological work, but the reworking of a series of conferences given to priests and seminarians in the hope of sharpening and strengthening their belief. Consequently one should not look here for a thought which is new, nor for the results of a scientific work. [32]

In this work De Lubac's theology of the Church clearly is not confined to the sacramental context. I shall gather elements which treat the Church as mystery, as sacrament, in what is passing and what is permanent, and in the relationship of the Church to the Eucharist.

"... The *mystery* of the Church is in resume the whole mystery. It is par excellence our own mystery. It takes us wholly. It envelops us, since it is in his Church that God sees us and loves us, since it is in it that he wills us and that we encounter him, and in it also that we cling to him and that he makes us blessed." [33] The Church is Jesus Christ continued, propagated, and communicated. [34] Like Christ, it is a great mystery and wonderful sacrament. [35]

The Church is the *sacrament* of our salvation. [36] "... 'The total locus of the Christian sacraments,' it is itself the great sacrament,

---

[31] *Corpus Mysticum*, pp. 126-129. De Lubac cites James of Viterbo's *De regimine christiano* as the oldest treatise on the Church (at the threshold of the fourteenth century).

[32] Cf. *Méditation*, preface, pp. 3-8. Yet the text is complemented by a multitude of notes, as many as ten to a page. Many of them are informative, for De Lubac is an erudite witness to a great part of the Catholic tradition. Yet some of the intended documentation is not accurate, and texts cited or quoted do not support the affirmations which they are meant to justify. This is unfortunate, since in most cases De Lubac's positions are beyond question, and the abortive efforts to document them distract from the movement of his thought. To save some readers a bit of eventual disillusionment, I shall point out a few instances of inadequate documentation. Where I judge it necessary, I shall indicate questions which remain concerning some aspects of De Lubac's thought.

[33] *Ibid.*, p. 36.

[34] *Ibid.*, p. 39, citing Bossuet.

[35] *Ibid.*, *magnum mysterium et admirabile sacramentum* (from the Roman liturgy for Christmas.

[36] *Ibid.*, p. 50, citing St. Leo's sermon on the birth of the Lord.

which contains and vivifies all the others." [37] It is here below the sacrament of Jesus Christ, just as he himself, in his humanity, is the sacrament of God. [38]

De Lubac's conception of sacrament is personal. "Every sacramental reality, 'sensibly perceptible link of two worlds,' presents a double characteristic. On the one hand, being the sign of another thing, it is necessary that it be traversed, not halfway, but totally. One does not stop at the sign; it has no value by itself; by definition, it is a diaphanous thing, it effaces itself before that which it points out, as the word which would be nothing if it did not lead directly to the idea. In this condition it is not intermediary, but mediator. It does not isolate, one from the other, the two terms which it is charged with uniting; it does not set a distance between them, but on the contrary unites them, by rendering present the thing which it evokes. But also, on the other hand, this sacramental reality is not just any sort of sign, provisional or changeable at pleasure. It is found in an essential relationship to our present condition, which is no longer inscribed in the time of pure figures, but which does not allow either the full possession of the 'truth.' Its second characteristic, inseparable from the first, will be therefore that it can never be rejected as having ceased to be useful. This diaphanous milieu, which one must traverse always and traverse wholly, one has never finished traversing. It is always through it that one attains that of which it is the sign. One can never pass beyond it, step over it." [39]

"The Church is the sacrament of Jesus Christ. That means, in other terms, that it is in a certain relationship of mystical identity with him.... Head and members make only one body, only one Christ. The husband and wife are one flesh.... [The Church] is at

---

[37] De Lubac does not identify the portion of this text which he sets in quotation marks. For what follows he quotes a fragment of the Council of Florence's decree for the Jacobites, concerning the necessity of being in the Catholic Church for salvation (DS 1351). The Council's text hardly bears the meaning of De Lubac's statement.

[38] *Ibid.*, p. 175. Here De Lubac cites for comparison two fragments: one from the Ambrosian Missal, preface for first Sunday of advent: "... manifestans plebi tuae Unigeniti tui sacramentum..." (manifesting to your people the sacrament of your Only-begotten), and the other from Augustine: "... Non est enim aliud Dei mysterium, nisi Christus" (for there is no other mystery of God but Christ) (*Epist.* 187.34: PL 38.845]). Here too his textual support for crucial formulae is dubious. In its context, Augustine's text concerns the reality which is the object of the same spirit of faith in the Old Testament and the New: the Incarnation of Christ, the *sacramentum* or *mysterium* which for the ancient saints was hidden, and for us our manifest Mediator made manifest (cf. the text in CSEL, vol. 57, pp. 112-113).

[39] *Ibid.*, pp. 175-176.

once his fulfillment and his fulness [plenitude].... If one is not in some manner a member of the body, one does not receive the influence of the head.... If one does not adhere to the unique wife, one is not loved by the husband...." [40]

The unique mission of the Church is to render Jesus Christ present to men. He must continue to be announced by us, to be transparent through us. [41]

It is not the Church which is passing, which will cease to be, but its figure, the form which it takes on in our eyes at present. [42] "... All that is of the sacramental order in the Church, adapted to our temporal condition, is destined to disappear in the presence of the definitive reality of which it is the efficacious sign. But that is not to be understood as the effacing of one thing in the presence of the other: it will be the manifestation of its 'truth.' It will be its glorious manifestation and its fulfillment." [43]

Until the second half of the twelfth century, the Eucharist was called the Mystical Body (*Corpus mysticum*). [44] The Mystical Body was the Mystery of Christ, according to Cyril of Alexandria. [45] It was a mystery in the sense of a sensible sign of a hidden divine reality. [46]

Paul linked the Mystical Body and the Eucharist (1 Cor 10.16-17. The Eucharist is *corpus in mysterio*, the body mystically signified and procured by the Eucharist, the unity of the Christian community which the "holy mysteries" realize in an efficacious symbol. [47] The Church is the *res sacramenti*, the ultimate effect of the sacrament. [48]

The relationship of Church and Eucharist is that of reciprocal causality: the Church makes the Eucharist, and the Eucharist makes the Church. In first case the Church is understood its active sense, in the exercise of its power of sanctification. In second case Church is understood in a passive sense, the Church of the sanctified. [49]

---

[40] *Ibid.*, pp. 181-182.

[41] *Ibid.*, p. 190.

[42] *Ibid.*, p. 54.

[43] *Ibid.*, p. 56.

[44] *Ibid.*, p. 107.

[45] *Ibid.*, p. 110.

[46] *Ibid.*, p. 112. One may note here in De Lubac's concept of *mystery* an echo of the thought of Isidore of Seville.

[47] *Ibid.*, p. 112.

[48] *Ibid.*, p. 113.

[49] *Ibid.*, p. 113. I strain the English word "makes" to bring out the word-play of De Lubac's French *fait*.

The hierarchical Church makes the Eucharist. [50] If the sacrifice is accepted by God, in its turn the Eucharist makes the Church. It is, St. Augustine tells us, the sacrament by which the Church in this time is united (*quo in hoc tempore consociatur Ecclesia*). [51] The Eucharist completes the work which baptism began. From the side of Christ sleeping on the cross flowed forth the sacraments by which the Church is formed (*Ex latere Christi dormientis in cruce sacramenta profluxerunt, quibus Ecclesia fabricatur*). [52] The Eucharist is the efficacious sign of the spiritual sacrifice offered to God by the whole Christ. [53] By the celebration of the mystery, in reality the Church makes itself. The holy and sanctifying Church constructs the Church of the saints. [54]

Reflection and evaluation. The element of De Lubac's thought which is most interesting for our present concern is his treatment of both Christ and the Church as mystery and sacrament in a broad sense. Two characteristics of his thought, however, make it difficult to assess the significance of what he has written. One is the defect of his documentation. Fragments of texts quoted do not in their contexts have the sense with which he uses them in the texture of his thought. The second is that *sacrament* and *mystery* are polyvalent in his usage. The meaning slides from the Pauline play on hidden and manifest, to Augustine's broad sense of sacrament/mystery which is basically Pauline, to the more limited sense of sacrament as sign, and on to De Lubac's rather poetic elaboration of the notions of sign and sacrament. At the end one is hard put to determine in what sense or senses, in De Lubac's thought, Christ and the Church are sacrament/mystery. I simply note here a need for a more thorough elaboration of the concepts of sign, symbol, and sacrament, admitting readily that such an elaboration was not called for in the non-technical work which I have been considering.

For his statement that the Church is Christ continued, propagated, and communicated De Lubac cites Bossuet. The thought is similar to that of Möhler in *Symbolik*, with which he is familiar. [55]

---

[50] *Ibid.*, p. 117.
[51] *Contra Faustum*, XII.20 (PL 42.265).
[52] Cf. Aug. *De Civitate Dei*, XXII.17, PL 41.779; St. Thomas, S.T. III. q. 64. a. 2 ad 3. *Méditation*, p. 129.
[53] *Ibid.*, p. 130.
[54] *Ibid.*, p. 131.
[55] Compare above, p. 78.

Finally, in his treatment of the relationship of Church and Eucharist, I note the apparent influence of Scheeben, whom De Lubac cites with approval in his *Corpus Mysticum*. [56]

(4) *Otto Semmelroth.*

Two works of Semmelroth are of special interest for our investigation of the broader use of *sacrament*, as it is predicated of both Christ and the Church. [57] I shall note these elements in his thought: (1) Christ as sacrament; (2) the Church as sacrament; (3) the complementarity in his personal conception of *sacrament*.

Christ is the exemplar (*Urbild*) of all sacramentality. Seemingly as his grounds for this affirmation, Semmelroth quotes De Lubac: "The Church here below is the sacrament of Jesus Christ, as Jesus Christ in his humanity is the sacrament of God." [58] Semmelroth takes *sacrament* in the sense of one of the formulae adopted by the Council of Trent regarding the seven sacraments of the Church, "the visible form of invisible grace." [59] Christ is the prime sacrament *Ursakrament*. [60]

In the New Testament Christ's manhood is the sacramental epiphany of the Son of God, the "visible form of the invisible God." In Christ there was the bodily presence of the personal God himself, the full realization of the objectification (*Vergegenständlichung*) of God in the sacrament. "He who sees me, sees the Father" (Jn 14.9; cf. 12.45). Beholding the bodily presence of Christ, the disciples behold the Word, and since the Word and the Father are one, [they behold] also the Father. The Word, eternally the image of the invisible God (Col 1.15), in the incarnation becomes also for us men the visible, tangible image, in whom the majesty of the invisible God becomes present. The Church has from the beginning considered this mystery of Christ as the Prime Sacrament its greatest treasure, and therefore has celebrated the Epiphany as the great mystery, which essentially stands alongside the Easter solemnity, since this,

---

[56] P. 293, note 45.

[57] Otto Semmelroth, S.J., *Die Kirche als Ursakrament* [2]. (Frankfurt am Main: Knecht, 1955); *Vom Sinn der Sakramente*. (Frankfurt am Main: Knecht, 1960).

[58] *Die Kirche als Ursakrament*, p. 39, with a quotation of the German translation of De Lubac, *Méditation: Betrachtung über die Kirche* (Graz, 1954) p. 137.

[59] *Ibid.*, pp. 39-40.

[60] *Ibid*, p. 40. I think that the term "Ursakrament," which has become common in German theological language, is best translated "prime sacrament." The English "prime," in my judgment, best captures the wealth of meaning of the germ "Ur-."

as return to the Father, is the completion of the Coming from the Father. [61]

Whoever calls the Church the Body of Christ, signifies it like Christ himself as sacramental. Moreover, whoever, like the teaching authority of the Church itself, grounds the visibility of the Church on the affirmation that it is the body of Christ, and thereby affirms that she is the mysterious bearer of an invisible-divine reality, which makes the unity of this Church more than moral, has pointed out very clearly that it is precisely from the sacramental point of view that the interpretation of the Church as mystical body is to be derived from the physical body of Christ.

Evidently the two "bodies" are not simply and in all respects alike. An analogy holds between the physical and the mystical body also from the point of view of their sacramental nature. That does not, however, diminish the fact that in both cases in a true sense there is question of sacramental realities. The right to call the mystical body of the Lord, as also the physical body, "sacrament" consists in this, that in both cases visible realities are sign and container of divine realities. Christ really bears in himself the second divine Person, and whoever comes in contact with him, touches the divine reality. The Church contains the divine reality so objectively and actually that one who stands in contact with the visible Church touches the divine reality contained in her.

However, in this containing the divine in a visible container there is evidently between the physical and the mystical Christ an essential difference which, beyond all likeness, may not be overlooked. Christ himself is "Sacrament" in the fullest sense, since the human nature of Christ has not its own proper subsistence [*Selbstand*], but belongs to the Godhead in the hypostatic union. In the mystical Christ the unity of the visible human container with the invisible divine content does not go that far. The Church, as a visible human society, has its thoroughly proper unique subsistence, and does not lose this to the divine reality contained in her. Hence only in an analogous sense can we express the sacramental nature of Christ and of the Church together. Yet the analogy does not make the expression untrue. What "sacrament" expresses, as we shall see more clearly, is realized in the Church in a true sense, and the more accurate investigation of the individual sacramental elements will clarify the knowledge of the Lord's mystical body. Therefore, "... at the beginning of the teaching of the sacraments one should treat

---

[61] *Ibid.*, pp. 41-42.

the Church, as the sign which comprehends all other signs in herself...." [62]

Like Christ, the Church is an *Ursakrament*. It is not to be
enumerated along with the seven sacraments of the Church, as if it
were an eighth. Rather the seven sacraments are formations derived
from the sacramentality of the Church. [63]

Semmelroth proposes a personal conception of *sacrament*
which must be considered apart from his general notions of Christ
and Church as prime sacraments. In these general notions he is
retaining a fairly common element in some traditional thought, as
we have seen. His personal conception of sacrament, going far
beyond "visible form of invisible grace," must be judged eventually
on its own merits or shortcomings.

Semmelroth thinks that some Catholic theologians have erred
in conceiving sacraments as involving a "downward" action (*von
oben nach unten*). He thinks that since Leo XIII and Pius XII
considered the sacraments as acts of worship, they must be thought
of as acts directed "upward." Yet there is a complementarity in the
sacraments. They involve God's expression to man, the revelation of
his invisible presence and grace, and the sacrament as an act of
worship, an act of man, in which the external expression of the act
is fixed by Christ. [64]

Semmelroth develops his concept of sacrament more fully in his
work *Vom Sinn der Sakramente*. The work of redemption begins
with descent of the Son of God, becoming man. The Father sends
his Son as an offer to sinful man of adoption as sons. He is the
Word expressing the offer of making men sons. To this coming
from the Father corresponds the return movement in sacrifice. The
Mediator as head of mankind brings man's answer to the Father. In
the incarnation he is God's word to man. In his sacrifice he is man's
answer to God. Redemption [deliverance] is a dialogic event.... This

---

[62] *Ibid.*, pp. 42-44. The closing quotation is from H. Stirnimann, O.P., "Die
Kirche und der Geist Christi," *Divus Thomas* 31 (1953) 16.

[63] *Ibid.*, pp. 46-47. Semmelroth points out Rahner's early term, "*Wur-
zelsakrament*" (*sacramentum radicale*) in his mimeographed manuscript "*De paenitentia tractatus historico-dogmaticus* (Innsbruck, 1955) p. 685; and his article,
"Die Gliedschaft in der Kirche nach der Lehre der Enzyklika Pius' XII, 'Mystici
Corporis,'" in *Schriften zur Theologie* (Einsiedeln, 1955) II. Band, 80. He cites
Oswald's term, "*das* christliche Sakrament" (*the* Christian sacrament), in *Dogma-
tische Lehre von der hl. Sakramenten* (Münster, 1894) 1. Bd. 12. What I have
translated as "formations derived from the sacramentality of the Church" is quoted
from M. Schmaus, *Dogmatik*[1-2] (München, 1941) Bd. III/2, 2: "*Ausformungen der
Sakramentalität der Kirche*".

[64] *Ibid.*, pp. 82-84.

process of the Christ event is what is set forth in the life of the Church as a symbol [*Bildzeichen*] of salvation. Therefore the life of the Church, analogously with the Christ event, is articulated in two mutually complementary services: to the Word of God, and to sacrifice.

Preaching is not mere informing, but participating the real mediating power of God's Word. In the historical work of redemption, incarnation is completed by sacrifice. So in the life of the Church the celebration of the sacraments is the opposite pole answering the Church's preaching of the word. [65]

Semmelroth thinks that the upward direction of the sacramental action is proved by the word which is an element of the sacrament: it is, he contends, always a prayer. So the word which animates and gives power to the sacramental sign is not like the word of preaching of God to men, but it rises as a plea of the Church in Christ's sacrifice: upward from below. [66]

Reflection and evaluation. Without presenting any independent documentation, Semmelroth repeats the witness to the broad sense of "sacramentality," in which Christ and Church are called sacraments. As I noted, he merely quotes De Lubac's formulation. In another place he quotes a fragment of Augustine, seemingly taken from De Lubac with a variation: "Non enim est aliud Dei sacramentum nisi Christus" [67]

Semmelroth's personal contribution is the term which has made a fortune: *Ursakrament*. It is important to note that this witness to the general truth of Christ and Church as sacrament must be taken with the weight which it bears with its very broad sense of *sacrament*. One might hold reasonably that *sacrament* would mean no more than the basic Augustinian "sacred sign." Semmelroth himself takes it in the sense of the formula chosen by the Council of Trent: "visible form of invisible grace."

As for Semmelroth's notion of the sacrament as human act directed "upward" to God, not "downward" from God, I reserve judgment for the present.

---

[65] *Vom Sinn der Sakramente*, pp. 44-46.

[66] *Ibid.*, pp. 49-50.

[67] *Ibid.*, p. 102 and note 81, p. 239. Semmelroth only approximates the actual text of Augustine, "... non est enim aliud Dei mysterium nisi Christus, ..." (*Epistula* CLXXXVII, n. 34, PL 38, 845 / CSEL 57, p. 113). Moreover, as I pointed out regarding De Lubac's citation of the same text (above, note 52), *mysterium* here has the sense of the Pauline mystery, the reality/truth at first hidden and then partially manifested, which for Augustine was the object of the same belief in both the old dispensation and the new.

(5) *Karl Rahner*.

I present here briefly Rahner's notion of sacrament as he
elaborated it in his work on the Church and the sacraments. [68]

Christ is both sacrament and *res sacramenti*. God's people
exists and is one prior to the institutional, hierarchical, juridically
organized Church. Its unity is that of the human race; not merely
the logical unity of nature, but the real, actual unity of a race
springing from one man, Adam, called to a supernatural end, with
one history of salvation and ruin. This unity of the race was
confirmed, strengthened, and made final through the Incarnation.
Jesus, a member of this mankind, consecrated it by the Incarnation
and by his death on the cross.

Christ himself is the historical real presence of God's mercy in
its definitive victory. Before Christ there was uncertainty about the
outcome of the dialog between God and man in the history of
salvation and ruin. Now the last Word has been spoken, as a word
of grace, reconciliation, eternal life. Christ is at once reality and
its sign: *sacramentum* and *res sacramenti* of the saving grace of
God. [69]

The Church is the continuation, the abiding presence of this
eschatological real presence of God's graciousness, of a grace
victorious and definitively established in the world in Christ. As
Christ's permanence in the world, the Church is really the
Ursakrament, the point of origin of the sacraments in the proper
sense of the word. From Christ, the Church herself has a sacramental structure: a historical perceptibility in space and time. By
reason of her permanent union with Christ, the Church cannot be
an empty sign. [70]

The sacramental structure of the Church is set forth and
perfected in the sacraments strictly so called. Like any society, the
Church must perfect herself, come to her full actuation, by acting.

---

[68] Karl Rahner, *Kirche und Sakramente* (*Quaestiones Disputatae*, 10) (Freiburg: Herder, c. 1960); *The Church and the Sacraments*. Translated by W. J.
O'Hara (New York: Herder and Herder, c. 1963). For an exposition and critical
evaluation of this work, see my article, "Reflections on Karl Rahner's 'Kirche und
Sakramente,'" in *Gregorianum* 44 (1963) 465-500. In footnotes I shall indicate the
pages, first in the German, then in the English translation. In my brief exposition
here I do not attempt to summarize Rahner's conception of symbol. I treated it at
some length in the article just mentioned, and I returned to consider the possibility
of "natural" or "essential" symbols in *Man the Symbolizer* (*Analecta Gregoriana*,
222, Rome: Gregorian University Press, 1981) pp.306-310. My critical evaluation
can be understood only in the context of that work.

[69] Cf. pp. 12-15/11-16.

[70] Cf. pp. 17-18/18-19.

The Church *is* fully, in the highest degree of her real essential perfection, *while* she teaches, witnesses to Christ's truth, bears his cross, loves God in her members, makes present cultically in the Sacrifice of the Mass the salvation which is hers, and so forth. Since all salvation is offered to the individual through some degree of positive relationship with the Church, and the Church herself has a sacramental structure (that is, the union of grace and its historically perceptible corporeality) every entry into the Church as means of salvation, and all reception of salvation from the Church, must be somehow sacramental, with at least a quasi-sacramental structure. [71]

When the Church, as means of salvation, officially, socially, publicly, explicitly encounters the individual in the final actualization of her being, then we have sacraments in the strict sense. The structure of such an act corresponds to the sacramental structure of the Church herself, the prime sacrament. This notion of prime sacrament (*Ursakrament*) is not a vague transfer from the notion of sacrament which is had in the rest of sacramental doctrine. Rather it is derived from Christology. As the salvific presence of Christ's grace for the individual, the Church is the prime sacrament. From it we can gain an understanding of the sacraments in general. [72]

We have a sacrament where the Church, in an absolute engagement, performs a basic act in which she fully actualizes her essence as the prime sacrament of grace for the individual in his decisive salvation situations. [73]

(6) *E. Schillebeeckx.* [74]

Christ is the prime sacrament. He is the Son of God. The second person of the most holy Trinity is personally man. Christ is God in a human way, and man in a divine way. Everything that he does is a divine act in human form, an interpretation and trans-

---

[71] Cf. pp. 18-20/21-22.

[72] Cf. pp. 21-22/22-23.

[73] Cf. pp. 85/96.

[74] E. Schillebeeckx, O.P., *Christ the Sacrament of the Encounter with God* [Translated by Paul Barrett, O.P.] (New York: Sheed and Ward, c.1963). I present here elements of Schillebeeckx's personal synthesis in this relatively early work. It seems to have been conceived as a tentative work, an intimation of what was to come in the often promised second volume of his *De sacramentele Heilseconomie*. Not contending that this early work represents Schillebeeckx's mature thought, I simply note here the conception of sacrament which he presented in this work, which is widely known.

position of a divine activity into a human activity. His human love is the human embodiment of the redeeming love of God, God's love in visible form. [75]

"... Because the saving acts of the man Jesus are performed by a divine person, they have a divine power to save, but because this divine power to save appears to us in visible form, the saving activity of Jesus is *sacramental*. For a sacrament is a divine bestowal of salvation in an outwardly perceptible form which makes the bestowal manifest; a bestowal of salvation in historical visibility.... Consequently if the human love and all the human acts of Jesus possess a divine saving power, then the realization in human shape of this saving power necessarily includes as one of its aspects the manifestation of salvation: includes, in other words, sacramentality. The man Jesus, as the personal visible realization of the divine grace of redemption, is *the* sacrament, the primordial sacrament...." [76]

"The human actions of Jesus' life as they come from above show us their character as acts of redemption of his fellow men; these acts, in the mode of human love, are the merciful redeeming love of God himself. As coming from below they show their character as acts of worship; these acts are a true adoration and acknowledgment of God's divine existence; they are a service of praise or cult, religion, prayer--in a word, they are the man Jesus' love of God.... Therefore Jesus is not only the offer of divine love to man made visible but, at the same time, as prototype (or primordial model) he is the supreme realization of the response of human love to this divine offer." [77]

The Church is the sacrament of the risen Christ. "... In his messianic sacrifice, which the Father accepts, Christ in his glorified body is himself the eschatological redemptive community of the Church. In his own self the glorified Christ is simultaneously both 'Head and members.'" [78]

"...Christ makes his presence among us actively visible and tangible too, not directly through his own bodiliness, but by extending among us on earth in visible form the function of his bodily reality which is in heaven. This is precisely what the sacraments are: the earthly extension of the 'body of the Lord.' This is the Church...." [79]

---

[75] Cf. pp. 13-14.

[76] P. 15.

[77] Pp. 17-18.

[78] P. 47.

[79] P. 41.

"The earthly Church is the visible realization of this saving reality in history.... the earthly sign of the triumphant redeeming grace of Christ.... Thus the essence of the Church consists in this, that the final goal of grace achieved by Christ becomes visibly present in the *whole* Church as a visible society." [80]

"In manifesting sacramentally its own holiness, the Church makes holy. Thus in the strength of its own being filled with the fullness of Christ--to which the Church gives ritual expression in the sacraments--the Church in its sacraments acts as a saving community.... Hence every sacrament is a ritual prayer of the whole Church, which thus infallibly confers on the religiously disposed recipient the grace prayed for...." [81]

"From this account of sacraments as the earthly prolongation of Christ's glorified bodiliness, it follows immediately that Christ's sacraments are not things, but encounters of men on earth with the glorified man Jesus by way of a visible form. On the plane of history they are the visible and tangible embodiment of the heavenly saving action of Christ. They are this saving action itself in its availability to us; a personal act of the Lord in earthly visibility and open availability." [82]

"... A sacrament, that is an act of the primordial sacrament which is the Church, is a visible action proceeding from the Church as redemptive institution, an official ecclesial act performed in virtue either of the character of the priesthood or of the characters of baptism and confirmation. Hence in this sense a sacrament is actually something more than that which we usually understand under the term 'seven sacraments,' but it is also something more limited than that which we have just called 'general visibility,' meaning sacramentality as an outward manifestation not of office, but directly of inward communion in grace (i.e., the outwardly visible holiness of the life of the faithful in the Church). It is, however, necessary to assess the seven sacraments in their proper place within the wider sacramental context of the entire Church. A sacrament is primarily and fundamentally a personal act of Christ himself, which reaches and involves us in the form of an institutional act performed by a person in the Church who, in virtue of a sacramental character, is empowered to do so by Christ himself: an act *ex officio*." [83]

---

[80] Pp. 47-48.
[81] Pp. 66-67.
[82] P. 44.
[83] Pp. 52-53.

"... [It] should be clear enough from all the subsequent discussion that the seven sacraments, although primarily an official action of the hierarchical Church (through the minister), are not this alone, but also an official action of the recipient who, in virtue of his baptism, by the intention he expresses in the actual reception of the sacrament truly and coessentially contributes to the validity, the full ecclesial realization, of the sacrament...." [84]

"... To receive the sacraments of the Church in faith is therefore the same thing as to encounter Christ himself. In this light the sacramentality of the seven sacraments is the same as the sacramentality of the whole Church...." [85] "... what takes place in the sacraments is the immediate encounter in mutual availability between the living *Kyrios* and ourselves. The sacraments are this encounter...." [86]

"... The sacraments are [Christ's] redemptive will itself in visible and tangible ecclesial form. They are thus the actual gift of grace itself coming and appealing to us in historical visibility. The sign itself makes the actual gift of grace here present. It is not of course as if the sign, as sign, could have an actual effect, but rather the other way about; the gift of grace comes in its own visibility; it makes itself here present visibly ... and therefore 'works' in visible presence...." [87]

Reflection.

Two general characteristics are notable in the thought of the six theologians whom I have considered in this chapter. First, every one in his own way stressed the general sacramentality of Christ and the Church. Second, if one looks to some sort of witness to a tradition, it can concern only the least common denominator in the thought of the six. That would be, I should say, a minimum notion of *sacrament*, perhaps best formulated in the broad formula taken over by the Council of Trent: visible form of invisible grace, or of divine reality.

Though Möhler and Scheeben were theologians who devoted great effort to patristic studies, neither they nor the other four present much accurate documentation for their broad conception of Christ and Church as sacrament or symbol. All six are notable for their elaboration of highly personal theological thought. Their

---

[84] Pp. 53-54, note 7.
[85] P. 54.
[86] P. 62.
[87] P. 74.

notions of sacrament, more or less sharply conceptualized, are personal, and anyone interested in critical evaluation would have to analyze and judge every one. That has not been my concern here. I am concerned simply in noting in these six theologians a common sense that Christ and Church are somehow great, prime sacraments.

Beyond this evidence of a broad common sense of Christ and Church as prime sacraments, all details of individual notions, for example of sacrament, worship, or efficacy may be more or less worthy of consideration as one would seek to develop a full sacramental theology.

With this minimum general reflection, I pass on to consider the notion of sacrament in the teaching of the second Vatican Council.

SACRAMENT IN THE TEACHING OF THE SECOND VATICAN COUNCIL

The Second Vatican Council took over the broad sense of *sacrament*, applied to Christ and to the Church, and in many of its documents contributed to what can be synthesized as an impressive body of doctrine. In my exposition I shall propose a synthesis of the elements which I have gathered from the documents.

The formal statement which perhaps is most significant is oblique, doubly oblique regarding Christ: "... Since the Church is in Christ as a sacrament or sign and instrument of intimate union with God and of the unity of the whole human race...." [88] The teaching is oblique concerning the Church, since it is in a subordinate causal clause. It is doubly oblique concerning Christ: *in* Christ the Church is a sacrament: implicitly its being sacrament is derived from Christ's being sacrament. Though the text should not be pressed beyond a general sense of sacrament, sign, and instrument, many fragmentary texts in several documents serve to provide a sort of commentary. The general sense of sacrament is gradually elaborated, and the themes of sign and cause are developed as they serve to give intelligible structure to many particular affirmations re-

---

[88] *Lumen gentium* (LG) Dogmatic Constitution on the Church, 1. In citing documents of Vatican II, in my first citation or quotation of a document, I shall give the traditional Latin opening words, the English translation of the title, and the numbers of the sections in the Latin document. Where it will be helpful, I shall add a period and numeral to indicate the paragraph of the Latin text, though such numbering is not given in the original text. In subsequent citations or quotations I shall give only the letters abbreviating the Latin opening keywords, for example "LG." Translations of the Latin are mine.

garding Christ and the universal Church, local churches and
parishes, and members of the Church.

I shall present this synthesis under three headings: Christ,
Church, and the sacraments.

(1) *Christ*.

As I have suggested regarding the significant text quoted, the
Council's oblique affirmation of the Church's being sacrament
implicitly affirms Christ's sacramentality. Other texts bear out this
interpretation and elaborate the ways in which Christ is sign and
cause, and what he signifies and effects.

Christ's "... humanity, in the unity of the person of the Word,
was the instrument of our salvation." [89] The Church's role is
illumined by the analogy with the human nature of the Incarnate
Word: "... As the nature assumed serves the divine Word as a living
organ of salvation, indissolubly united to him, so in a manner not
unlike this the social structure of the Church serves the Spirit of
Christ which vivifies it, for the growth of the body." [90]

Christ's role as sign is implicit in the opening words of the
document on the Church: "Since Christ is the light of the
nations...." [91] and in the account of his manifestation of the
presence of the Kingdom. In the word, works, and presence of
Christ the kingdom of God shines forth to men. His word is
compared to a seed. His miracles prove that the Kingdom has
already come on earth. Above all however the kingdom is
manifested in the very Person of Christ, Son of God and Son
of man. [92]

Most efficacious of all that Christ did and suffered was the
whole paschal mystery: "This work of human redemption and
perfect glorification of God, to which the divine wonders in the
people of the Old Testament had been a prelude, Christ the Lord
fulfilled principally through the paschal mystery of his blessed
passion, resurrection from the lower regions, and glorious ascen-
sion. By this mystery he 'destroyed our death by dying, and by
rising restored our life.'" [93] It is from the paschal mystery that all
sacraments and sacramentals draw their power. [94]

---

[89] *Sacrosanctum Concilium* (SC) Constitution on the Liturgy, 5.
[90] LG 8.1.
[91] LG 1.
[92] Cf. LG, 5.1.
[93] SC 5.1.
[94] SC 61.

Christ continues to be present and active in and through his Church. "To complete this great work, Christ is always present to his Church, especially in liturgical actions: He is present in the Sacrifice of the Mass, not only in the person of the minister [in which it is] 'the same now offering by the ministry of priests who then offered himself on the cross' [Council of Trent....], but also and most of all under the eucharistic appearances. He is present by his power in the sacraments, so that when anyone baptizes, Christ himself baptizes. He is present in his word, since he himself speaks as the holy Scriptures are read in the Church. Finally he is present as the Church pleads and sings, he who himself promised, 'Where two or three are gathered in my name, there I am in their midst' (Mt 18.20). In this great work, by which God is perfectly glorified and human persons are sanctified, Christ really associates with himself his Church, his beloved spouse, which invokes him, and through him worships the Eternal Father." [95] "In any community gathered about the altar under the sacred ministry of the bishop, there is shown the symbol of that love and 'unity of the mystical body without which there cannot be salvation.' In these communities, though often small and poor, or living in dispersion, Christ is present, by whose power the one holy catholic apostolic Church is united." [96]

(2) *The Church*.

"... It pleased God not to save men individually, without any mutual bond, but to constitute them a people, which would acknowledge him in truth and serve him in holiness...." [97] The Eternal Father planned to call together in the holy Church those who believe in Christ. This Church, "... prefigured from the beginning of the world, wonderfully prepared in the history of the people Israel and the Old Covenant, was manifested by the outpouring of the Spirit, and at the end of time will be gloriously consummated." [98]

The genuine nature of the Church is "...to be at once human and divine, visible with invisible endowments, fervent in action and free for contemplation, present in the world and yet a pilgrim, and in such a manner that there is an order and subordination of what is

---

[95] SC 7.1. For his presence in performance of the divine office, cf. SC 83, 84.
[96] LG 26.1; cf. 21.1.
[97] LG 9.1.
[98] LG 2. For other statements regarding the phases of this process see LG 13, 48.2, 59; SC 5.

human in her to the divine, the visible to the invisible, action to contemplation, and the present to the future city which we seek...." [99] "Christ the sole Mediator established and continually sustains his holy Church, a community of faith, hope, and love, as a visible structure, by which he spreads truth and grace to all.... The society equipped with hierarchical organs and the mystical body of Christ, the visible assembly and the spiritual community, the earthly Church and the Church endowed with heavenly goods, should not be considered as two things, but they form one complex reality, which is comprised of a human and a divine element..." [100]

Several times the Council returned to the basic conception of the Church as sacrament, sign and instrument. "...That messianic people, though it does not actually include all men, and often seems a small flock, still for the whole human race is a sturdy sprout of unity, hope, and salvation.... Established by Christ as a communion of life, love, and truth, it is also assumed as an instrument of redemption of all, and is sent out to the whole world as the light of the world and the salt of the earth.... The assembly of those who look with faith upon Jesus as the source of salvation and the beginning of unity and peace, God has called together and established as a Church, to be for all and for each a visible sacrament of this saving unity...." [101] "Christ, raised from the earth, drew all to himself; rising from the dead, he sent his vivifying Spirit to his disciples, and through it established his Body, which is the Church, as a universal sacrament of salvation...." [102] The Church is "... an ensign raised up to the nations, beneath which the scattered children of God are to be gathered into one, until there be one sheepfold and one shepherd." [103] "... Every good which the People of God in the time of its earthly pilgrimage can give to the family of men flows from this, that the Church is a 'universal sacrament of salvation' [LG, 48], at once manifesting and effecting the mystery of God's love for men." [104]

By its teaching on the liturgy, the Church's public worship, the Council brings out both the importance of the Church's broad sacramental role and the unique place of the sacraments

---

[99] SC 2.

[100] LG 8.1 The Council continues here with the text which I have quoted above, concerning the analogy between the roles of the human nature of Christ and of the Church.

[101] LG 9.2-3.

[102] LG 48.2. Cf. *Ad gentes* (AG) 1, 2, 5.

[103] SC 2. Cf. AG 36.

[104] *Gaudium et spes* (GS) 45.1.

within the life of the Church. In my treatment of the teaching on Christ as sacrament I have quoted the great affirmation concerning Christ's multiple presence in his Church, especially in liturgical actions. The Council continues by setting forth its understanding of what the liturgy is. "Rightly therefore the liturgy is considered as the exercise of Jesus Christ's priestly ministry, in which through sensibly perceptible signs the sanctification of human persons is signified and is accomplished in a manner proper to every one, and full public worship is carried out by the mystical body of Jesus Christ, that is by the Head and his members. Therefore every liturgical celebration, as a work of Christ the priest and his Body, the Church, is eminently a sacred action, whose efficacy no other action of the Church equals with the same title and degree." [105]

Christ sent the Apostles not merely to preach the Gospel to every creature, but also "... to carry out the work of salvation through the Sacrifice and the Sacraments, about which the whole liturgical life turns...." [106] The liturgy is the peak to which the action of the Church tends, and the source from which all its power flows. [107] Through the liturgy, most of all in the divine Sacrifice of the Eucharist, "the work of our redemption is carried out." The liturgy contributes in the highest degree to this, that the faithful by their lives express and manifest to others the mystery of Christ and the genuine nature of the Church. [108]

In liturgical actions in the local church, Christ is present, and the Church is present. [109] Liturgical actions are not private, but celebrations of the Church, which is the "sacrament of unity," that is, a holy people united and ordered under the bishops. Therefore they pertain to the whole Body of the Church, and manifest and affect it. [110] The principal manifestation of the Church is had in full and active participation of the whole holy people of God in the same liturgical celebrations, especially in the same Eucharist, in one prayer, at one altar at which the Bishop presides, surrounded by his priests and ministers. [111]

---

[105] SC 7.2-3.

[106] SC 6.

[107] Cf. SC 10.

[108] SC 2. The quotation is from the Roman Missal, for the ninth Sunday after Pentecost.

[109] Cf. LG 26.

[110] SC 26.1-2.

[111] SC 41.

Working out many of the implications of the Church's being a sacrament, the Council indicates particular roles of local churches and of all of the members of the Body. [112]

(3) *The Sacraments.*

I gather here some of the elements of the Council's teaching on the Eucharistic sacrifice and the sacraments, beyond what I have cited in treating the liturgy.

"... As often as the sacrifice of the cross, 'by which Christ our Pasch was immolated' (1 Cor 5.7), is celebrated on the altar, the work of our redemption is carried out. At the same time, by the sacrament of the eucharistic bread, the unity of the believers is represented and accomplished. They constitute one body in Christ (cf. 1 Cor 10.17)...." [113] The Eucharistic sacrifice is a "...sacrament of devotion, a sign of unity, a bond of love, a paschal banquet 'in which Christ is eaten, the spirit is filled with grace, and we are given the pledge of future glory.'" [114] The Eucharist is the sacrament by which the unity of the Church is both signified and effected. [115] To priests the Council makes a special recommendation: "... In the mystery of the Eucharistic Sacrifice, in which priests fulfill their principal office, the work of our redemption is carried out continually. Therefore its daily celebration is earnestly recommended, which, even if the presence of believers cannot be had, is an act of Christ and of the Church...." [116]

"Sacraments are intended to sanctify men, to build up the Body of Christ, and finally to worship God. As signs moreover they

---

[112] I shall not attempt to set forth the details. For those who wish to trace the lines of development of the theme, here are most of the classes mentioned: Peter and the Roman Pontiff (LG 18, 23); bishops (LG 21, 23); priests (LG 28.2; and PO, *Presbyterorum ordinis*, Decree on the ministry and life of priests, 12); lay persons (LG 30-35, 38; AA, *Apostolicam actuositatem*, Decree on the apostolate of lay persons, 1, 2, 6, 13, 16, 20; AG, *Ad gentes*, Decree on the missionary activity of the Church, 21,41); in particular women (AA 9); the married and family members (LG 35; AA 11, 16; GS 47-51); martyrs (LG 42); virgins and celibates (LG 42; PO 16.2); religious (LG 39, 44, 46; PC, *Perfectae caritatis*, Decree on the appropriate renewal of religious life, 1; AG, 18; and finally a summary treatment of many (LG 41; AG 11-12, 15). On the missionary activity of the Church, involving many members, see AG 5, 9, 11, 15, 23-27.

[113] LG 3.

[114] *...sacramentum pietatis, signum unitatis, vinculum caritatis....* SC 47. The quotation is from the Roman Breviary, the antiphon for the *Magnificat* in second vespers of the feast of Corpus Christi.

[115] UR, *Unitatis redintegratio*, Decree on Ecumenism, 2.

[116] PO 13.2.

pertain to instruction. They not only presuppose faith, but by words and things also nourish, strengthen, and express it. Hence they are called sacraments of faith. They confer grace indeed, but their celebration also best disposes the faithful to receive that same grace fruitfully, to worship God fittingly, and to practice love." [117] In the Mystical Body "... Christ's life is spread to believers, who through the sacraments in a secret and real manner are united with Christ who suffered and was glorified...." [118] The apostolate of lay persons flows from the Christian vocation. They share in Christ's priestly, prophetic, and regal office. By baptism and confirmation they are assigned to apostolate. By the sacraments, especially the Eucharist, they are nourished inlove. [119]

---

[117] SC 59.
[118] LG 7.
[119] Cf. AA 1-3.

CHAPTER V

THE STATE OF THE QUESTION

At the end of our long review of the process of conceptualization of *sacrament*, one may sense bewilderment. Certainly the process has not come to term, nor will it ever come to term. No one will ever "define" the Christian sacrament in such a way as to convey an understanding in which all theologians, or all inquiring and reflecting Christians, could rest content. From the beginnings of Christian reflection recorded in the New Testament we witness an untiring effort to probe aspects of the Mystery. Far from registering failure, the record of these struggles to understand helps us to appreciate both the fruits of continued effort and the incomprehensibility of the Mystery.

In the long history, of which I have traced some lines, we find revealed truth and a succession of insights, all of which contribute some degree of understanding. We cannot hold a cluster of insights, or form a sort of mosaic of insights, which together would constitute an adequate conceptualization. We may hope, however, to ponder them, hold those portions of the truth which they express, evaluate them for their contribution to theology, and seek to expand our grasp of the field of relationships in which alone we may deepen our understanding of the Christian sacrament.

To facilitate such a further reflection, we may gather what seem to be noteworthy contributions to an eventual deeper understanding. In this chapter I shall first present the revealed data and what I consider important insights into the nature of the Christian sacrament and then indicate further questions. In the chapters which follow I shall prepare the elements which I regard as helpful in the task of a further elaboration of a definition of the sacrament. Then I shall present my own definition, and finally reflect on the implications of my thought for further elaboration of some themes of classic sacramental theology.

A CLUSTER OF INSIGHTS

(1) *The configuration of actions in baptism.*

In its entirety the NewTestament teaching on baptism serves as a rich, powerful catechesis which illumines the ceremony by setting

it in its place in the history of salvation, the Mystery. Within that
catechesis we may discover a significant configuration of actions,
some of them perceptible, others known only by revelation of what
the Divine Persons are doing in the total event. Reflection on the
configuration of these actions yields some initial insight into
significant relationships.

(a) Preaching. The saving event begins with preaching, proclamation of the word of revelation, which is absolutely necessary.
By it alone are hearers given the first clue to the "world" of
salvation history within which their baptism will have meaning. On
Pentecost Peter set the events of Christ's death and resurrection,
and of the outpouring of the Spirit whose effects the multitude had
just witnessed, in the pattern of promise and fulfillment, in the
history of salvation. Through baptism, those who believed would
receive the Spirit, and their change of heart would include
commitment to a new way of life. Baptism is a saving event,
intelligible only as an act in which God's saving action reaches this
man or woman here and now, and effects an enrichment and
transformation.

(b) Belief. Preaching alone could not make baptism intelligible.
Without the gift of belief, those who heard the word could not
understand. Faith is demanded, and it has a role which in later
terminology would be called that of a disposition. It is required
because it is intrinsically necessary to the whole saving event. Faith
involves not just a human act, but also a divine illumination. Only
by inner illumination does a man or woman enter into the world
within which alone baptism is intelligible. Without it, no one can
really grasp who is or are really acting principally, and what is really
happening within the person who is baptized. Of themselves the
perceptible symbolic elements of the whole event would be utterly
inadequate to convey the unique meaning of baptism in the
Christian mystery. At most they could suggest some sort of
death/rebirth or purification or other effect which they vaguely
represent in rites of other religions.

Both elements of the act of faith are essential. The illumination
by the Spirit opens the "vision" of a new world of reality. The
personal act of belief, itself at once gift and free personal acceptance, is a leap beyond what could be naturally evident, a personal appropriation of the new life which is offered.

(c) Repentance, change of one's way of life, commitment to
continuing effort to live a new life also contributes to understanding
the meaning of baptism. It is the beginning of a process which is to

lead to final fulfillment of the promise, to the full salvation which is the Christian's goal. The Christian has been saved, and is being saved, is being created anew and built into the living temple of God.

(2) *Who is, or are, acting?*

One of the most important elements of New Testament teaching on baptism is that the principal agents are Father/God, Son/Christ, and the Spirit of God and of Jesus. As I have pointed out, this truth is retained in a few of the Church's documents. A relatively adequate theology of the Christian sacrament must give proper emphasis to this truth.

(3) *What are they doing?*

Evidently through human agents They are performing external symbolic actions. The meaning of these external actions can be grasped only by belief in their imperceptible effects. I have spelled out these effects in the biblical terminology regarding baptism. [1] From patristic thought through the long history of theology grasp of the relationships grounded in these effects pertains to the theology of the Christian sacrament. Sacraments have a twofold function. One is cognitive: they represent, and mediate some understanding of, the event in which God's saving action is coming to term here and now in this man or woman. The other is causative: the sacrament somehow mediates the enrichment and transformation which God effects in the recipient.

(4) *Inchoate conceptualizations.*

Looking back at the stages of conceptualization which I have sketched in preceding chapters, I should say that all of the efforts to conceptualize the Christian mystery-sacrament have yielded modest results.

(a) The term *mystērion* means little more than hidden, absolutely or relatively. What understanding we reach from reflection upon Pauline or patristic use of this term comes not from a definition, but from the intelligible relationships which can be traced in the total field of all that is called *mystery*.

One element of Chrysostom's thought, however, is worthy of note. It is his distinction between *aisthēton* and *noēton*: that which is sensibly perceptible, and that which can be known only by the

---

[1] See Chapter I.

power of faith, with "spiritual eyes." I shall indicate the significance of this distinction after having recalled a similar one in the thought of Augustine.

(b) *Sacramentum* in Augustine's thought marks a degree of progress in conceptualization which has served western theology and Church teaching through the centuries. Yet his definition of *sign*, his distinction between *signum* and *res*, and his formula *sacrum signum* for the sacrament as a divine sign, are a very modest achievement. The sign is a *thing* which, being known, causes another thing to come to thought. Apart from the vague distinction between natural and "given" signs, he offers no theory of the origin of "given" signs. In my judgment, all of the teasings of Augustinian and near-Augustinian formulae contribute little to the understanding of the Christian sacrament. Augustine's sign and his various formulae which entered into the effort to define the Christian sacrament are bits of vague conceptualization, free to float in many inchoate intellectual worlds.

The notable distinction in Augustine's thought, similar to that marked in Chrysostom's, is between that which is seen and that which our faith teaches. As I shall point out, these two distinctions may occasion some fruitful reflection on later "definitions" and on the notions of visibility, perceptibility, and sacramentality as they are common in modern and contemporary theological thought and language.

(c) Classic "definitions" or descriptions in medieval and later theology and in Church documents. At the outset of my exposition of the attempts of medieval theologians to define "sacrament," I set forth "complicating factors," more than a broad hint of my judgment of the results of the long succession of efforts. [2] None of the classic "definitions" has won general acceptance. None deserves it. This judgment is confirmed, I think, by the fact that the Church, in its teaching regarding the sacraments, nowhere offers what could be regarded as a definition. Rather, it selects elements from the many classic formulae of patristic and scholastic thinkers, and often modifies the formulae or blends them in an eclectic manner. Ironically it is the Second Vatican Council, whose purpose was pastoral rather than dogmatic, which offered some stimulating formulae and many elements of a rich teaching.

As for the formulae and elaborations of modern and contemporary theologians, I regard them as suggestive, but hardly

---

[2] See Chapter III.

advancing beyond the "dialectic of opinions." Much remains to be done. I shall not proceed by critical analysis and evaluation of others' offerings. I shall attempt to assemble some elements to be kept in mind, and I shall propose my own definition.

(5) *Salvation history.* [3]

Like any other history, salvation history may be conceived of as either process or human knowledge of that process. As process, it is the gradual realization of God's eternal plan to bring men and women to fulfillment in and through Christ (cf. Eph 1.3-14). "Salvation" may be defined here broadly as a twofold divine action: deliverance from the misery of the state of sin which followed upon human rejection of a prior divine gift, and enrichment by a second gift which transcends that which was lost. In its positive aspect, it is a God-given fulfillment by a share in the divine life, transcending all merely human perfection. I should say that we can distinguish two conceptions of the history of such salvation.

One would embrace the whole of human history, as it is viewed in the light of Christian revelation. We believe that God's will to save is universal. Consequently he gives to all men and women grace sufficient for them to reach the fulfillment which he offers. I should say, however, that "history" so understood is history as process, not as human knowledge. We can acknowledge that in this conception the whole of human process is one in which the God whom we believe is offering the grace of a share in his life and fulness of being. If, however, we consider history as human knowledge, we must admit that we do not have the data for the elaboration of such knowledge. We can affirm our belief in that process. We can do no more than conjecture the course of its realization in the vast majority of the human race: those who do not have an explicit knowledge of, and belief in, Jesus Christ.

The other conception is paradoxical in its apparent limitations. As process, it seems to be a segment of total human process, that which concerns God's action on behalf of the people which he formed as his very own, and then his action in and through Christ and in the new people which is the Body of Christ. As knowledge, it is grounded in the revelation given to the patriarchs and the many who received the word in Israel, and it was completed in God's

---

[3] For my earlier treatment of this theme, see *The Mystery*, regarding Israel, pp. 84-98; regarding Christ and life in Christ, throughout Parts II and III, "The Mystery: Christ"and "The Mystery: Life in Christ." Further, the whole of *Telling About God*, Volume I, *Promise and Fulfillment* is concerned with salvation history.

revelation in his Son. It was by the knowledge of the history of
God's action on its behalf, formulated in the classic recitals of its
scriptures, that Israel defined itself as a people. It is in the great
recitals of the continuation of the process of salvation, of the
fulfillment of the promises in Christ, that we identify ourselves as
the new Israel.

In what sense do I say that this conception of the history of
salvation is paradoxical in its limitations? As knowledge, it regards
directly what has been revealed to Israel and to us. As process, it
seems to regard that segment of human history in which God is
acting on behalf those who received and believed that special
revelation. Yet by this special revelation alone do we know that
God's will to save is universal, and that the whole of human process
is borne by God and directed to human fulfillment in a share in
divine life in and through Christ. By special revelation we know the
process in which we are involved as we live in Christ. Yet we know
too of the universal will to save. We know that God is offering his
life to all. We do not know by what ways he is acting on behalf of
the vast majority of men and women who do not know Christ and
will not in their lifetimes.

As Peter explained on Pentecost the meaning of the baptism which he exhorted his hearers to receive, so we can explain our sacraments as part of the mystery which is being realized
in us: by situating them in the history of salvation, the mystery of
Christ. In doing so, we are finding some understanding of our
sacraments in their relationships within the whole world which we
know only by special revelation. There remain some tormenting
questions regarding whether and how they are related to the men
and women who have been saved and will be saved with only
intimations of that transcendent world of which we have explicit
knowledge.

(6) *The sacramentality of God's saving action.*

Sacramentality is a theological concept, elaborated first in a
reflection on salvation history in the Old Testament, then extended
to God's saving work in Christ, and finally to the continuation of
that work in the Church. Beyond that development, one can
recognize a universal sacramentality, coherent with the truths of the
universality of both God's will to save, and the history of salvation.
The universality and analogy of such sacramentality raise further
questions, which demand consideration in any relatively adequate
search for an intelligible account of the Christian sacraments in
their setting.

Evidently the word *sacramentality* in this theological context is correlative to *sacrament* taken in a broad sense as *sacred sign*, and understood in the broad sense as it has been taken in the western theology since the middle ages. In this sense a sacrament has two functions: to make known the sacred, and to effect something of the sacred which it signifies.

The whole conception is based on belief of the truth revealed to Israel and then through Christ. Without such belief, the notion of the sacramentality of God's saving action is unintelligible.

What, then, is involved in the concept of sacramentality and the elaboration of a theory of universal sacramentality? It is the reflection which I have mentioned, proceeding in four stages, regarding four stages in the understanding of salvation history.

(a) In Israel. In his saving action on behalf of those whom he made his own people, God somehow manifested what he was doing. Humanly speaking, he broke into human history by word and action. Both word and action are important. God somehow appeared and spoke to Abraham and the patriarchs, to Moses and the prophets. We cannot conjecture the psychological structure of the experiences of those who received God's word. We know simply the tradition that they were convinced of having received his word, and that they somehow understood the meaning of his action as it was revealed by his word.

With regard to God's action, the theological sense of "action" in this context obviously is not the divine action in itself, identical with the divine essence, but its term, the perceptible effect of the action.

When Abraham asked how he was to know that he would possess the land which God had promised, the answer came in a symbolic covenant ritual with an explanatory word (Gn 15.8-21). In the series of actions by which God delivered his people from Egypt, word and action were essential elements. By his word God predicted his action and explained its meaning. The purpose of his actions was to convince Moses and the people that God had spoken (Ex 4.2), to compel Pharaoh to let them go (Ex 3.20), to make the Egyptians acknowledge that he is Yahweh (Ex 7.3-5; 9.14,16), and to bring Israel to acknowledge him (Ex 10.2; 11.7). Later God ordered the prophets to perform symbolic actions, sometimes signifying, and seemingly effecting, punishment for sin. Through the prophets he announced marvelous works in the restoration of Jerusalem: signs for the conversion of all nations and the gathering of Israel (Is 66.7-23). Gathering Israel, he would show forth his holiness and power, to bring the nations to worship in Israel (Ez 20.40-44; 28.25-26; 38.23; 39.21-29).

Obviously there is a difference between history of past action and prophecy of future. Yet the relation of word to action is the same in both. God is not visible. Nor would his action be perceptible or intelligible simply from external effects in themselves. Salvation history is known as such only by belief in the word of special revelation which gives the clue to its meaning. Symbolic action heightens the vividness of the message. Yet without a word of revelation the meaning would not be apparent, nor would God's saving action be "perceptible."

There is what can be called a second order of sacramentality of God's saving action: it is the complex sacramentality of Israel's public worship. I should say that it involves three elements.

First, one element of that worship was the recital and ritual commemoration in a symbolic enactment of Yahweh's great saving actions. The feasts of the Passover and of the unleavened bread were meant to be memorials. They involved symbolic actions whose meaning was to be explained by the recital of salvation history (Ex 12.26-27). The rite was meant to be a sign, to remind Israel of Yahweh's great act of deliverance, and to move her again to a response of faith. In covenant renewal the theophany of Sinai was re-enacted symbolically, and the covenant pledge was relived. [4]

A second element was the essential religious response, the heart of the act of public worship, which rendered perceptible the saving action reaching its relative term in personal response. If the rite had any real meaning, it was not in the mere external symbolic action of the participants, but in their full reliving and appropriating the original experience.

A third element was the whole system of the sacred. An altar (Gn 12.7-8) or a pillar (Gn 28.18) or a monument of twelve stones (Jos 4.1--5.1) marked the spot of a divine intervention, reminding Israel and others of Yahweh's action in Israel's favor. In cultic institutions sacred persons, places, things, and times served to signify Yahweh's presence and to move the Israelites to a religious response. The purpose of the whole cultic system and of the Law of

---

[4] I am not suggesting that such commemoration should be understood as some believe, as a rendering present of the past event in its full reality. Such an interpretation, in my judgment, is fantasy. Rather, as I understand the matter, the symbolic reenactment served to revive memory and stir vivid imagination, and thus to move the people to recall and make their own the experience of their ancestors. As the first Israelites did when the covenant was struck, so later generations, moved by the vivid representation of that event, made that history their own, and committed themselves in their turn to covenant union and fidelity. So they themselves found their identity by acknowledging their place in the sacred history.

Holiness (Lv 19-26) was to consecrate a people truly holy, intimately united with the covenant God, and manifesting the further effect of his saving action in their lives.

Beyond the limited realm of worship there was a third order of the sacramentality of God's saving action: the whole life of Israel, which was to be a sacred sign, showing the holiness of Yahweh, and drawing other nations to worship him (cf. Ez 20.40-44; 28.25-26).

Obviously in the whole range of things, natural phenomena, actions, persons, and places there is a broad analogy of sacramentality. In theophanies, when God used fire or wind or thunder to symbolize his presence, power, and action, when he somehow "appeared" and was "heard," the things and actions and persons which serve to manifest him were purely signs and instruments, utterly diverse in themselves from the divine reality which they somehow signify. God cannot be seen or heard, and sensible manifestation is not a dimension of the divine operation itself. God's use of signs, and the "sacramentality" of God's saving action is a matter of pure condescension. Until the Son of God takes human nature in the mystery of the Incarnation, "sacramental" action is not "natural" to God, and cannot be explained in terms of phenomenology, except by a projection of human needs and the manner of human encounter.

In the sacramentality of the human response and of the cultic system of Israel, a distinction is needed. There is a whole order of signs, sacred persons, things, places, and times which are completely distinct both from God and from the worshipper. They signify the sacred, and call for a religious response, but they are in a sense part of neither. Even in the case of consecrated persons, what is involved is an "ontological" holiness, of "things" set aside to serve as signs. Quite different is the sacramental dimension of the human act of worship, in which the person and the community show in external, perceptible action the full flowering of devotion. Their "sacramental" action is not a thing, a mere sign, completely distinct from them. Rather it is the culmination in outward manifestation of the whole human act of devotion which involves spirit and body. This is the sacramental action and the sacramentality which can be explained in part by the phenomenology of human encounter.

With regard to the notion of encounter, which some have used to explain sacraments, a reservation is called for. "... The various kinds of sacramental action are moments in the encounter of man and God, but none of them can be simply identified with the encounter, or with the salvation which is the purpose and the term of the encounter. The external action by which God offers salvation--whether in the original saving act or in its symbolic

re-presentation--is the first moment of the encounter: external
manifestation of the divine offer and invitation. The external
dimension of the human response to grace is an element of the full
human reply, which is the final moment of the encounter. Both the
divine and the human external action are sacramental and pertain
to the encounter: they are not simply the encounter, which
involves both of these and much more. On God's part, saving
action is imperfectly expressed in an external symbol which is by
nature simply alien to the divine reality which it somehow
signifies. Moreover his saving action goes beyond the moment of
the external sign of offer: God operates within the human spirit,
fashioning the human response which is the work of God and
man, of God in and through man. On man's part, the sacramental
dimension is but one of many, and it cannot express fully the
reality of the human response, which rises from the spiritual
powers of man; which at times reaches its peak of intensity not in
the moment of external manifestation, but in silent, secret prayer
heard by God alone, and never to be adequately expressed in the
poor words and gestures of external worship.

"What I have said of the relation of sacramental action to
encounter implies what must be noted explicitly: the imperfections
and the limitations of sacramentality. This is a complement to
what I have observed concerning salvation history as world
process and as knowledge. The whole process of the divine saving
action is only partly perceptible, visible, sacramental. Neither God
nor man can express it adequately in human word and gesture.
Salvation history as knowledge must remain imperfect because it
can never grasp the full reality which is its object. Proportionately,
sacramental action, expressing the action of either God or man or
both, must remain inadequate to grasp and express the whole
reality of the divine offer and the human response in which it
terminates." [5]

(b) In Christ and in the Church. I simply recall here the
insight of modern theologians and the teaching of the Second
Vatican Council. Sacramental theology is enriched by the grasp of
the broad notion of the sacramentality of God's saving action in
Christ and in the Church. [6] Later I shall elaborate the roles of
Christ and of the Church in the diversity of its members.

---

[5] *The Mystery*, pp. 102-103.

[6] On Christ as the great sacrament, sign and instrumental cause of eternal life,
see *The Mystery*, pp. 178-186. On the Church and individual Christians, *ibid.*, pp.
347-353.

(7) *Worship*.

From the whole context of Augustine's treatment of some sacraments, clearly there is question of rites of worship, in the Old Testament and in the New. St. Thomas situates the sacraments in his theology of worship. Pius XII, in *Mediator Dei*, and the Second Vatican Council develop their teaching of the sacraments as acts of public worship of Christ in and through his Church. Worship is one of the themes which must figure explicitly in any definition and theological elaboration of an understanding of the Christian sacrament.

These, in my judgment, are important insights and bits of conceptualization which must be part of a more adequate theology.

REFLECTION

I suggest here some thoughts concerning three elements of the historical sketch which I have presented, regarding the scholastic definitions, the role of Church documents, and contributions to a further understanding of the sacraments set in the context of the broad sense of sacrament.

With regard to the classic scholastic definitions, I offered some implicit critical reflection when I pointed out complicating factors in the whole process. [7] One might characterize the whole effort as an ingenious shuffling of words, without any serious attempt to conceptualize. The Augustinian notion of sign is utterly inadequate to afford the conceptual resources necessary to elaborate an intelligible structure which accounts for all of the factors which are involved in the complicated data concerning the Christian sacraments. Recall Augustine's distinction of things and signs, and his quasi definition of sign: "Some things are not used to signify anything, for example wood, a stone, a sheep. Other things are also signs. What, then is a sign? It is a thing which, besides the appearance which it brings to the senses, causes something else to come to thought." [8] First, I suspect that if anyone had given Augustine a minute or two, he could have reversed himself and suggested how wood, a stone, or a sheep could signify or symbolize something else. But more serious, how do certain things come to

---

[7] See above, chapter III, pp. 46 ff.
[8] See above, chapter II, p. 38.

cause something else to come to mind? Nowhere in the whole history of patristic and scholastic use of the term sign is there any serious effort to explain really what a sign or symbol is, how it comes to be, and how it functions in the interpersonal worlds in which alone it somehow is. The field of agents, or persons affected, of conditions, of effects, and of the historical context in which all are somehow intelligible shatters the Augustinian notion of sign. And the implicit scholastic notions of definition and of the method which could give some hope of relatively satisfactory results condemned the whole effort to frustration.

What is the role of the Church documents, which I have cited, in chapters three and four? They do not offer any advance in conceptualization. Rather they employ eclectically fragments of patristic and scholastic terminology. Nevertheless they play an important role. As occasion demanded, the Church fixed some elements of dogma and common teaching which set out clearly some of the data which must be accounted for in any sacramental theology. The elements of the teaching of the Council of Trent, of Pius XII, and of the Second Vatican Council are particularly important.

With regard to the soundings which I have taken of modern and recent theologians' contributions to the broader concept of sacrament, to a sense of the relevance of the notions of symbol and of encounter, I have made some very limited critical observations in this work. I do not intend to proceed by further critique of any of these offerings.

What I shall present in the remainder of this work is the result of my own study and reflection and gradual elaboration over a period of more than twenty years. [9] I am seeking to understand, and to share what hopefully will be intelligible to others. If it is intelligible, if it accounts for all of the data, affords an intelligible structure, and is open to further questions, if in short it rings true for some, no more can be asked. In such an effort one does not proceed by refutation and demonstration, but by patient reflection and elaboration of the complex written conceptual symbol which is a work of theology, intended to communicate what has been understood.

I turn now to setting forth the results of this effort.

---

[9] I do not include in this period my earlier work, resulting in my *De Sacramentis in Genere*, Rome: Gregorian University Press, 1957, 1960, 1962.

Chapter VI

HUMAN SYMBOLIZING

Symbolizing is an aspect of properly human operation, and symbols are properly human products.[1] They can be understood, therefore, only in their setting in the human world--in the many personal and interpersonal worlds which are uniquely human. In my judgment, the best way to approach their understanding is by a reflection which involves two stages. First, within the concrete whole of human conscious experience, we can discern and differentiate the principal human operations (and powers, as some would hold). Second, we can consider an aspect of such conscious operations which analogously is common to them: symbolizing and the symbols which are produced.

I acknowledge that this chapter is long. I find no other way to make clear that the two steps are intimately connected. As I reread *Man the Symbolizer*, I had the impression that two sets of six chapters, on human experience, and on symbolizing and symbols, might seem to fall into what could have been two books. That would be unfortunate. More than ever, I regard symbolizing and symbols as pertaining to the heart of the mystery of the human way of being. To make that clear, I reconsider essentials of the book here in a single chapter. After all, whether it is presented in one chapter or two, the whole thought must be developed before I pass on to what is distinctively new in this work: divine-human symbolizing and symbols. There is no inexorable law regarding the length of chapters. Nor is the same thought more or less formidable as it is presented in one or two chapters.

---

[1] I have treated the matter of this chapter in my work *Man the Symbolizer*. The thought developed there is an indispensable preparation for my consideration of divine-human symbolizing in the remainder of this work. Here I shall attempt to present concisely the essentials of that book. I am not, however, simply compressing its contents, but seeking to refine the thought.

Three Preliminary Considerations

(1) *Human experience.*

Human experience is a small segment of total process in the universe of bodily being. Like all that is bodily, we are involved constantly in the infinite interplay of forces and agents in the universe. Like all living things, we have a specific range of susceptibility to stimuli which, in our case, evoke a properly human response. That specific mode of susceptibility and response is a function of the organization which is characteristic of our highly complex human way of being and operating. Because we are in a bodily way, there is a bodily, "physical" element in both stimulus and response as they figure in all of our experience. At the higher levels of human operation, both stimulus and response are within the realm of human consciousness, awareness.

(2) *Conscious and consciousness.*

First, note that we are concerned with *human conscious* experience. Whatever may be known about animal consciousness at levels other than the human, I am focussing on human consciousness, characterized by uniquely human modes of knowledge and appetite. Second, I am approaching the matter by reflecting on our waking consciousness, not concerned here with the distinction between waking and dream consciousness.

What do I mean by *conscious* and *consciousness*? The notion of consciousness is simple and irreducible. To be conscious is to be aware. We may become "aware of awareness" if we reflect on our waking experience. We may concentrate on seeing what is before us, and turn to focus on other objects, and be aware of those objects, and of our seeing, and of shifting our visual perception from one object to another. We may listen attentively to one sound among the many which we hear, and shift to listen to another. We may feel the coolness of the tabletop, and then move to feel the heat of the teapot. We may reflect on our seeing and hearing and feeling. In every act we are aware "of" some person or thing or event. And as we are aware of them we may attend to our awareness of ourselves, "caught in the act" of our being aware of another. We may attend to our naming of what we perceive, and knowing at least vaguely what it is or they are. We may affirm, "This is a table. That is a dog." So at different levels, with different degrees of immediacy, we are aware of what we perceive and recognize by name and affirm to be; we are aware of our acting, and of ourselves caught in the act.

More vividly, we may become aware of awareness when we "come to" after having lost consciousness by fainting or by anaesthesia. Daily we can reflect on waking consciousness as we awake from sleep, and on the differences between waking consciousness and dream consciousness, at times by reassuring ourselves of being really awake after a terrifying nightmare. Pressing against the solid wall beside our bed, feeling our body, turning on the light and viewing our room, we contrast all these bits of "solid reality" with the substanceless fantasies of the dream, and free ourselves from the terror which they begot in us.

(3) *Twofold basic intentionality.*

Before undertaking the discernment and differentiation of our conscious operations and their products, we may note briefly an important aspect of all of them. They are somehow *of* the *other* or *others*. In philosophical terminology which has become common since the work of Husserl, this characteristic of our conscious operations is called *intentionality*. [2] We are in a universe of bodily beings, involved with all the rest in the continual interplay of agents, forces, or whatever we may prefer to call them, and in our conscious operations we somehow regard the other or others. Considered as regarding the other, our operations are *intentional*. Yet this common characteristic is realized diversely in two broad classes of operations. One mode of intentionality is *cognitive*. The other is *emotive/volitional/motor*.

There is a cluster of operations in which we react to the world in which we are by holding something of what we see, hear, feel, smell, taste; and within our seeing, hearing, feeling, smelling, and tasting we have from the outset some grasp of relationships, which are not sensibly perceptible. Within this whole cluster of operations our knowledge gradually develops. This is the realm of the operations which we call cognitive, among which gradually we distinguish different modes of sensing, and of understanding and judging, which are radically diverse from all modes of sense perception. In all cognitive operations and their products, the knowers, remaining themselves, somehow hold within themselves the mystery of the other.

---

[2] In using the terminology, I do not enter a Husserlian world of thought. The terms are used freely now, and my meaning is to be drawn from my brief explanations and the context of my own thought, as I have presented it principally in MS, pp. 13, 26-27, 84, 113-116, 125-134, 139-140.

There is a second broad class of widely divergent operations which presuppose knowledge of some sort, and by which we react to the other as good or bad for us. In this class of operations the basic intentionality is a love of all that is vaguely sensed to be good for us, and a tendency to union with that good. This love grounds our hatred of evil, and all consequent fear of it and shrinking from it.

DISCERNING AND DIFFERENTIATING OUR CONSCIOUS OPERATIONS

I shall consider first our cognitive operations, then our emotive, volitional, and motor operations.

(1) *Perception.* [3]

All sense perception regards what is present to us here and now: it is of *this*, or *these*, *here* and *now*. I cannot see or hear or feel now what was yesterday and no longer is. Nor can I see or hear or feel what is present now to you, but not to me. I have defined perception thus: "... an act of sense knowledge, primitive and immediate, objective or subjective, global and unitary, resulting in an image which itself is a complex configuration." [4]

As I perceive, I may be looking and listening and feeling by touch, and smelling, all at once, and what I am regarding is a complex field within which I may be roving from one object to another, and dwelling on one sensible aspect after another. I may be regarding a scene which is relatively motionless, or birds in flight, or drifting clouds, or swirling smoke, wondrously dynamic. But all is present to me, here, and now. The image is not like a fixed snapshot, but rather shifting and ever varying. As I gaze and listen and feel and smell I have an ever varying object. In our perception, as in all of our being, we are in space and movement, but always at the present moment in what we may call the flow of time. Moreover, in our perceiving we are ever grasping objects in somewhat different ways, as we shift our position and point of view. Our perceptions vary according to our perspective. If we are standing with others who are perceiving the same objects, we can, by comparing our experiences, verify the slight differences in what we

---

[3] See MS, pp. 32-40, 144-145.

[4] MS, 33. I observed there that the notion of an image is rejected by empiricist and so-called objective psychologists, and I indicated clearly the world of thought in which alone my whole theory of human operation and of symbolizing is intelligible.

all perceive from our varying points of perception. All perceiving is relative to our position, and to our personal worlds, the personal setting of every perceiver. All perceptions are characterized by the perspectivism of the many perceivers who themselves are continually changing position, and who are unique in the personal worlds within which they perceive.

(2) *Memory.*[5]

Memory is another kind of knowledge, involving the partial retention of what we have experienced. It is not a function of our external senses, but is performed somehow within us. Its object is unique: some segment of past personal experience. It differs from the retention of facts which we have learned. Thus I may remember many dates and events and personal qualities of historical persons, all of which I have been told, or have learned from study. Such retention and recall differs from what I retain and recall of my own personal past experience, whether it be of what I have seen or heard or felt or smelled or tasted, or of what I have come to know by discovery, or have judged to be true after examining the evidence, or what I have felt by emotion, desired, or shrunk from in repugnance, or what I have decided to do and have done. Knowledge of what we have learned and retained, but have never experienced personally, lacks the wealth of memory of past personal experience, the blend of images retained from perception and from all the other aspects of total concrete personal experience. This difference is significant for subsequent consideration of symbols and their functions. I shall return to it at the proper moment.

Memory is not like a collection of snapshots, which we can shuffle and by which we can recall fixed, rigidly limited images similar to those caught by a camera. Rather it is the retention, and possibility of recall, and actual recall, of a complex segment of personal experience. It affords a range of different kinds of images. Some are like the images of perception, but they are somewhat partial and faded, and continue to fade as time passes. Some are like images of the experience of desiring, of the act of inquiring, of understanding, of affirming, of resolving, of acting. They are not isolated, detached images, but belong to the context of a complex past personal experience, imperfectly retained and ever fading, but allowing a probing and testing to determine whether we are remembering or imagining. With others who have shared ex-

---

[5] See MS, pp. 41-47, and for the role of intellect in memory, pp. 146-149.

periences in similar settings, we can compare our memories, and together we can recall details which every one of us has experienced in a unique personal way, but which everyone has forgotten partially.

Like perception, memory is of the particular: it holds and can recall what is always individual, particular: *this* or *that* or *those*. But, unlike perception, which is of the *here* and *now*, memory holds what was *there* and *then*.

"Like perception, memory holds me to my full personal reality. It affords an extension of my personal horizon, a broader horizon within which I can locate individual events in my personal history, and which helps to guarantee my sense of the unity and continuity of my experience and of myself.... I know myself, in part, by being able to locate myself in the history, the personal history, which somehow defines me. This I have been, this I have done, this really bears on my present life: it is no mere imagining, no dream...." [6]

What I have written here concerning memory and its difference from acquired knowledge of a past which I have never experienced personally, suggests a helpful distinction which I have drawn elsewhere, and a further theological development of memory as it functions in transcendent life, a participation in the life of Father, Son, and Holy Spirit.

Take "history" in two senses: as past world process, especially past human experience; and as knowledge of that process. [7] In both senses there is a history which has a bearing on the meaning of my life. Considering history as process, I can recognize that at a certain point I have become part of it. By natural human conception and birth I have entered into life within a family and in a larger situation in the human race and human process; and all that preceded my entry into the process somehow affects my personal being. Moreover, by faith and baptism I have been begotten and born anew, and have entered into a vastly enriched life. Within that life, by faith in the whole new transcendent interpersonal world which I have entered, I am enriched by experience which begins not with perception, but with belief in imperceptible transcendent reality. Of both natural and transcendent process we may have knowledge, in part by memory, in part by what we have learned and retained.

There may be a rich blending of knowledge of history, and what may be called commemoration and appropriation. What, then, are the distinctions between history, commemoration, and

---

⁶ MS, p. 43.
⁷ See *The Mystery*, pp. 87-91.

appropriation? Knowledge of history, like any other knowledge, enhances my personal being, and the recognition of the significance of past events is a part of wisdom. Beyond such enrichment, we may be further enriched by commemoration and appropriation of historical events, by which we deepen our understanding of the importance of such past events, realize their importance for us, and are more powerfully influenced by them. Commemoration involves both recall and a kind of intense reliving of a great event or series of events of the past which antedated my life, but whose importance I acknowledge and whose influence on my own life I wish to enhance. It may be a civic act, in the celebration of a national holiday on which some great event in our nation's past is recalled and somehow relived. It may be religious, as in a Christian liturgical celebration, principally the Eucharist, celebrated with a sense of reliving the uniquely efficacious act by which Christians believe they were saved. Further, by participation in such a commemoration, I may appropriate the salvation history culminating in Christ's saving act and really present in its unique representation. I make it my own. [8] By appropriation I am enriched in my present life, and I begin to live a fuller life, in which I have a memory of personal experience of Christ and of Father and Spirit grounded on their continuing saving action in me and my belief and full response to them. Memory within such an enriched life has the fulness which characterizes all retention and recall of past personal experience, cognitive, emotive, volitional, and motor. It is unique in ways which we shall consider as we develop our understanding of the nature and functions of religious symbols. It is such memory which I call "transcendent memory." [9]

(3) *Imagination*.

This is a third kind of cognitive power and experience. Like perception and memory (to the extent that memory concerns sensibly perceptible aspects of our past experience), imagination regards images, sensibly perceptible likenesses: they are always particular, portraying *this* or *that* or *these* or *those*. They differ in not being fixed to the *here* and *now* of perception, or the *there* and *then* of memory. By imagination we experience a flow of images which are free of all relationships to time and place and actual fact. They have no existential index, no verifiable link with any real

---

[8] MS, 44-45.
[9] For further consideration of memory see MS, pp. 46-47 and 147-149.

experienced object, present or past. Though I am aware of my actual imagining, and that I am actually imagining this or that, I cannot affirm that what I am imagining is or ever was.

What is the source of the images? It seems necessary to recognize a twofold source. First, if we consider what may be called the material with which we work, seemingly it is the fund of all of our images of the sensibly perceptible, formed and held by all sorts of perception, external and internal, and by memory: all that was not only focal and explicit, but also the marginal, implicit, barely noticed. Moreover, by imagination we draw not only on our cognitive experience, but also on our emotional and volitional and motor actions, and on our vaguely sensed body image, or body set. All of these are only the raw materials of imagination. [10] They alone do not suffice to explain imagination. When we imagine, we do not simply call up a fund of images. By imagination we work creatively, and fashion from the raw materials worlds of images of objects which we have never perceived, much less remembered. There is a distinct function, or set of functions, involved here, which seem to be intelligible only as being rooted in a distinct power by which we work freely and creatively.

Consequently we sense reverberations of imagination in our whole conscious life. As we may be stirred to cognitive or emotive or volitional or motor action by what we perceive and by what we remember, so too what we imagine can influence us powerfully by thrusting us into imagined worlds which often impinge upon us more forcefully than the objects which we encounter in "real" life.

Note the difference in the roles of imagination in the cases of our knowledge of history or other facts and our memory of past personal experience. When I remember my past experience, I do not imagine: I do not freely create images from the materials provided by all past perception. The images retained in memory are not the work of imagination, but the portions of actual past experience which I retain. On the contrary, when I learn the history of persons and places and events which I have not experienced personally, imagination supplies the images, which may be judged eventually to have been more or less plausible. In such cases, I may have a sort of surrogate experience of the unexperienced past, more or less rich in proportion to the vividness of the symbols which mediate my knowledge and stimulate my full response. Thus a moving picture portraying the Civil War can affect me deeply if the symbols are effective. Thus too the whole range of symbolism of architecture,

---

[10] Cf. MS, pp. 51-56, 150-151.

sculpture, painting, music, dance, and, most powerfully, word--and at times dramatic silence--may enhance my response to a liturgical representation of sacred history which I never witnessed. Of such past events themselves I have no images from memory: I have never seen or heard or in any way perceived the actual historical reality. My images are those of my own imagination, stimulated by the variety of symbols used to represent the sacred history.

Imagination, then, supplies a great need, and enriches our life immeasurably. By its very nature, however, as a creation, a sort of fabrication, at times it calls for a careful critique. [11] It is supremely important to be able to distinguish between what truly *is* or *was*, and what we imagine to be or to have been.

(4) *Insight*, *conception*, and *judgment*.

These are cognitional operations of an order diverse from the kinds of sense knowledge which we have been considering. We may approach this matter by reflecting that in the preceding discernment and differentiation of perception, memory, and imagination, we have been performing operations far different from perceiving, remembering, and imagining. We have been doing a sort of phenomenology of perception, memory, and imagination; and phenomenology of these operations is not done by perceiving, remembering, or imagining. It involves insight, a grasp of relationships which are not sensibly perceptible; conception, a gradual sharpening of our formulation of the relationships which we have grasped; and judgment, affirmation or denial of the truth of what we have observed.

Our reflection on structures of perception, memory, and imagination is possible only because intellect permeates all conscious operations: we can observe, reflect on, discern, and differentiate these operations only because our internal operations are part of the field of intellect. All of our internal operations are present to us in consciousness. We have a massive, implicit awareness of them, within which it is possible for us to direct explicit intellectual operations, to inquire, to conceptualize, to affirm. Our awareness, or consciousness, of our acts and of ourselves is, in a sense, part of our implicit, marginal knowledge. When we reflect on the acts and on ourselves, we direct explicit intellectual operations to them. We make them our objects, "objectify" them. And in the intellectual operations which we perform, we transcend the whole order of sense knowledge.

---

[11] See MS, pp. 150-151, 160-166.

But much more is involved than this symbolic role of intellect in the reflection on our operations. From the outset of our conscious life, as we perceive, remember, and imagine, within those operations we are vaguely aware that the "world" *is*, that these and those *are*. We are vaguely aware of relationships between objects. We are at the beginnings of intellectual life, as of all conscious life. Consciousness, of objects and of our acts and ourselves, is a marginal knowledge. It is part of the mystery of knowledge, permeated by intellect.

In dealing briefly with insight, conception, and judgment, I shall reflect on explicit conscious acts, in which what is distinctive of the three may be grasped clearly. Then I shall move to a consideration of the mystery of primordial consciousness, in which all conscious intentional acts are present in an initial, amorphous, implicit manner. Reflection on our primordial consciousness, in my judgment, helps us to understand how our explicit acts of all types evolve, and how all modes of symbolizing develop from a common matrix.

(a) Insight should be considered as a distinct act, a moment in the movement toward understanding. It consists in a flash of intellect in which, within our wonder at a vast world of objects and vaguely sensed relationships we suddenly fix upon one relationship which stands out clearly. It is a beginning of understanding, a vivid experience which comes suddenly, unprogrammed. It is a stimulus to search further, to make out more clearly the relationship which we have seized, to fix and hold what we have grasped. We do not grasp and understand instantly the object which we have been perceiving or remembering or imagining. We are not pure spirits, which could grasp all in a flash. We are in movement, in our intellectual life as in all the rest. Beyond insight, there is a further, unending movement of inquiring intellect, of intellectual and rational persons seeking to come to a fuller life by understanding and the attainment of truth.

(b) Conception is another distinct act, a moment in the drive to understand, to answer the basic implicit question: *what* is it, or are they? Perception, image, question, insight, a gradual process of conceptualization, and the concept which is its product are related as moments in a particular thrust of the person seeking to understand. Concerning an object which we perceive we may ask different kinds of questions, and reach different modes of understanding. I have worked out two such lines of questioning and conceptualization concerning a wheel which we would have seen

and wondered about.[12] One line of questions could rise concerning
its shape, its roundness, and could reach ultimately a definition of
the circle: a concept in the world of mathematics. By another line of
questions we could search to understand the uses of the object, the
reason for its roundness, the way in which it functions in human life
and society.

The point of all this is that questions, insights, conceptualization, and concepts involve more than clear perceptions and
vivid imagination. Insights give an initial grasp of relationships.
Relationships are determined more clearly, fixed, and held in
concepts, one or more. Relationships cannot be seen or imagined:
they can be understood. The term of the movement toward
understanding, whether of true roundness or of real wheels, is the
concept or definition. The concept is a distinct achievement in our
striving to reach our potential relative fulness of life as human
persons. It is not, however, a work in which we can rest. One
concept can evoke further questions, and a continuing effort to
refine our answers, to understand more fully. It marks a stage in
our movement; it is not the goal we seek to reach. Nor would a
vast array of concepts fulfill our intellectual desire. There is a
further level ofachievement, in acts which are unique.

(c) Judgment is the act by which we affirm truly that what we
have grasped *is*, or *is such*. It is only in affirming that things or
persons *are*, or are of such or such a kind, as they truly are, or
denying that this or that is *such*, as is actually the case, that we
reach truth. We could have countless concepts, but if we never
ventured to join two of them as subject and predicate, and to affirm
that X is Y, we would never come to what is regarded as the
principal human intellectual achievement, truth. Nor would we risk
the principal failure, falsity.

If we reflect on the pattern of development of our knowledge, it
seems reasonable to affirm that judgment, like conception, rises
from primordial consciousness, the matrix of all of our conscious
operations.[13] From the outset of conscious life, as we vaguely
perceive, and vaguely sense relationships, so, within these beginnings of understanding, we are vaguely aware that *they are, it is*. A
massive, vague, primordial affirmation of existence holds us to the
task of inquiring into objects and their relationships, and grounding
eventually the certain judgment that *they* are in the relationships

---

[12] MS, pp. 64-68.
[13] On primordial consciousness see MS, pp. 76-80.

which we have grasped, that our concepts fit the objects as they really are.

Conceiving and judging are discernibly different acts, and the latter is far more momentous than the former. What, then, is the proper object of the act of judging? "... Every judgment, explicitly or implicitly (with regard to the verb form used, or the equivalent of a verb form in a given intersubjective setting) regards the act *to be*. Affirmative or negative, the judgment may be expressed by using form of the verb *to be*, or by another verb expressing a state or action, or by a single word or gesture which in a given context is taken as expressing assent or denial. In any case, the underlying sense of the judgment is that in one way or another, with or without indication of a particular manner of being, something *is* or *is not*, *is* walking or *is not* walking, *is* standing or *is not* standing." [14]

The firm judgment *It is* is not reached by a sort of syllogism, conditional or other, in which the conclusion can be affirmed only if the premise expressing the condition is affirmed. In any such paradigm of judgment, the question would return: how is the premise affirmed for sure? Unless we recognize that human intellect is ordered by its very nature to two diverse acts, which regard two diverse objects; and that the second act of intellect, judgment, affirms directly that the very subject in question *is*, we can give no intelligible account of affirmation, or of truth attained by human intellect.

Thus far I have considered only cognitive operations and their products, in which analogously we hold something of the mystery of the being of others. A reflection seems opportune here. Even cognitive operations and the variety of knowledges which we attain through them do not terminate entirely within us, in the manifold images which we hold. Even knowledge reveals a structure of stimulus and response which thrusts beyond the knower. Knowing, we seek to share our knowledge: we communicate, or at least fashion instruments capable of communicating, our knowledge. Those instruments, as we shall see, are symbols. They function both in the development of our knowledge and in our communicating or trying to communicate with other persons, and our influencing them in properly human ways in the interpersonal worlds which we share.

I turn now to consider intentional operations of the second broad class which I have indicated.

---

[14] MS, p. 75.

(5) *Emotion.* [15]

I define emotion thus: "a conscious act responding to what is known by the senses to be good or bad, pleasing or displeasing for the agent." [16] Part of the response is a felt change in the body, a resonance, varying according to the object and the relationship of agent to object. I distinguish two classes of emotions: simple and complex.

Simple emotions regard the sensibly known good or bad, pleasant or unpleasant, attractive or repulsive. The two basic emotions are love and hate. A further differentiation is based on the presence or absence of the good or bad. Desire is the response to an absent good; joy or pleasure, to the present good; aversion, revulsion, and flight, to an absent evil, present only in image; pain or sorrow, to the evil which is present.

Complex emotions, presupposing the diversity of the perceived good and bad for the subject, are differentiated in terms of another factor: relative difficulty in attaining the good or avoiding the evil. Hope regards an absent good which is judged to be attainable, though not without difficulty; despair, an absent good judged to be unattainable; daring, an absent but imminent evil which can be warded off; fear, an absent but imminent evil which seems unavoidable; anger, an evil which is present.

(6) *Volition.* [17]

Though there are many roles of intellect in human emotion, in response to a good or bad which is sensibly perceptible, there are higher reaches of human action in response to good and evil which are not sensibly perceptible as such. This is the proper realm of volition: the response to good or evil known by intellect. An act of volition is an act of rational or intellectual appetite, will. Its objects are diverse from those of sense appetite, and they pertain to a diverse order of appetitive intentionality. I can sense that a food or drink is good, pleasing. I can know by reason or intellect that it would be better for me to not to eat or drink it, for reasons which are not sensibly perceptible. I know, but cannot sense, that abstaining from either or both is better for my health. When I am

---

[15] See MS, pp. 84-93 and 151-158, for a treatment of emotion and its involvement with other factors of experience, and an indication of the relationships of my account to others.

[16] MS, p. 87.

[17] See MS, pp. 93-103 and 158-160.

attracted by a sensibly pleasing object, and yet judge that it is better for me not to enjoy it, I am choosing between two diverse values.

"Volitional action regards values: objects known to be not merely good or bad in themselves according to their kind as sensibly perceptible, but good or bad for the person who is attracted to them, or repelled by them, for reasons which often are not sensibly perceptible...." [18] Whereas classic moral philosophers considered human acts as good or bad, regarding objects which are good or bad in themselves, more recent moral philosophers and theologians have recognized the importance of the notion of value. A person or thing is *good* to the degree that it has a relative fulness of perfection according to its kind, its proper mode of being. *Value* is an attribute of a person or thing which is not simply good in itself according to its mode of being, but judged to be good for human persons generally, or for a particular person. What is valued "counts" for something in the world of the one who values it.

Values differ greatly, and moral philosophers have attempted to work out a hierarchy of values. I present this one, a modification of that proposed by Joseph de Finance, S.J. [19] (1) *Infrahuman*, good not only for human persons, but for animals, though animals do not know them as such. This class, in the order of increasing value, includes objects pleasing to the sense; and biological or vital values: all that regards the maintenance, success, and expansion of animal life, according to the perfection of the species. (2) *Human, but inframoral*, of various kinds: economic (prosperity, success, riches), intellectual, aesthetic (beauty, grace, elegance, sublimity), social, perfection of will (energy of character, constancy in undertakings, ability to rebound from failure). (3) *Moral*, which is one, and unique in relation to all lower values. "These ... are some of the characteristics of moral value. First, it is a quality of a human *act*: persons are good or bad morally because they act well or badly. Second, it is worthy of esteem, lovable, desirable for itself, not as conducive to some other value. Third, it differs from other 'spiritual' values (intellectual, aesthetic, or pertaining to the will) in that it can never be surrendered for another value.... Fourth, it is the very reason for living: it gives sense to life. It is the proper value of a person, the personalizing value par excellence. It is individual in the sense that no one can provide it for me: I must realize it by my

---

[18] MS, p. 94.
[19] *Essai sur l'agir humain* (Rome: Gregorian University Press, 1962) pp. 372-379, and *Éthique générale* (Rome: Gregorian University Press, 1967) pp. 69-74 and 183-184. Cf. MS, pp. 95-103.

own action. Yet it is universal in two regards: acts which are morally good or bad are so for all persons; and right moral judgment in any situation deserves to be approved by all who could understand the situation.... In what, then, does moral value consist? It is the agreement of both the volitional act and its object with right reason: reason faithful to itself and open to the ideal, the fulness of good, ... the absolute good." [20] (4) *Religious*: objectively regarding the sacred, the divine, and in its supreme degree God, the ultimate foundation of all values; subjectively consisting in religion, respect, submission, confidence, piety, personal holiness. Religious value regards the subject's relation to the source of being and of the whole order of values. There is no morality without religion, no religion without morality.

I have offered a critique of this proposed hierarchy of values. [21] Here I note again one serious defect: the lack, throughout the scale of values, of a distinction of personal, social, and inter-personal. The sense of the distinction between personal and social is evident: any value can be of importance to one person or to some social group. The distinctive quality of interpersonal value is not evident, and it deserves consideration. Beyond all other manners of fulfillment by the attainment of values, there is a unique fulfillment to be attained in mutual interpersonal knowledge and love and sharing of any or all of other values. Truly interpersonal fulfillment in mutual knowledge and love is a value of a diverse order. It does not consist simply in this, that two persons help each other to attain a greater share of some value than they could by unaided striving. Rather there is question of a fulfillment which is possible only in love and fellowship, as a distinct and supremely human mode of being. Mutual knowledge and love, and the sharing of other values in a union of love, is a human achievement which no person can attain alone. It is the supreme purely human value. I say "purely human" to allow for a transcendent interpersonal union of love, which in my judgment can be affirmed and somehow understood only in the light of revelation and faith. I shall consider this later in the treatment of divine-human symbolizing.

As in acts of emotion, so in those of the will, there is an order of intelligibility. "As love is the basic emotion or passion, and all other emotions are somehow intelligible in their relationship to love, so at the level of volitional response to good and evil, love is the basic act, and it is somehow the source of all other volitional acts.

---

[20] MS, pp. 96-97.
[21] MS, pp. 97-103.

Not only do intellect and will permeate and subsume emotions, but volitional acts parallel emotions, responding to aspects of the good and evil known only by intellect. So love, desire, joy, hate, aversion, sorrow, hope and daring, fear and despair, and anger have their counterparts at the level of will. In a sense they are not 'counterparts,' not another set of responses of 'pure spirit' to a good or evil known only by pure intellect. All of our intellectual and volitional acts are enfleshed. All intellectual grasp is conditioned by, and accompanied by, some image derived from perception. All action, even in the pursuit of the loftiest ideal grasped by the most powerful act of intellect, is in the concrete, in the world of existing persons and things. Our ... human response to good and evil is fully human: with the blend of all elements which together characterize the human mode of being. We are... [human persons]..., not angels with bodies." [22]

(7) *Motor action.*

"One element of human action remains to be considered: motor action. Since I *am* in space and time, I must *move* in space and time to attain a distant good. In fact I must move even to think about it or desire it, for I am in a humanly bodily way, and I am by being in movement continually in countless ways. Emotion involves a conscious motor impulse toward the attractive good, or away from the repugnant evil. Volition is not the act of an angel, not even of an angel inhabiting a body. It too has its bodily factor. Not only can I not will without expending energy, but I cannot do anything about the good which is my goal without acting; and I act by moving somehow." [23]

FURTHER CONSIDERATION OF HUMAN CONSCIOUS EXPERIENCE

To this point I have discerned and differentiated human conscious operations. This analysis must be complemented by a reflection on what characterizes the concrete whole of our experience. Only thus can we understand the interplay of all elements, and prepare to understand symbolizing and the functions of symbols. The term "concrete whole" may seem strange. Obviously

---

[22] MS, p. 100. In what follows there, pp. 100-103, I offered some other reflections on love which I omit here only to respect the reasonable limits of my present exposition.

[23] MS, p. 103.

we cannot hold it present in its entirety, for we are experiencing as we continue to live in our continuous extension in space and movement in time. Nor can we conceptualize it without considering one aspect after another. So, like our consideration of operations one by one, our reflection on the whole from different points of view necessarily will involve a succession of linear movements of reason. Ironically, then, even when we seek to turn from the abstractive consideration of one operation after another, our attempt to characterize the concrete whole is also abstractive. All movement of discursive reason is composite. Every stage of a rational discursive account is linear. At the end we can only seek somehow to gather up what we have determined along every line of our consideration.

(1) *Unity and continuity*.

Our experience, or any segment of it which may be regarded somehow as a unit, is a whole in which many elements are blended: all of our cognitive, emotive, volitive, and motor operations. Our perceptual experience may be continually shifting, as we are attracted by one object after another, or one after another facet of the same object. We may deliberately concentrate for a time on one mode of intentional activity, regarding one object. But we never shut out completely other objects present in an ever shifting, varying marginal awareness. At different levels or modes of consciousness, waking or sleeping, or in rare cases of successive waking consciousness and unconsciousness, we recognize the unity of our consciousness. We personally are aware of the succession of modes of our own consciousness, except to the extent that our rational powers may fail us, for intervals or in our eventual decline.

(2) *Figure-ground structure*.

In the whole of our experience we can observe a constant, analogous structure of what can be called figure-ground, or focal-marginal, or object-field/horizon/world/sphere. When we are fully aware, usually we concentrate on one object of one operation in one intentional mode. We are perceiving this rose, or dog, or garden, or library--or whatever--bit by bit, and at any moment we can perceive only by focussing on minute portions of the whole as we halt our roving eyes or strive to listen to this word or phrase of this voice, or to this phrase of this music, shutting out what for us at this moment is the surrounding noise. When we are drawn to a person, we may respond to his or her beauty and goodness in an act of love, forgetful for the moment of any effort to inquire and to understand. While we concentrate on one object in one operation in one mode of intentionality, that object and that operation are figure against the ground of all other types of operation regarding all other objects continually presenting themselves to us. Or, by other metaphors in phenomenological terminology, all that is present to us in our awareness, but is not engaging us at the center of our conscious operation, is marginal in relation to what we are focussing on, or is like the field or horizon or world or sphere in which the object is situated. [24] Since all of our intentional operations, and all of the objects which we may attend to in the world of which we are aware, are somehow in continuity for us, we may be drawn--or turn deliberately--from one to another, and any one object may evoke any mode of reaction to any one of the other objects which somehow are associated in our experience.

In a sense, the ground, or the marginal/field/horizon/world/ sphere seemingly contains us. And, as it contains us, it is what we may call the external, objective guarantor of the unity of our consciousness. It is within our ground, field, horizon, world that we are aware of being, and that we live. It is the continuity of this external world as it figures in our awareness that somehow affords us the all-embracing objective setting which makes possible a continual vaguely recognized verification of the unity of our consciousness. Through all of my conscious operations in *my* conscious world *I* am one and the same person. In a sense all of us dwell in our own personal worlds, which no one else can share completely; and our hold on *our* world is our guarantee of wholeness and sanity. As long as that personal world is whole we are whole, poor as we are.

(3) *We ourselves as persons unifying all elements of a complex dynamic interrelationship.*

From what precedes one might be inclined to regard our being in our worlds as being passive to a great extent, undergoing the influence of many forces or agents which account for many diverse elements in our awareness; and then as if being drawn to, or actively choosing between, operations and objects, much as we would press buttons to choose many possible spectacles to contemplate or

---

[24] Concerning ground, field, horizon, world, and my own term "sphere," and the relationship of such phenomenological terminology to strictly scientific terminology on the one hand and fully philosophical terminology on the other, see MS, pp. 108-111.

delight in, or many possible activities regarding objects offered for our choice. It is not so that we live. We undergo many influences, but in the whole of our conscious experience we are active in the many modes of our intentional operations. We act. We are persons, and all impact on us is received in us as persons, and we react as persons. Moreover the countless varied images which we form, and by which we hold something of others, and the many impulses and full acts by which we react to them as good or bad for us, are involved in an inconceivably complex dynamic interrelationship. *We* perceive and imagine and remember and gain insight and fashion concepts and judge; and what we hold in these various modes of knowledge affects us, so that we are attracted or repelled, and act, at times impulsively, at times with full deliberation and free choice. We are affected by our own perceptions and imaginings and memories, and stirred to emotions, desires, and deliberate acts. We, knowing and judging and willing, can control emotions and desires within limits. We personally are the base of all of our conscious life, and we monitor and, within limits, can control the interaction of all elements of our conscious life.

(4) *Our intersubjective world.*

But we are not isolated every one in his or her personal world. We are in many particular personal worlds. We are together with all "others" in the physical universe which we share in many ways. Most importantly we are in a world of persons, every one unique as we are, and every one involved in the inconceivably complex process of being acted upon and acting, most significantly in intersubjective life. Of all of the "objects" which we encounter as we live in our part of the vast universe, most important and most precious are other human persons. When we act and interact in manners fully human, the manners are far different from those in actions in which we encounter other objects. At the minimum, we recognize their dignity as persons, and are aware that we should treat them with the respect which they deserve. At higher levels, we truly meet them as persons, in I-thou relationships, [25] and we engage in many modes of interpersonal activity by which we may communicate, come to mutual knowledge and love, and reach a fulfillment which no person can possibly attain alone. In our interpersonal life, we affect one another by our intentional operations. We make a difference to one another. Our effects in one another's lives are *real.*

---

[25] On the differentiation of acts, and the human intersubjective world, see MS, pp. 125-134.

The human intersubjective world is the vast complex of human persons who live and act in their uniquely human way, in the intelligible order discerned in their interplay as persons, acting upon persons and things by properly human operations, with the effects and relationships which result from such operations.

We share a universe in ways in which only human persons can share. We share insights which we have gained in great part by mutual stimulation and suggestion. We share feelings, will, and effort to transform the world's resources as known by the natural sciences. We fashion properly human works. Science itself is our work, a properly human creation. All of our culture, our social and political structures, our laws, our formulations of rights and duties--all are part of properly human organization, an intelligible order discerned, elaborated, and effected by human persons sharing a universe, organizing their own efforts and the operations of the resources of the universe whose laws have been grasped, and whose activities have been managed, to the degree to which we have advanced in science and technology.

Properly human action can be understood only as it is situated in the whole of this intelligible order of human operations, effects, and relationships. Human persons are intelligible to human persons alone in the universe of bodily being. Human works and human interpersonal relationships have meaning for human persons alone in the totality of bodily being. [26]

(5) *The reality of the intersubjective world.*

Is the intersubjective world *real*? "... The question can come hesitantly from a man or woman with a common-sense view of the realities of the world in which we live. It can be pressed relentlessly ... by a contemporary empiricist thinker, for whom persons and things are dissolved, and all that is 'really real' is readings upon a four-dimensional manifold. The man or woman of common sense may be impressed with the obvious reality of the geographical or physical world, and of the persons and things visible and palpable in their physical being and operation. The empiricist thinker, reducing all reality to what can be accounted for in terms of physics, will have banished persons and things as illusions of common sense, and will have progressed beyond all representations of particles and forces to pure relational concepts." [27]

---

[26] MS, p. 134.
[27] MS, pp. 135-136.

What is *real*? Whatever *is*, in any manner whatsoever. It *is*, it *operates*, it *counts*. Its operations are real, and its effects are real, for they are part of the mystery of the universe. Everything that *is* is and operates according to its own way of being.

From the moment at which we began our human lives as persons, we *were* in a distinctly human and fully human way: fully constituted in our basic human manner of being and acting. We were not yet all that we could become, but we were acting to attain a fuller degree of being. Our operations were real. Their effects in us and in others were real. Our knowing is a mode of being. So is our loving. So too our feeling emotion, and willing, and tending toward the object which we desire. So are all other human operations, and their effects, and the relationships grounded upon them.

Our human way of being is characterized by transcendence. We *are* such that by our properly human operations we tend somehow to transcend ourselves, to go beyond "ourselves," and by doing so to become more fully what we can be. We do so most of all as we become true by knowing and affirming the true, and as we become better by loving the good.

We do not do so alone. We are persons in society, and none of us could ever achieve much alone.

(6) *The many roles of intellect.*

Only after a first consideration of the acts of intellect can we complement our initial treatment of other intentional operations, for the most profound reflection on them involves the roles of intellect in their functioning. Moreover, only in this second consideration of the other intentional operations can we approach a more adequate understanding of the roles of intellect, and prepare to probe the mystery of symbolizing and symbols. [28]

As we have seen, consciousness is part of the mystery of knowledge. *We* are conscious, and we *know* it. Our conscious life is complex, but one and continuous in all of its ever varying modes. From the outset of our conscious life, as far as we can have intimations of its beginnings which are consistent with our experience of the patterns of our development, by intellect we penetrate and permeate all of our conscious experience. All lies continually on the margins of our awareness, and we can direct explicit intellectual acts to probe all.

"It is the wide range of intellectual intentionality which grounds the notion of the permeation of all conscious operations

---

[28] I have treated this matter extensively in *Man The Symbolizer*, pp. 143-181.

by intellect. All of our conscious, intentional operations are permeated by a twofold intellectual factor: massive existential affirmation holding us to the total reality of the world and of
ourselves, and a massive initial grasp of relationships and tendency
to discern and differentiate, which drives us continually to understand the world and ourselves, and to affirm explicitly what we
have understood...." [29]

This penetration and permeation by intellect is far more than
what might be regarded as a sort of monitoring of all other operations. By intellect alone we accomplish much of what we would be
inclined to attribute to other cognitive operations and powers, and to
aspects of our emotional, volitional, and motor action.

As we perceive, we are aware of the perceptive field in which
we are acting in our many modes of sense perception. That
perceptive field is not perceived, but understood from personal
experience. I know that as I look northeast from my window, I am
limited by that window in my visual perception, and limited in
hearing by the walls and surrounding building. I could turn to my
right and see my bed, the south wall, and my corner closet. I know,
but do not perceive here and now, that I could move around my
desk, through the door and out of my room into a corridor, where
again I could choose to move in one or other direction, and open
other partial fields of perception. I do not perceive my perceptual
field: I know it from a pattern of movements in my surroundings,
immediate and remote, from memory, from gradually deepening
insight into the broader world within which at present I am
perceiving this or that. I know and understand my perceptive field
by intellect: penetrating my present perception and appraising my
potential.

Besides our perceptual field, these are other elements of our
conscious experience which must be attributed in part to functions
of intellect: our awareness of space and time; our memory as
retention and recall of our past personal experience known precisely
as such, and discernible from imaginings; in imagining, a certain
sense of pattern, a critique of adequacy, and a multiple instrumental
role of imagination in the service of intellectual operation; in
emotion, and analogously in volition, a role in the judgment of what
is good or bad for us; in motor action, a sense of the shape of our
action and of its aptness; the integration of our knowledge; all grasp
of analogy; and knowledge of the singular. [30]

---

[29] MS, p. 143.
[30] MS, pp. 145-181.

(7) *Imaging*.

Thus far we have discerned and differentiated our conscious operations, considered their unity and continuity and manifold interrelationships, and the unique roles of intellect, which permeates our whole conscious being and complements our other human powers at all levels of operation.

One more aspect of our human way of being remains to be considered. It is all-important for a deeper understanding of our human mystery, and of our transcendent mode of being and operating as we share the divine life. In particular it is essential for a deeper understanding of the Christian sacrament.

It is the analogous sensuous imaging and images which characterize all of our human conscious operations and their terms. This imaging, as we shall see, is the analogous range of operations by which we fashion the meaningful sensuous images which function both in holding (in knowledge) something of the "other" which impinges upon us, and in responding to it as good or bad for us; and by which we can communicate to others the knowledge which we have, and affect them in other ways possible in the interpersonal world.

Thus we make a transition to symbolizing and symbols: for, as we shall see, the imaging is symbolizing, and the images are symbols.

Basics of the Consideration of Symbolizing and Symbols

To help to focus on what we are observing and seeking to understand, I propose this nominal definition of symbol: "a meaningful sensuous image." [31] The three operative words call for some explanation, along with two other concepts. To this explanation I turn now.

(1) *The "habitat" of symbols*.

To avoid disastrous confusion, I affirm at the outset that symbols *as such* are and have meaning only in the worlds of human conscious experience. A piece of rock with a certain shape, whether formed by the chance play of natural elements or shaped by a human artist, has meaning only for human persons. As a rock, it

---

[31] In MS I offered two other variations, pp. 215, 218, 293, and then introduced the notion of image.

has its distinctive physical qualities according to its kind and its individual characteristics. If for some it is a symbol, its meaning as such does not pertain to the realm of geology. If the song of a cardinal to me is like the name of a friend called with a certain insistence, that likeness does not concern any scientist interested in the nature and operations of cardinals. In probing symbolizing and symbols, therefore, we are not considering "things" or actions which as they are by nature can be observed and classified by any natural science. As symbols, they are real and have meaning only for us, though, as we shall come to recognize, they may function instrumentally in human worlds and have very real effects, of far greater importance than those observed in the realms of rocks and birds.

(2) *The sensuous.*

Again, in considering the sensuous as such, we are treating something which is not the concern of the physicist or chemist or any other natural scientist, and so, in their estimation, is not "really out there." The sensuous is that which pertains to our senses: consequently it can be defined only in relation to our human experience.

"Sensuous" refers to what is sensibly perceptible in the bodily world in which we are; to the sense powers by which we have different modes of knowledge and of response to what we perceive sensibly to be good or bad for us; and to the terms of our sense operations, which themselves in turn are somehow sensibly perceptible.

The basic principle regarding the sensuous is this: there is a sensuous element in all of our intentional operations, cognitive, emotive, volitive, and motor. The matter is evident regarding our knowledge by perception. It is easily recognized in memory and imagination, where "images" retained and fashioned creatively resemble those which we have by perception. In emotion, and in much of volition and motor action, we are responding to what appears to us through our senses to be good or bad for us, and we have an interior feeling of our operation.

With regard to our intellectual and volitional operations, not only do they occur in the blend of our total human conscious life, which involves the sensuous in the elements which I have just discussed, but there is a sensuous factor from which they cannot be separated. Classic philosophers affirm that the phantasm is a constant principle of our knowledge, and that we gain insight "into" phantasms. It is only as we are perceiving, remembering, and

imagining that we gain insight. Only within the experience of visual
and audible images do we grasp relationships, which themselves are
not visible or audible. Only by fashioning an inner word do we form
a concept. We have no "imageless" concepts, no purely spiritual,
disembodied thought and acts of will. The most severely abstract
thought, and the most refined scientific or philosophical language
has its residual traces of intuitive origins, with suggestions of the
images which accompany human thought from beginning to end.
This is not an affirmation that our thought is "picture thinking." It
is not. Relationships are not perceptible by any sense power, nor in
any sense operations, as I have noted in differentiating concept from
perception. But there is always a sensuous factor in our thought and
speech, and in all of our symbolizing. As we think, we fashion or
adapt sensibly perceptible symbols, linguistic or other, internal or
external. Without expression in some external symbol our thought
or act of will cannot have any effect in the interpersonal world.

(3) *Image*.

An image is a likeness, which has a similarity of form with that
of which it is an image. No image in human experience is a perfect
likeness of that which it images: it is not a full replica of the imaged
reality. Rather the imaged reality is filtered, so to speak, in the
operations by which a human person encounters and responds to
the world.

To begin with, what I said concerning the "habitat" of symbols
is true of the "image" and "form" which I am considering now.
Physiological or other types of empiricist psychologists may ridicule
or simply dismiss images or forms as fabrications. They are concerned with only what pertains to their "formal object"--for them
another meaningless term from "perennial philosophy." Rightly so,
from their point of view. In all of their observation and correlation
of measurable aspects of human being, they find no trace of the
images we know in our experience of men and women. What I have
been referring to as experience makes sense only for a science or
serious reflective and systematically, coherently organized body of
knowledge which begins with a reflection on structures of human
conscious response to the multiple stimuli within the range of our
susceptibility to the impulses which we undergo in the play of agents
or forces in the physical universe.

In perception we grasp and hold fleeting configurations of tiny
portions of the object which we are regarding. We have a continuous succession of such configurations which fuse in what we
fashion as we rove over the object which we see or hear or feel by

touch, or taste, or smell. The degree and vividness of such effects within us vary according to the power of the individual senses and their mode of contributing to our global knowledge of the object or objects.

Our visual images are remotely analogous with photographs; yet a comparison of the two may help to make clear the fragmentary and extreme inadequacy of both to "hold" the full imaged reality. Every photographic image, whether a single still photo or a succession of photos flashed in succession to give the illusion of a "moving picture," portrays a configuration of portions of one or more objects, fixed rigidly in a relationship in which they were for an instant, as seen from a given point of view chosen by the photographer. Even the photographic "image" is non-existent on the film or on the paper on which it is printed. There it is only an aggregate of particles of the substances used in photography and printing. *We* see the image. We do so by fashioning and "beholding" it in the inscrutable mystery of human vision, within the whole of our marvelously organized conscious human being. Beyond the limitations of the accuracy of the representations of portions of the object, the photograph locks its object forever in what we behold as an unchanging image. No one has the illusion that the camera has caught the full reality of its object.

If we could suppose an "individual" visual or auditory perception, caught in its momentary existence in our vision or hearing, as we scan an object or a field, it would have no existence or subsistence beyond the flash in which we fix our gaze on one minute portion of the object. It does not hold somehow the very "appearance" of the object, as if that appearance were part of the objective reality of the person or thing or multitude. So our image is a fleeting reality within us, far from holding its object in its full reality, as it continues for a time to be and to function in the physical universe.

Given the ever fading character of memory images, which hold imperfectly only traces of images formed by perception, clearly they are utterly inadequate likenesses of what we originally experienced. As for the freely creative work of imagination, whose images offer no basis for affirming the reality and substance of its representations in the world of bodies, evidently they could not be claimed to hold fully any objective reality. No image is a full replica of a person or thing.

What is to be said of intellectual "images"? A concept holds not the full reality of the thing conceived, but only a correlation, a relationship which has been grasped, and which is grounded in the reality of the thing as it is in the physical universe. We do not picture such concepts. We fashion them to express the insight which we have gained as we sense and remember and imagine, and we fashion them only as we express them in a linguistic symbol. We do not have the "intelligible appearance" impressed upon our intellects, nor an expressed intelligible appearance, if either be regarded as a perfect likeness of the very essence or nature of the thing known. We form concepts in a succession of efforts, in each of which we grasp relationships more accurately, or grasp other complementary relationships which we hold in a less inadequate concept. We shall turn soon to consider the process of the formation of our images: symbolizing.

Do we fashion images analogously in our other intentional operations: emotional, volitional, and motor action? Yes, in the sense that every portion of an act of emotion, or of will, or of motor action, somehow stands for and expresses the whole. A single violent word or gesture can portray strong anger. Regarding acts of will it is necessary to distinguish between purely interior action and the communication of our will in community. In our own inner life, the image involved may be simply the inner "word" by which we express inwardly our free determination to act. To communicate our act to others, some external word or other perceptible sign is necessary. A single stride may portray clearly enough the general sense of my movement by which I seek or shrink from an object of emotion or of will. In every such case the part stands for the whole. It is somehow an image of the whole. It is necessary for the completion of the act of emotion, will, or motor action, which must be somehow perceptible in order to be effective in society.

An analogous sensuous imaging and images, then, characterize all of our human conscious operations and their terms. Tentatively we may say that symbolizing is the analogous range of operations by which we fashion the meaningful sensuous images which function both in holding (in knowledge) something of the "other" which impinges upon us, and in responding to it as good or bad for us; and by which we can communicate to others the knowledge which we have, and affect them in other ways possible in the interpersonal world. Symbols are the images which we produce, instruments in a vast network of communication and influence, intrapersonal and interpersonal.

Earlier in this section on images, I linked image and form. What I have affirmed concerning the habitat of symbols and images is true of the "forms" which are similar in the objects and in the terms of our intentional acts. They are not "principles of being" of persons and things as they are in the universe. Take as an example a perception of a hill from a certain point of view. It may have the

shape which from here looks like a hog's back. Perceived from
another point of view, it could seem to have any of several other
shapes. Does that mean that the "form" of the hill is really part of
the hill? Hardly. If we would multiply the perceivers, situated in
many places, we could have to account for numberless "forms."
The absurdity is evident. First, a hill is not a "thing" with its
natural mode of being, existing as an individual of some natural
species. It is an accumulation of animate and inanimate "things,"
and it would be utterly futile to seek to determine how many
"things" of how many kinds are heaped up in it. Rather, the
"form" of the hill is the image produced by whatever impinges on a
particular perceiver in a particular local relationship to the hill.
How the process occurs from physical impression to conscious
human response is part of the mystery of our unique human being.
"Forms" and the "images" which are somehow like them are not
emanations of the being of the person or thing existing in the
physical universe. They are terms of our conscious intentional
operations. The verification of the likeness of the shape of the hill
perceived from this position and the image formed within us can be
had simply by repeating the experience, and by having others look
and share their experience. There is no further court of appeal. [32]

(4) *Meaning* and *meaningful*.

The meaning of these terms may be found only by untangling
the many senses of "mean" and "meaning," The verb *mean* and the
verbal noun *meaning* have clusters of meanings which seem to bear
ultimately on the sense of a sort of intransitive verb and its
corresponding verbal noun, and then a derivative transitive verb.
When I say that X means Y, or that the meaning of X is Y, I am
saying that the answer to the question "What is X?" is "Y."

Once removed from this basic sense of *mean* and *meaning*, there
is a transitive verb and its corresponding verbal noun. They are
involved in questions or statements about what I mean by my words
or gestures: what am I trying to express and communicate. When I
say X, my word means Y. I mean Y, and my word means Y. Y is
the object of my act, in this case a purely cognitive act.

Another sense of *mean* and *meaning* presupposes knowledge,
but expresses directly an act of the will: intention. By the act of
intending I *mean* to accomplish something beyond what I am doing
immediately. My meaning or intention in doing X is to accomplish
Y. Here too there is a question of a sort of intelligible relationship.

---

[32] On the "critique" of perception see MS, pp. 162-164.

The action X is understood to be performed in order to accomplish Y: the act is understood in relation to its object.

Besides these instances of intellectual and volitional acts, any other intentional act, of emotion or of motor action, also has a meaning: it is understood as bearing upon its object. Consideration of *meaning* and *meaningful*, then, bring us back to the field of the intentional. All intentional acts are meaningful, analogously, every one according to its own structure, its own type of relationship to its object or term. Symbols, then, in a first tentative nominal definition, are meaningful sensuous images, immediate terms of intentional operations.

(5) *Representation*.

Since the symbol is a meaningful sensuous image of the reality which it images, it can stand for that reality, or represent it, and mediate its influence on the human world. Its functions may vary. It may be prevalently cognitive, communicating knowledge of the reality represented. It may be predominantly emotive, volitional, or motor, or a blend of some or all of these. A single external act of love can express the whole of a rich emotive and volitional state, and evoke a response of love. A single violent word or gesture can express the whole passion of anger, and evoke fear or provoke a violent reaction. We act fully and function in human society through symbols which represent our inner disposition and action. They are part of our whole action: its sensibly perceptible aspect.

Symbolizing

(1) *One person, one symbolizer*.

Since there is an analogous sensuous imaging which ranges through all of our intentional operations, one might be tempted to suggest that our eyes, and ears, and all of our organs of sense, external and internal, and all of our other powers, cognitive, emotive, motor and volitional, are symbolizing in widely different ways. Thus, every person would seem to be a cluster of symbolizers. Not so. As I observed above, [33] *we* undergo multiple impulses of the world in which we are. As we see and hear and feel by touch, and taste, and smell, and remember, and imagine, we are aware of

---

[33] "We ourselves as persons unifying all elements of a complex dynamic inter-relationship," pp. 128-129.

all, focally or marginally. Our total conscious experience is permeated by intellect, for consciousness is part of knowledge, and
intellect has a role in all of our other intentional operations. Only as
we are aware intellectually of our sensuous images do they have
meaning. We symbolize fully, therefore, as full persons. Consequently, to understand the process of symbolizing, we may begin
most profitably by studying its intellectual core.

(2) *Primordial experience.*

At crucial points in the elaboration of my theory of symbolizing
and symbols in *Man the Symbolizer*, I emphasized the concept of
primordial experience. [34] What is the origin and basis of this
concept? I should say that it is neither a postulate of some state which
is beyond recall, nor a reflection upon any gradual conceptualization
of such a postulated state, nor a hypothesis to be verified. I am not
engaged in an empirical science, nor is my thought meant to be
demonstrative. I am seeking to understand within the mystery of
human experience, to provide a base for the understanding of the
analogy of Christian experience. Obviously we cannot return to our
experience in the womb, at the first awakening of consciousness, and
reflect on the structures--or lack of structure--of our experience at
that moment. Yet we can recognize patterns of relatively primordial,
implicit conscious experience, succeeded by and contrasted with more
explicit, subsequent experience. And it seems reasonable, from that
pattern of process, to gain an insight into what must have been the
pattern of all of our development in conscious experience.

What, then, is primordial experience? It is the whole of our
immediate experience of the world and of ourselves which has not yet
become the explicit object of any act of knowledge or will, affectivity
or motor activity. It is the whole of the background, the marginal, the
'horizonal,' which has not been fixed as an object, does not figure in
explicit imagination or memory, but is part of our total experience,
and can figure later, whether in dream or in unexpected images or
memories whose origin seems so mysterious. Primordial experience is
the great, uncontained flow of our basic experience of the world and
of ourselves, or rather the whirling, surging, blending flow of many
streams which fuse into one. It is the stuff of all symbols. Its fulness
explains the marvelous range and variety of symbols, and the variety
of their adequacy and efficacy. [35]

---

[34] Definition, MS, p. 26; importance, p. 27; matrix of subsequent acts, p. 80;
massive primordial sense of our situation in the world, 316.

[35] Cf. MS, p. 26.

Primordial experience is marked by a twofold basic intentionality, cognitional and emotional-volitional-motor. Cognitional
intentionality involves primordial perception: the vast, vague,
implicit sensible awareness of the world and ourselves. This is the
matrix of all explicit perception, and the beginning of all knowledge.
Yet from the outset an intellectual factor pervades and transcends
all primordial perception. This also is twofold. There is a vague
grasp of relationships as intelligible, and a drive to grasp them more
firmly and fix them. Second, there is a massive existential affirmation of the world, which holds us to a sense of our situation in
the world, and to the task of understanding and of explicit affirmation.

The basic emotional-volitional-motor intentionality is a love of
all that is vaguely sensed to be good, and a tendency to union with
that good. It is the love which makes us cling to life, and desire to
understand the good and embrace it and hold it more firmly. It is
the radical response to the good as understood. It grounds hatred of
evil, and consequent fear of it and shrinking from it. [36]

Primordial experience is a constant challenge to transcend our
present achievement, to extend our understanding and affirmation
of truth, to become more true as we are enriched in this aspect of
our being; to grow in goodness as more and more we love the good,
and are united more and more with all that is good, and with the
source of all goodness.

In a sense it is the guarantor of our wholeness and sanity.
Beyond all of the potential atomizing and fragmentation of human
knowledge and of our world as we grasp it, the massive primordial
existential affirmation of the world, and of ourselves in our world,
holds us to the task of probing within a universe which holds
together. A corresponding primordial love of all that is vaguely
sensed to be good, beyond all conceptualization and attainment of
particular goods, tends to the full reality of the good which is loved,
and to union with the all-fulfilling source of all good and goal of all
striving. [37]

(3) The process of symbolizing.

Since we produce meaningful sensuous images by all of our
intentional operations, and the manners of doing so in cognitional
operations alone are many and diverse, it may seem strange to
entitle this section as if there were a single process. My reason for

---

[36] See MS, pp. 26-27, 316.
[37] See MS, p. 80.

doing so is this. There is an analogy which runs through all symbolizing, and a multiplicity of functions of symbols, which can be the relative terms or products of many distinct operations. A single act may terminate in a meaningful sensuous word or gesture which has a multiple intentionality. I may break forth with a strong "Yes!" by which I express understanding of what has been proposed, great joy, firm assent, and readiness for action. That word may change my life and the lives of others. Thus it may have real effects in the interpersonal world. There is an analogy in the manner in which I utter that word, which proceeds from my intellect, my emotion of joy, my will, and the beginnings of a vaguely sensed imminent motor action.

The multiple act begins with an insight, [38] for some knowledge precedes emotion, will, and motor action, and all fully human knowledge begins with insight, the flash of intellectual grasp of an intelligible relationship, which in the illustration which I have just given would be a grasp of the desirability of a proposed action and its object.

How, then, do we move from insight to a symbol terminating an intentional operation? I shall begin by considering the cognitive factor in symbolizing and symbols, and then indicate how emotional, volitional, and motor operations somehow terminate in a symbol.

With regard to the cognitive factor in symbolizing and symbols, we may distinguish two contrary ways of symbolizing, and two kinds of symbols. [39] One is conceptual; the other, intuitive. I consider the conceptual first, since the intuitive is understood more easily in contrast with it.

Conceptual symbolizing proceeds gradually from an initial insight to a sharper, more accurate determination of relationships, and their formulation in concepts, which eventually constitute a system or world of meaning. The elaboration of concepts has its sensuous factor: it is inseparable from the shaping of a sensuous medium. For the most part the medium is articulate vocal sound, constituting a language, and its derivative written signs expressing the language. In specialized thought, such as mathematics, other written signs are developed in a system which to some degree bypasses speech and the polyvalence of the spoken or written word in ordinary languages. In some cases, not without the sacrifice of wealth and suppleness in expressing concepts, the sensuous medium may be visible gesture, in sign language.

---

[38] See MS, pp. 184-186.
[39] Cf. MS, pp. 186 ff.

Conceptual symbolizing involves moving from the vagueness and polyvalence of common-sense language toward an ever sharper expression of relationships clearly grasped. It is abstract in several ways. First of all, it tends toward the exclusion of all non-cognitive elements of common experience: and to the degree in which it succeeds it is purely cognitive. Second it isolates one by one every particular relationship, differentiated from all other relationships which were vaguely associated in common experience. Even in common-sense thought and language, conceptual symbolizing tends to cut through figurative expressions to the plain, unadorned, simple literal expression of relationships. Third, the process continues and intensifies in the development of technological, scientific, and philosophical language, or in a substitute system of symbols, such as in mathematics. One goal, attainable with considerable effort at distinction and definition, is that in any given discourse a term will be understood to have only one meaning, one relationship which has been grasped. The unattainable goal of the tendency of conceptual symbolizing would be a purely relational language, with no trace of its origins in common, intuitive experience.[40] It is unattainable because it would be freed from all links with the human mode of being and operating. All human speech, however technical or scientific, has its sensuous base, its moorings and launching ramps in the world of perception, and it is "vulnerable": the purity of its abstract, univocal meaning is constantly threatened. Even mathematical language can be read aloud in the common languages of those who use them, and must be read or spoken or written to be introduced and explained. Its antiseptic mathematical shield is penetrated, and it is vulnerable to infection by the polyvalence of 'function' and 'funzione' in spoken English or Italian.[41]

Conceptual symbolism is linear and successive. It cannot hold and exhibit its object simultaneously, as does the painter or sculptor. Michelangelo could portray Moses as he imagined him, to be contemplated as a whole, present to the beholder. On the contrary, one who seeks to define must discern and distinguish, and move slowly along a single line of thought, then along another, word after word, proposition after proposition, as he or she fixes and formulates many relationships, and fashions a linguistic conceptual symbol which must be read and pondered with a similar linear, discursive operation.

---

[40] See Ernst Cassirer, *The Philosophy of Symbolic Forms*, III (New Haven: 1957) p. 385; and concerning physics, p. 479.

[41] MS, pp. 187-188.

Effective by dividing its task and making several linear movements of thought to discern, explore, and fix successively every significant relationship, such symbolizing is rigid and limited in its achievements. It tends to produce symbols which are ever sharper and thinner. It is poor even in its cognitive function, which is its sole concern.

I take "intuitive" here in the sense of pertaining somehow to the order of sense knowledge. Intuitive symbolizing begins with experience of some vivid visible form, or audible sound, or striking movement, or shocking accident--or whatever may evoke a deep sense of the feeling suggested by what is seen or heard or felt. The movement then from insight to the fashioning of a symbol is diverse from that of conceptual symbolizing. Though we have insights in the total experience, we do not seek to isolate and fix relationships. Rather we exploit the wealth of our primordial experience, seek sensuous analogies in what we hold by memory and create from imagination. We hold not merely the cognitive factor in the initial experience, but its total impact and evocative power. We fashion a sensuous image, a likeness, a semblance of the object which has impinged upon us and evoked a manifold response.

In its own way, intuitive symbolizing is an abstractive process, for only essentials are retained, to condense and heighten the expressive power of the meaningful form. Thus what is shaped captures a significant form, concrete, sensibly perceptible as the original, but somehow more vivid, "bigger than life." It is involved in the humblest verbal account accompanied by gestures more or less graceful and appropriate. In the work of a skilled symbolizer, in the many arts differentiated in part by their media and by the kinds of abstraction which they effect, the symbolizer produces an image of life or other objective reality often more vivid than nature itself. Intuitive symbolizing and symbols somehow image the whole of the sensibly perceptible reality which is portrayed, and express insight into the "shape" of the feeling which has been felt, the shape of another's feeling, or of deep feelings common to us in infinite variations. They do not express a sharply elaborated concept. They enable us to behold a sensuous likeness of the original phenomenon and share the perceiver's response.

Some intuitive symbolizing is analogous with conceptual in being linear and successive. All linguistic symbolizing has this characteristic, whether it be common narration or description, or one of the art forms such as poetry or other literature. Music and dance, too, create their images by successive elements.

Finally, we must note some truths which could be overlooked in beginning with the cognitive factor of symbols. First, as I noted in treating image, we form sensuous images by all of our intentional operations. [42]

Second, as I noted in considering meaning, in our intentional operations we express several kinds of meaning, cognitive, emotive, volitional, and motor. [43] We must not, therefore, suppose either that only conceptual symbols have a cognitive meaning and a function of communicating knowledge, or that only intuitive symbols have emotive, volitional, and motor meaning and can evoke corresponding responses. Great literature, prose and poetry, can hold and portray a profound understanding of human nature and the mystery of human life. Great works of philosophy and theology, for example of Plato or St. Thomas, can have a beauty, a splendor of form, which stirs emotion no less than a work of art. There is a marvelous blend and continuity in the endless ever varying ways of human symbolizing.

Third, the distinction between conceptual and intuitive symbols does not enable us to divide all symbols into exclusively conceptual or intuitive. Rather, it is a distinction of two manners of symbolizing which may characterize some symbolizing and symbols as prevalently of one type or the other. No symbol is purely conceptual or intuitive. We are all symbolizing continually, mostly without significant achievement. Most of our symbolizing is a matter of employing symbols which have been developed and adapted in the long history of our culture, cross-fertilized by elements of other cultures, more or less blurred in meaning, more or less expressive of thought, feeling, velleity, or will. When I distinguish and differentiate modes of symbolizing and symbols, I am referring to the significant achievements which reveal much of our human potential.

In my treatment of conceptual and intuitive symbolizing, I declared my intention of dealing first with the cognitive function of symbols. Much of what I have written, however, implicitly indicated what is to be said of the emotive, volitive, and motor intentionality. In forming symbols, meaningful sensuous images which somehow represent and communicate thought, we show forth analogously the shape of our feeling, will, and motor action. Take as an example a man who has been involved in an accident, in which he has been injured, and which he is convinced happened through the fault of the other. His vehement words, facial expressions, gestures and dangerously close approach to physical violence portray not only his thought, but the shape of his feeling, emotion, and movement. All are symbolized in the blend of a composite sensuous image,

---

[42] See above, S6, p. 26.
[43] Above, S6, p. 29ff.

meaningful with all the intentionalities involved in his total experience.

TOWARD UNDERSTANDING SYMBOLS

There is a certain ambiguity in the title of this section. It could mean understanding what *symbol* means. It could mean grasping and understanding the meaning of a given symbol: for example, baptism. I am taking it here in the first sense. We are moving toward a deeper understanding of what a symbol is.

(1) *The integration of part into whole.*

In all symbolizing a single function is being performed analogously: a particular, a part, or an aspect is integrated into a whole, in which alone it has full meaning. [44] In predominantly conceptual symbolizing the whole is an intelligible field, a world of thought. In intuitive symbolizing, a simple gesture or an exclamation, is grasped in its setting in a particular human world of shared experience, hopes, struggles, joys and sufferings. Only one who knows that world can grasp the meaning of the symbol, cognitive, emotive, volitional, and motor. This law of integration of a part into a meaningful whole is observed variously as the worlds and the media of symbolizers vary.

There is a further analogy in the integration of part into whole. In discursive linguistic symbolizing a word has its definite meaning, or its suggestive fulness of meaning, bursting any effort to define, as it is set in a sentence or meaningful phrase, and further into a whole linguistic symbol. In a painting, one detail in the composition, or one bit of color, has its meaning as it is set in the whole. In both cases, analogously, the symbolic element has meaning as it is grasped in context. So the law of integration applies first to the parts and whole of the symbol itself.

Second, at another level, the symbolized reality can be grasped only to the extent that it is a partial image of the world of the symbolizer: intellectual, emotional, volitional. A philosopher's proposition can be understood only in the whole world of philosophical thought of the symbolizer. A painting will be more meaningful to the extent that the perceiver knows the whole life of the person portrayed, and the artist's world of thought and feeling.

At this level, I am referring to integration not of the symbol, but of the symbolized reality, into the total reality of the sym-

---

[44] See MS, pp. 193-194.

bolizer's world. What do I mean? Take baptism as an example of integration of part into whole. At the first level indicated above, the symbolic immersion or pouring or sprinkling is one part of the indispensable symbolic action. The pronunciation of the prescribed words is the other. Each must be held in a total composite action which is the symbol. Each is a part of the symbol, integrated into a whole meaningful sensuous image. At the second level, the symbolized reality is the total effect of baptism: union with Christ in the mystery of his death and resurrection, forgiveness of sins, and so on. If this reality is to be intelligible, it must be integrated into the total symbolized reality: the world of the symbolizer, partially portrayed by the symbol. In the case of baptism, this total symbolized reality is the total transcendent reality of the eternal divine plan, and the agents and actions and effects which comprise the history of salvation, the gradual realization of the divine plan, coming to fulfilment in this human person here and now. Baptism has its relatively full, distinctively Christian meaning only as it portrays partially the whole transcendent reality.

At a third level, the imaged reality will have potentially infinite subtle differences of meaning as it resonates in the unique personal worlds of many perceivers. Thus the meaning of a symbol is modified as it is received and appropriated by the perceiver. As the full meaning of the symbol in the world of the symbolizer can be grasped only partially, so its meaning for any individual perceiver can be conjectured, but never comprehended. Every person wraps a mystery.

A perceived symbol will communicate a meaning which is conditioned by the unique world of the perceiver. As it is perceived, even a conceptual symbol, and far more an intuitive symbol, is somewhat indeterminate and polyvalent. The culture, personal endowment, and experience of the perceiver determine what could be called spontaneous or connatural meanings of symbols. Consequently, the symbolizer or someone else who is concerned with the communication of the symbolizer's meaning, must introduce the perceiver into the world of the symbolizer. As we shall see in the following chapter, the need of such an introduction is greatest in the case of divine-human symbolizing. Here the symbolizer's world is from the outset completely new, and unless the perceiver is introduced into that world, the whole set of symbols will be alien to the perceiver, who will be unable to grasp the meaning intended by the symbolizer.

I should indicate two considerations here. First, to the extent that the worlds of symbolizer and perceiver are different, some modification or expansion of the perceiver's world is necessary for effective communication. Second, even when the perceiver has been introduced to the symbolizer's world, his or her spontaneous and connatural meanings, suggested by the symbol, will remain part of their personal understanding, even if only as marginal or subliminal. They will not be obliterated. Any attempt at inculturation must take account of the fact that the message will be somehow modified, and will be unique as it is received into the world of the receiver's total experience. Moreover, the receiver will not be the only one to be affected by the encounter. The messenger too, meeting the demands of communication, will be affected by the interpersonal encounter, and may come to a deeper respect for the potential full meaning of the original symbol.

(2) *Kinds of symbols.*

As we move toward a better understanding of the symbol, it is helpful to recall my nominal definition of symbol: a meaningful sensuous image, [45] and the range of operations by which we fashion such images. I simply distinguish here the various kinds of symbols which we form. At this stage of our consideration, I employ the nominal definition. With this notion in mind we can recognize that all of the following analogously are symbols.

At this point, I am focussing on the symbol itself, the image. I shall proceed next to consider the functions of the symbol, with regard to the symbolizer and to others in the human interpersonal world; and the relationships which are grounded on those functions. Finally I shall attempt to define symbol, holding at the core the symbol itself, and setting it in the field of intelligible relationships in which alone it can be understood.

I shall merely enumerate the kinds of symbols which I have considered in detail elsewhere. [46] My ground for presenting these as symbols is the analogous imaging which we found in our reflection upon the range of our conscious operations. My first division is between internal and external symbols. The division suggests from the outset the great diversity of symbols and the impossibility of a relatively simple classification.

(a) Internal symbols as such remain within the subjective conscious experience of the symbolizer. We are aware of them "within" ourselves, as they occur in the flow of the conscious experience which characterizes humanly bodily being. Though empirical science, with delicate instruments, can detect bodily factors

---

[45] Above S6, p. 24, line 19.
[46] MS, pp. 222-267.

of such experience, the experiences themselves, as conscious, and the symbols in which they terminate cannot be detected. They are not expressed or projected. They do not have an existence and a consistency outside the subject. They do not serve to communicate meaning in an intersubjective world.

These are internal symbols: (1) images in perception, memory, imagination, and dream; (2) conceptions, reasonings, and judgments which remain unexpressed in external signs, verbal or written or other; (3) emotions, acts of will, and motor impulse, insofar as they remain incomplete, unexpressed, unexecuted; (4) body image: all that pertains to our awareness of our body, our sense of position, bodily tone, needs, and physical and intersubjective surroundings as they affect our personal bodily being.

(b) External symbols, though they terminate operations which we perform by the various powers which we have discerned and differentiated within our conscious experience, are manifest, sensibly perceptible, to others. They have at least some fleeting existence outside us, even if it be only the visible appearance of a grimace, or the ringing of a cry. They function, or are capable of functioning, to communicate meaning to others in an intersubjective world.

I propose a basic division of such symbols: elementary symbols, which may be recognized in their relatively simple forms, and which can figure in varying ways in more complex symbols; and complex, or developed symbols.

These are examples of elementary symbols: (1) facial expression, gesture, and elements of what has come to be called body language; (2) vocal sound, whether articulate or inarticulate; (3) instrumental sound in a broad sense of sound produced and shaped in various ways by use of either bodily organs (for example, clapping) or instruments in the strict sense; (4) formed external material, shaped to a meaningful sensuous form.

These are some of the principal kinds of complex or developed symbols: (1) speech or language, the most widely ranging of all; (2) conceptual symbols in science, mathematics, and philosophy, and in a unique way theology; (3) intuitive symbols: works of art. [47]

(3) *Functions.*

Continuing our effort to understand what symbols are, we must go beyond the notion "meaningful sensuous image." A symbol

---

[47] For a fairly full study of these symbolic forms, see MS, pp. 227-267.

is not a thing in nature. It is the term of a multiple human intentional operation, which functions in the human world, intrapersonal and interpersonal. We must, therefore, determine what its functions are, fix the relationships grounded on these functions, and then seek to formulate a definition which may hold reasonably well the field of relationships in which alone it is intelligible.

(a) Actualizing the symbolizer. First, by "actualizing" I mean contributing to the realization or actuation of one's potential. Since we symbolize by all of our conscious operations, we affect our own relative fulness of being as we symbolize. Ideally, in the mystery of human transcendence, we enhance our being by our operations. By perception, memory, imagination, insight, concept, judgment, emotion, will, and motor action to attain a desired good, we can enrich ourselves by acts which increase our knowledge, respond to the good known and possessed, and attain it. By loving, desiring, and attaining the good, we ourselves are better. On the contrary, we may engage in intentional operations by which we come to sense knowledge which only stimulates further activity which is evil: falsehood and the desire of and attainment of what is not good for us and diminishes our being. In either manner, symbolizing affects the symbolizer for better or for worse. A symbol is either the sensibly perceptible aspect of our intentional act, or its sensibly perceptible external term. Examples of the first type are words or gestures; of the second, a written word, a painting or a piece of sculpture.

With regard to the actualization of the symbolizer, I should observe first that as human persons we are actualized not by a series of discrete, discontinuous realizations of our potential, but by a process of continuous manifold actualizations of diverse kinds. We are bodily in a human way, and consequently we *are* by being in movement. That may seem to be contrary to what some might conceive to be the manner of our intellectual and volitional acts. They might seem to occur in a flash, in a discrete act, as if instantaneous, punctuating our continuous being. I should say that such a notion of our "spiritual" operations would be a misconception. We are in continuous being, in a manifold process, in which we can designate quasi instantaneous intellectual acts, such as insight or the flash of understanding. Yet all such acts occur in the flow of our being, in time. They are all moments in the continuum of our conscious experience. We are imaging by all of our conscious operations, and the innumerable successive images of all kinds play their roles in the total process of our development, personal and interpersonal, or intrapersonal and interpersonal. Insight and conception are examples. As I have maintained, [48] insight is not an achievement in which we rest, a sort of angelic act of understanding, complete, timeless. It is the beginning of another in a series of successive thrusts toward understanding. Analogously, the concept is not a punctual, instantaneous, perfect grasp of the "essence" of whatever we seek to understand. It is a moment in a process, an incomplete grasp of some aspect of the reality which is its object, and it will occasion further questions and probing to the person who continues to think.

We must distinguish the roles of internal and external symbols. As we have considered, we are imaging continually by all of our conscious intentional operations. Moreover, there is a continual, manifold interplay among them. Perceptions continually enrich memory and imagination. All three may evoke acts of emotion, will, and motor action, which in turn intensify a total experience and subsequent memory and imagination. All are factors in a total experience which is somehow understood. Insight, understanding, judgment, and will come to be only in the matrix of our total sense knowledge, and are conditioned by emotion. The patterns of combination and interrelationship are beyond conception. By our manifold intentional operations, then, we ourselves come to a higher degree of actualization of our potential, even without consideration of our external acts by which the operations are completed. We are actualized, therefore, by a wonderful complex of operations by which we are imaging, symbolizing, internally.

In so far as we consider ourselves solely as persons in the presence of God, we can recognize an important fulfillment in such inner acts, terminating in one or more internal symbols. Yet as human persons we do not come to fulfillment in a human solitude. We live fully when our minds and hearts are revealed in acts which affect other men and women. The gauge of our love of God is our love of our brothers and sisters, a love which must be expressed in word and deed.

Acts which come to a relative term in an internal symbol are but a stage in our full actualization. As we live in our interpersonal world, we cannot function in community, and cannot come to our relative fulness of being, except by acts which terminate in sensuous, externally perceptible acts and, in many cases, perceptible meaningful products of our acts. Our actualization as persons living in community is not just a plus-value, without which we could do quite nicely. We cannot live fully as persons without opening on the inter-

---

[48] See above, S6, pp. 10-11.

personal world. Anyone who tried for long to live closed in on self, with all thought and feeling unexpressed, would be in danger of serious personal derangement, and eventually in need of special care.

(b) Revealing the symbolizer's world. A symbol is a proximate term of a process which began with insight. That process may involve one or more modes of intentionality: cognitive, emotive, volitional, and motor. It is a proximate term, not the ultimate term. Symbols continue to function in the life of the symbolizer and in the lives of others in an interpersonal world. I distinguish two sets of these further functions. One regards the symbol in relation to the process by which it came to be, and the world of the symbolizer from which it proceeded. The other regards its further functioning in affecting the symbolizer and others. I am considering here the first of these two sets of functions.

A symbol is the meaningful sensuous term of a human operation. It is a shaped sensuous image of the thought, feeling, will, and purposeful movement of the symbolizer. The imaged reality is a fragment of the full personal reality of the symbolizer. It can be understood only as it can be set in the whole personal world. If the symbol is a blend of gestures and words, it is a particular image in which, for example, intense anger reaches its full expression. It is more meaningful as it stands out in the flood of passion, and its relatively full meaning could be grasped only by one who knew the mystery of that person, of the injury suffered, of the personal, family, and total tragic world.

Every symbol serves as a partial revelation of the symbolizer and of the world into which he or she had an insight and responded from his or her situation. It gives some inkling of a personal world, objective and subjective: that is, of the surrounding world as he or she faces it; and of the world of personal experience in which this particular experience is set.

To whom does the symbol reveal the symbolizer's world? We must distinguish according to the kinds of symbols. Internal symbols reveal something of the inner personal world of the symbolizer. In the example which I have given of response to injury, the internal symbols may be perception, flashes of memory of related incidents, insight, flood of passion, strong will to ward off further attack and to punish the attacker, images of possible defense or reaction, strong impulse to strike the offender. All of these internal images are part of the total conscious experience. All make the victim aware of what is happening and how he or she is responding. They are a series of readings on the total experience. They reveal the person's situation, grasped in the context of previous patterns of experience. In the total concrete experience the succession of images are a sort of inner revelation, a series of running readings, all occurring within the victim. As far as they remain purely internal, they reveal nothing to spectators. When the victim breaks into angry words and actions, these external symbolic elements together begin to portray the inner response of the victim. External symbols are the "face" of the symbolizer in this interpersonal world, the meeting point of two worlds, that of the symbolizer and that of the perceiver.

External symbols, then, reveal the symbolizer to the extent that the imaged reality is grasped in the setting of his or her personal world. They mediate all interpersonal communication and influence. Every such symbol is representative: the part stands for the whole. A concept expressed is grasped as it is set in a whole world of thought. A single act of love partially reveals a full life and love. A determined act of will expressed in a decision or command is a thrust of a free man or woman shaping the world. A poised body, or a single initial segment of a movement stands for the whole subsequent action. The whole race is symbolized in the tense body of the sprinter poised against the starting blocks, and in every stride along the course, and in the final thrust to break the tape.

(c) Affecting the human world by a multiple efficacy. Three terms call for a brief note here. First, I say "human world" to include both the intrapersonal world of the symbolizer and the interpersonal world which he or she may affect. Then, using the terms "affecting" and "efficacy," I proceed without considering it necessary here to vindicate the general notion of causality, or the particular order of reality, influence, and causality which figure in the intrapersonal and interpersonal worlds. I have treated these matters concisely in this work, and amply elsewhere. [49] Knowing and loving are ways of being. They are real. When we grow in knowledge, and in the affirmation of truth, and when we love the good, we grow in truth, in goodness, in the relative fulness of our potential being. When we contribute to others' growing in knowledge and truth and goodness, we influence in some way their relative fulness of being and truth and goodness. When we grow in mutual knowledge and love, we reach a fulfillment which is unattainable for men and women by their solitary powers. Symbols figure in the total intrapersonal and interpersonal worlds in which these enrichments occur. [50]

---

[49] For more ample treatment of "real" and "reality," see MS, pp. 135-140, 219-220, 271, 281-282; for "causality" in this context, see MS, pp. 282-290.

[50] On the efficacy of symbols, see MS, pp. 280-290.

A Definition of *Symbol*

With the insertion of one word, *meaningful*, I retain the definition which I proposed in *Man the Symbolizer*: *a symbol is a meaningful sensuous image which terminates a human intentional operation, represents the imaged reality, and may affect the human world with a manifold efficacy.* [51]

No exposition or explanation of the definition should be necessary: the whole preceding development of thought in this chapter has prepared the elements of the definition, which is merely a formulation of relationships which should make "symbol" intelligible.

All of our imaging is symbolizing, and is itself symbolic of our human way of being. Every effort to hold something of the mystery of the other, and every thrust to attain what we desire or to flee what we dislike, is symbolic of our being: diffused in space, in movement, measured by time, we *are* only bit by bit, in a diffused being, every bit of which is symbolic of the whole. We are by being continually in movement, striving toward a greater fulness of the realization of our potential. So our intentional operations, imaging, symbolizing, are as a whole symbolic of the mystery of our human transcendence, our tending toward a greater fulness of being, truth, and goodness.

So it is at the level of our purely human being and operation. As we go on to consider our elevation to a higher level of being, in the share of the divine life, we find the mystery of divine-human symbolizing, itself symbolic of our divinely given thrust toward a transcendent fulness of being. To that we now turn.

---

[51] MS, p. 294.

Chapter VII

DIVINE-HUMAN SYMBOLIZING

One cannot move from the consideration of human symbolizing to any discourse about divine or divine-human symbolizing by simply taking the theory elaborated in the preceding chapter--or any other conception of human symbolizing--and applying it to a new set of symbolizers. If a symbol is a meaningful sensuous image, and symbolizing is the process of elaborating such a symbol, then it may seem from the outset that divine symbolizing is inconceivable. If one succeeds in establishing an analogy by which it is possible to conceive of divine symbolizing, then another challenge remains. What sort of hybrid conception is expressed by the term divine-human symbolizing? What is the human role in such an operation? Does the theory of human symbolizing apply to this human role, and if so how?

The passage to the consideration of divine and divine-human symbolizing is similar to the passage which I worked out in seeking to understand God: a movement from a metaphysical phase to a theological phase of the consideration of divine being, truth, goodness, and unity. [1] The movement here too is from philosophical to theological thought. The difference is that here we must make a twofold passage. Regarding God and divine symbolizing, we move from a metaphysical to a theological consideration of God as true and good. Regarding the human element in divine-human symbolizing, we are moving from a philosophy of the human way of being to a theological understanding of a transcendent human way of being, a theological anthropology.

In both passages we face an arduous challenge. We can think analogously of divine symbolizing only by a rigorous purification of the notion of symbol. The challenge may be even greater regarding our elaboration of the human role in divine-human symbolizing. The reason is that we must avoid yielding to the temptation to work out our account without attending to the almost equally rigorous demands of the theological analogy which is involved. What I call a transcendent human way of being regards the utterly new world and

---

[1] See *Telling*, III.

level of being to which we are raised when we come to be in Christ, sharing the divine life in the experience of the Mystery of God's way of bringing us to relative fulfillment of his eternal plan for us. To understand the human role in divine-human symbolizing demands a reexamination of every aspect of the theory of human symbolizing.

There is a broad analogy of divine symbolizing, within which we must locate and determine what is proper to divine-human symbolizing. Within the latter, in turn, it will be necessary to distinguish several modes, only one of which is proper to an understanding of the Christian sacrament, which we seek.

First, I use *analogy* in a strict sense, which, in my judgment, applies only to similarity-in-diversity of being, one, true, and good, the so-called transcendentals. Analogy in this sense differs from mere metaphor, by which the name of one is applied to another which is simply different in nature. When metaphor is used aptly, there is a remote likeness which is hit off by a comparison based on a similarity of form, or manner of action, or whatever else may strike the coiner of the metaphor. The man who is called "fox" is no more a fox then he is a horse or an airedale. On the contrary, in the case of analogy all those of whom an analogous term is predicated, really are somehow alike intrinsically, despite their radical diversity.

Using the term analogy in this strict sense, I should say that, with proper distinctions, we may speak by analogy of God as a symbolizer. Human symbolizing pertains to the mystery of human transcendence, by which we tend somehow to go beyond our present degree of fulness of being, truth, and good. We do so by knowing and affirming the truth, and loving the good. [2] What pertains to attainment of truth and good by cognitive and volitive operations in symbolizing allows of analogical affirmation concerning truth and goodness in God. By contrast, what pertains to emotive and motor acts in human symbolizing could be affirmed of God only metaphorically. A further limitation is necessary in thinking of divine symbolizing. What may be affirmed of God as symbolizer regards the perfections of true and good, not the mystery of human transcendence, the process of going beyond our present level of perfection. All that pertains to the human process in symbolizing is grounded in the limited manner of human being: we cannot project the process itself into divine symbolizing. Yet, as we shall see, when we consider divine-*human* symbolizing, all that we

---

[2] For my earlier treatment of the analogy of symbolizing, and divine symbolizing, and our part in it, see MS, pp. 330-337; and at greater length, *Basics of a Roman Catholic Theology*, "God the symbolizer: metaphor or analogy?" pp. 49-62, and "Some consequences and further questions," pp. 62-70

have determined concerning human symbolizing is relevant to the roles of the human persons through whom God symbolizes and in whom his symbols have their effects.

I shall consider first briefly the range of divine symbolizing, in which there is a broad analogy, from the "inner life" of the Trinity to the great variety of ways in which God symbolizes in this bodily world.

THE RANGE OF DIVINE SYMBOLIZING

(1) *The processions within the Trinity of divine Persons.*

I shall not attempt to compress here what I have worked out at length elsewhere.[3] Briefly, as I have pointed out in the places just cited, theological reflection on the Son as image of the Father is grounded on Col. 1.15: "... He is the image of the invisible God, the firstborn of all creation;...." Implicitly he is the image both as God and as man. It is not a long step to the concept of the Son as symbol of the Father: perfect image as God, imperfect as man. Some Greek Fathers affirmed that the Holy Spirit is the perfect natural image of the Son, his seal, his exact representation. Once we have elaborated the concept of symbol, it is reasonable to apply it analogously to eminent symbolizing and symbols in the Holy Trinity. Obviously, in the necessary purification of such thought regarding God's eminent symbolizing, both the process of human symbolizing and the notion of *sensuous* image are denied.

(2) *Creation as universal revelation, a phase of God's self-manifestation.*

By all that God has made he shares and shows forth something of his own fulness of being and good. By all of his visible creation, in which his creatures are somehow sensibly perceptible, he symbolizes, representing something of the "world" of the prime symbolizer in a wonderful variety of sensuous images. All that he has made is a faint image of himself, representing his perfection, and capable of moving men and women to acknowledge him and move to him as the source and goal of their being.

---

[3] Concerning the analogy of the true, and hints of interpersonal knowledge of the three Persons, see *Telling*, III, pp.184-194. Concerning the analogy of the good, love, and interpersonal love, see *ibid.*, pp. 231-240. I have proposed my complementary model of a transcendental trinitarian theology, *ibid.*, pp. 325-343.

What is the purpose of this symbolizing, which thus is capable of affecting only human persons? I should reply differently than I did formerly. Then I spoke and wrote of a merely natural knowledge of God, a sort of inchoate metaphysics or ontology. Now I should say that in his universal revelation God is symbolizing vaguely, very imperfectly, the Mystery of his plan for us. Eternally there is only one divine plan, and it is salvific, directed to bringing men and women to a fulness of life in the share of the life of God. Yet the meaning of this bodily world is known by faith alone. Consequently I should say that only a Christian theologian can read the universal revelation as it is illumined by the special revelation of the Old and New Testaments.

For the phenomenologist of religion the bodily universe leads only to a natural knowledge of "god," intimations of a power or being on which the visible world depends, a sort of inchoate ontology. The Christian theologian, believing that there is one universal process, one divine plan, recognizes that even in the most obscure universal revelation God is offering the possibility of a knowledge and acknowledgment which can lead to the fulness of life to which he calls us. This distinction of two levels of understanding of the same reality in universal process makes sense only to the Christian theologian who maintains it. Yet that is part of the mystery. The Christian world view, and the Christian interpretation of the situation of all men and women in this one economy of salvation, make sense only in the light of revelation and faith.

Only the believer, like the psalmist in Ps. 104, reads the transcendent meaning of the perceptible universe. Yet in the vague intimations of God which are possible without explicit special revelation, men and women are drawn to acknowledge the only God, and to move by dark ways to find a fulness of life in him. Heaven and earth and all that is in them show forth, symbolize, the one God who made them and us, and who moves us to come to life in him. The functions of God's symbols in creation are cognitive and volitive: he gives some knowledge of himself, and draws men and women to find their full good in him. As these symbols resonate in the men and women who perceive them, they have emotive and motor dimensions. Thus the universal divine symbolizing has a multiple impact and efficacy in the human world. The obscurity of the knowledge of God, and of the ways to fulness of life, are tormenting. Yet this symbolizing is part of the one divine plan. [4]

---

[4] I have touched this mystery in *Telling*, II, "*In History*," pp. 47-75, especially 74-75; and I shall return to it in dealing with Christ and Church as Prime Sacra-

In his universal revelation through creation, God symbolizes through sensuous, sensibly perceptible persons and things which are meaningful to men and women who penetrate their mystery sufficiently to find some likeness of the God who made them. They are symbols, meaningful sensuous images. They do not involve a special participation of men and women in the process of symbolizing, except that in the whole of their own being and operating human persons, like all else that God made, share and show forth something of God's perfection.

What are the grounds for the Christian theologian's affirmation of a deeper meaning of universal revelation than is affirmed by any phenomenologist of religions? The base is our belief in the universality of God's will to save. Consistently with that belief, we affirm that God offers to every man and woman the grace necessary for salvation. Consequently we must hold that the knowledge of God which is possible for all without explicit special revelation is sufficient for salvation. I should say that the explanation must lie in the twofold intentionality of universal revelation which I have indicated, cognitive and volitive. Though the knowledge which is mediated by the universal revelation is scant and obscure, God moves men and women interiorly, within their pondering of the mystery of the world about them. Within their obscure knowledge, they receive the grace, the movement of their wills, which suffices to draw them to act according to their consciences. Doing this, they are saved by the grace of God. If they reject the judgment of their own consciences, they reject the grace which has been given them. [5]

(3) *Revelation and inspiration.* [6]

I mention these two manners of divine-human symbolizing simply to indicate their place in the range of divine symbolizing, and to note briefly what is proper to each. Both involve a human mediatorial role. God's special revelation occurs by somehow communicating his truth to men and women, by whatever form of sensibly and intelligibly perceptible reality may be employed in a

---

ment. For a fairly ample treatment of universal revelation, as distinct from special revelation, see *Basics*, pp. 43-48.

[5] What I affirm here I have elaborated in two related contexts. One is the experience of God in history, in *Telling*, II, pp. 56-75, in which I considered the paradox of Christ and the Church as prime sacraments, a theme to which I shall return later. The other is the theological development of the truth regarding God's eternal decree and its execution, in *Telling*, III, pp. 263-313.

[6] See *Basics*, "Revelation," pp. 71-93; "Inspiration and its Term: the Bible," pp. 94-118.

given case. Moreover, the human mediator of special revelation must use symbols, sensuous images which are meaningful and which pass on the divine word to others. Inspiration involves God's moving human authors to write or dictate the works which preserve the divine word. God is the prime symbolizer, the author of the individual inspired work, and of the whole of the Bible. The human author serves as mediator of the divine word, preserved in the Bible. Both revelation and inspiration, then, in the instrumental human role, involve sensuous images of some sort. They are possible too only through the free participation of the human recipients of the divine word. Moreover, they are limited by the personal potential and the culture of the recipients. The human mediatorial function seemingly does not in all cases involve a deep religious commitment or holiness.

(4) *Israel as a sacrament*.

In God's revelation and realization of his saving action in Israel, we can distinguish three manners of divine-human symbolizing. First, by his word of revelation he foretold his actions, explained their meaning, and continually reminded Israel of what he had done on their behalf. Second, in his action, God showed both by his perceptible deliverance and blessing of his people and by his recurrent punishment of their infidelities that he is the kind of God that he promised to be. Third, in Israel's worship and life of fidelity, it is God who was bearing them by his grace, and showing forth an image of the fulness of the blessings promised for fidelity.

When Israel was faithful to God's law, and when its worship was pleasing to him, the human role in the divine-human symbolizing in Israel involved a life of deep religious commitment and holiness. They were to be holy as he is holy. He symbolized through them only as they were somehow an imperfect image of his holiness and his plan for those who would believe and respond to his offer.

(5) *Christ the sacrament*.

In Christ divine-human symbolizing is supreme. In his perfect human nature and powers, his fulness of the Spirit, and his full human response to the Father's will, Christ images the Father and the fulness of life which the Father and he offer. In Christ as man we have not a perfect image of the Father, for Christ's human nature and powers and acts are finite, inadequate as are all symbols to express the full reality which is imaged. We have, we might say without irreverence, the best that even God can do in human nature. In the Incarnate Word we have human nature and operation raised to its highest possible role in the divine-human symbolizing by which God shows forth and effects the realization of his plan to raise us to a share in his divine life and blessedness.

(6) *The Church as sacrament.*

Jesus Christ in glory is not sensibly perceptible. Through the Church--the whole Church--he continues to act, and is somehow perceptible. In its public worship, the Church participates in Christ's worship of the Father. Ministers of sacraments and of the Eucharistic sacrifice act perceptibly and are believed to be acting in the name and power of Christ, the only High Priest. In its teaching and preaching the Church continues to make known in the world today the word of salvation. In the whole of their life in fidelity to the new covenant, Christians are perceptible and are believed to be members of Christ, who continues to show forth in them a partial realization of the Mystery. Sharing in the sacramentality of the Church, men and women living in Christ share in the human role of God's continuing divine-human symbolizing.

(7) *The paradox of Christ and Church as sacraments.*

There is a multiple paradox in the sacramentality, the symbolizing, of both Christ and the Church. It regards the strange manner in which the concept of symbol may be applied to them. I recall the definition which I proposed at the end of the preceding chapter: a symbol is a meaningful sensuous image which terminates a human intentional operation, represents the imaged reality, and may affect the human world with a manifold efficacy.

First, obviously Christ and Church as divine-human symbols terminate both divine and human intentional operations. As divine symbols, they are the sensibly perceptible terms of God's operation by intellect and will, showing forth as they realize the partial accomplishment of his eternal plan. As human, they are the sensibly perceptible terms of the multiple intentional operations of Christ and of the men and women in whom the Church is sensibly present at any one time and place.

Second their meaning is unique, not to be gathered simply by perceiving and understanding, as is the case in ordinary human symbols. The meaning of these symbols, prime sacraments, is God's meaning. They image God and the eternal divine plan for bringing all to fulness in Christ. They cannot be understood, nor can they have their full effect on the human world, without God's special revelation and the gifts of faith and of the grace by which men and women are drawn to respond to God's offer. During Jesus' public life even his closest disciples did not understand who and what he was. Only after the pentecostal gift of the Holy Spirit did they believe, and somehow understand, and respond more fully.

As for the Church, its sole visibility is in its living members. The Church through the centuries does not manifest its meaning to all who perceive the men and women who are members of Christ. We see them in their sensibly perceptible human reality. Only in so far as we believe what has been revealed concerning the Church and them do we believe that they are members of the Body of Christ, and that somehow obscurely they show forth the mystery of Christ within them, and influence the human world about them. Only in so far as we know by faith the mystery of Christian life do we sense the reality of the inner life which their external behavior somehow represents. The external, sensibly perceptible aspect of their lives is the meaningful sensuous symbol of the inner reality, surmised only by those who know of the Christian way set forth in the Gospel and witnessed to in the *Acts* and the letters, especially of Paul and John.

Third, there is a paradoxical disproportion between their being sensuous, sensibly perceptible, and their efficacy in mediating grace to all men and women. We believe that Christ reconciled us to the Father, and that all grace comes through him. We believe too that the Church, in Christ, is a universal sacrament, mediating life and union to all who receive it. Yet consider the limits of the sensible perceptibility of Christ and of the Church. Jesus was perceptible only during his life on earth and, to a few at rare moments, in his apparitions after the resurrection. Even during his public life and in his appearances, Jesus was perceptible as man, not as God. Seeing is not believing. Even when Thomas saw, he had to believe. Christ is the Prime Sacrament, the universal sacrament of salvation for all men and women of all times. Only through the salvation which he somehow manifested and which he confers are men and women of all ages saved. Yet he was perceptible for only a short time to relatively few men and women. His perceptibility is severely limited. His efficacy is universal.

Similarly the Church's perceptibility is severely limited. In what sense, and to whom, is the Church perceptible? We cannot see the whole Church. We see only men and women whom we believe to be members of the Church, of the Body of Christ. We may see the man who is the pope. We can see him as he is dressed distinctively and as his position and actions in relation to others, for example in worship, suggest that he is special. We cannot see his papal dignity as such, any more than we can see his hidden life in Christ. So with regard to other members of the Church, seeing these men and women, we believe that they are of the Church. We believe that they have some special role in the Church, corresponding to one or more consecratory sacraments which they have received. For us, in so far as they are perceptible and show forth something of the Mystery, they are sacraments, sharing in the unique divine-human symbolizing of the Church.

For most men and women, the vast majority of the human race which has lived from the beginning of the Christian era, the Church has not been, and is not, perceptible as the mediator of Christ's grace. They did not, and do not, recognize the transcendent reality of the Church, which is not perceptible in any case. The Church can be perceptible only in its members, and they can be perceived only as these men and women: their life in Christ, their dignity and role in the Body are imperceptible. We believe the reality of their lives as Christians, but we do not perceive it. For those to whom what we believe is neither attractive nor credible, in no sense do members of the Church manifest the Mystery. Indeed, some members of the Church occasion or cause some men and women to judge the Church adversely, and to reject any notion that the grace of Christ comes to them through the Church. Again, the perceptibility of this sacrament is severely limited.

After all of these negatives, we should miss the wonderful mystery of the Christ and his Church as sacraments if we did not emphasize their transcendent meaning and efficacy for those who have received the Christian revelation and do believe in Christ and the Church. Their meaning and power are unique, and they enrich Christian experience wonderfully. I say Christian *experience*: our consciousness, awareness, of the realization of the Mystery within us personally and in our community of believers. The more we ponder God's promise and fulfillment, and respond in belief and love and hope, the more Jesus means to us, and the more we wonder at the beauty of those who witness to us the richness of life in Christ.

Christ and Church are paradoxical sacraments: there is a bewildering disproportion between their sensible perceptibility and their efficacy. [7] For us who believe they are uniquely meaningful and powerful.

(8) *Divine-human symbolizing?*

If we consider the range of symbolizing which I have sketched, the question can occur: how much of this is human symbolizing,

---

[7] See *Telling*, III, pp. 60-75, esp. pp. 70-75.

and how much divine or divine-human? When men and women are taken up into God's saving action, and participate in the realization and manifestation of the richer life which they share, it may seem that it is human symbolizing which is involved, not divine-human. Yet Israel's symbolizing in its worship and its fidelity to the way set by God was a manifestation of God's work in them. Christ's symbolizing as the Prime Sacrament is the supreme instance of divine-human symbolizing: God's was showing forth and realizing in Christ his eternal plan of loving mercy, reconciliation, and bringing to fulness of life in Christ. All of the human symbolizing in the process of salvation history is borne by God's grace. God is realizing in and through Christ, and now in and through us, his eternal plan. God is the prime symbolizer.

The whole of authentic Christian life and worship is divine-human symbolizing. Yet it is marked by peak experiences in acts of worship which are consecratory, making men and women sacred to God, holy in a unique way. The rest of their life and worship is a flowering of the life given through these acts of consecration. Sacrament and sacrifice constitute the people, consecrate and sanctify individuals, and engage them in their prime sacramental actions, in which they, as Church and as individual members of the Body of Christ, show forth most vividly what they have become. They are the supreme symbolic, sacramental actions of Father, Son, and Holy Spirit, sanctifying these men and women here and now. Within the human frame of that sanctifying action, they are the acts of Christ, God and man, filled with the Spirit, worshipping the Father, reconciling us to him, bringing us to a greater fulness of life in himself.

These acts of divine-human symbolizing, then, are unique. They must have all the wealth of ordinary actions of Christian life in which we are sacraments, symbolizing the Mystery. In addition, they have another dimension, by which their efficacy is not dependent on the perfection of the personal divine-human response of the individual symbolizer. To the mystery of this unique divine-human symbolizing in sacrament and sacrifice we now turn.

(9) *Christian sacrament and sacrifice.*

Until the recent revival and development of the concept of Christ and Church as sacraments, the term sacrament was reserved normally for the seven principal rites of Christian worship. Even now that Roman Catholic usage has extended the use of the term to the whole range of realities which I have sketched, the seven sacraments have a unique role, and a distinctive intelligible structure as divine-human symbols. The seven sacraments, including the Eucharist as sacrifice and greatest of the sacraments, are the principal acts by which Christ continues to honor the Father in and through his Body. They are the actions in which Christian life comes to a peak, in which the Church and individual participating members show forth most fully what they are.

Any act of public worship of the Church is a complex event. Christ, the eternal high priest, is acting in and through his Church. Depending on what rite is being performed, the members of the Church who are physically present participate diversely. In the liturgy of the hours, though the participants may differ in dignity, the act of worship does not depend on the exercise of the power of the sacrament of orders. A bishop or abbot or priest may lead the worship, but his prayer, like that of the other worshippers, has a value and efficacy proportioned to his own faith and love and reverence. Like the prayer of all others, his is borne by Christ in this perceptible act of public worship performed in and through his Body. Participation demands a share in the universal priesthood of Christians, grounded on baptism and confirmation. Since the Church's public worship is not a private matter, those who participate physically present somehow represent the whole Church, believed to be present and acting in and though them.

When we attempt to understand the special dignity and efficacy of the sacraments and the Eucharistic sacrifice, we must reckon with a greater complexity and diversity of powers, functions, and efficacy. Valid performance of baptism and matrimony do not require the power of orders in the minister. The other sacraments and the Eucharist do. They are divine-human symbols in which God is the principal symbolizer, and the human minister functions instrumentally in a complex act by which God is honored and human persons are consecrated or sanctified. Christ exercises his priesthood diversely in the Eucharist and in the individual sacraments, and at the proper place we shall have to consider this. It is, however, the role of the minister of the sacrifice or sacrament which is most difficult to discern and differentiate. Historically this difficulty has occasioned the elaboration of a sacramental theology which has focussed on essentials, on what is necessary for validity of the minister's action and of the sacrament or sacrifice performed. Often the stress has been on this, to the neglect of the full perfection of the minister's action. Dealing with human roles in divine-human symbolizing, I shall attempt to develop a conception of the full perfection of the minister's act of worship.

Human Roles in the Christian Sacrament

(1) *The incarnational principle.*

In the human share in divine-human symbolizing, it seems right to read an unfolding of implications of the mystery of the incarnation as characterizing the whole of salvation history. This is what I term the incarnational principle in the mystery of our salvation.

What is the principle? God takes human nature and human persons seriously in the history of salvation. Eternally God knows and wills salvation in and through Christ: through the mystery of the assumption of human nature into the union of one person, the Son, the Incarnate Word. He wills to effect our salvation in and through one who is of our very nature, by the supreme achievement of one who is human as well as divine. This involves in Christ full natural human perfection, the fulness of grace, and the supreme actualization of the Son as man in the work of our redemption. In his whole work, culminating in the paschal mystery, Jesus manifests the coming of the reign of God, the salvation of our fallen race, in a worship which honors the Father as it marks Jesus' own full human achievement.

In the whole of the redemptive incarnation, God symbolizes in Jesus, showing forth and effecting his reconciling of the world to himself in Jesus. He could not symbolize without some sensuous image. He symbolizes most wonderfully in the human being and operation of Jesus.

According to the analogy of faith, we may find an extension of the principle of incarnation. In a broad sense, without extending the hypostatic union beyond the historical Jesus, we may say that God performs the whole of his saving action in history in and through men and women, through human nature and operation by which he symbolizes, represents the imaged reality (the whole of the Mystery being accomplished), and effects the salvation of those who will receive his offer of life.

So, to the extent to which his saving action is known by revelation, analogously in his People of the Old Covenant, and in his new Israel of the New Covenant, God saves in and through men and women, through their grace-borne action, all somehow an unfolding of the salvation wrought by Jesus Christ, the Incarnate Word.

In a Christian interpretation of the history of Israel, we may see that God's saving action preceding the incarnation is somehow a series of types and anticipations of what is realized in Christ and then continued in the Church and in Christian life. The Old Testament is "all about Christ," as Augustine recognized. The Servant is a figure of Jesus. So too are all of the prophets and great figures. In all of them, their own personal fulfillment is symbolic of what God is effecting.

In a unique way in the whole Christ, in Jesus and his members, the whole work of salvation is effected in and through human nature and operation. God is symbolizing in and through us, as he did in and through the human nature and operations of Jesus. Jesus is worshipping the Father in and through us, taking us up into the full worship which he offered to the Father throughout his mortal life and especially in the paschal mystery. As the Father sent Jesus, Jesus also sends us.

Manifesting the full implications of the principle of incarnation, God takes seriously the role of human persons, members of Christ, continuators of his mission and work, symbolizing as they themselves achieve their relative fulness of being in Christ. Christians, living in Christ, show forth in their whole being, and especially in their participation in Christ's public worship of his Father, what they are all about: they are themselves images of the reality being achieved within them and through them: the Mystery, the eternal divine plan at work and being realized here and now in these men and women. To the extent to which men and women live fully, are fully actualized as they symbolize, they realize God's purpose in them: to continue in and through them, as continuators of Christ, the reconciling of the world to himself.

Full divine-human symbolizing, then, beyond the strict mystery of the hypostatic union and of Christ as prime symbol, involves full human actualization, full personal achievement and fulfillment of men and women who at once come to their own fulness of life in Christ, and show forth in the whole of their being the mystery at work in them. They symbolize, as they continue the symbolizing of the Incarnate Word who has taken them up into his Body and lives in them and continues to honor his Father and to establish his reign in and through them.

In a broad sense, then, all Christian life is a form of divine-human symbolizing. Since all of our being and operation in Christ is borne by the grace of Christ, it is all part of the transcendent instrumentality by which we serve to bring about the realization of God's plan in others. We symbolize: God and Christ symbolize through us. We serve to manifest and to effect the continuing new creation.

The Christian sacrament and the Eucharistic sacrifice are unique instances of divine-human symbolizing in the Christian mystery. In seeking to understand them, it seems important to insist

first on the full actualization of the human person who is symbolizing in sacramental action. The reason is that only in relatively
full actualization of the human person as minister is the privileged
role of human nature taken seriously.

When this factor of the ideal fulness of the human sym-
bolization has been taken into account, we may turn to consider
what is utterly unique in sacramental action: the divine power and
action and efficacy at work within sacramental action, and the
unique effect attributable only to that unique dimension of divine
power and operation in the sacrament.

Only thus is the extension of Christ's action in his members,
and their full role, taken seriously. One who performs a sacrament
does not perform simply the "essential rite" as a sort of slender
purely instrumental action within which the divine power and
operation is at work.

(2) *Roles of the human nature of Christ.*

We must distinguish between the institution and the use, or
repeated performance, of the sacraments. Though the eminent
intentional operation from which the symbol proceeds, and which it
terminates, is the divine knowledge and will, truth and goodness,
still there is a whole range of analogous application to Christ, the
Church, and human ministers.

Christ, instituting the sacraments, knows the whole eternal
plan, the Mystery. In commanding that a sacrament be performed
through the ages, he knows the whole of the ensuing history of
salvation, and in the moment of institution he wills the performance
of every sacramental act. In every sacramental act Christ, by his
human nature, and acts of intellect and will, is the prime instrument
of the divine will. He is present and acting in every act of public
worship of his Church, in every performance of every sacrament.
That unique presence is intelligible only if we consider Christ as
God and man. As man, he is the prime instrument of the divine
action. That he be present and acting in every act of public worship
to the end of time is due to his divine nature and power and
operation. In the unity of the operation of Father, Son, and Spirit,
he manifests and realizes his/their will that through this symbol here
and now this man or woman be sanctified.

The full reality which the sacrament represents is the Mystery,
the saving action which culminates in him, and which continues to
the end of time in and through the Church and the individual
ministers of every instance of the performance of every sacrament.
The full potential efficacy of the sacraments is the fulness of life

which he offers, and which will be received by individuals according to their dispositions.

(3) *The Church*.

It is the Church which by its teaching, and by its supervision of the formation of the full rites in which the essential action is set, interprets the sacraments. The Church, by the catechesis which it disposes and inspires, teaches what the symbols represent, and what is their potential effect upon men and women who perceive and receive them. The Church, present in every act of public worship, is, in Christ, the second instrument of the divine action.

The universal presence of Christ and Church in the administration of the sacraments must be understood in the context of their instrumental causality. Both the humanity of Christ and the Church, each at its own level, function in the present conferring of grace through every sacrament only insofar as they are instruments of the divine nature. What is involved here is more than an enduring act of Christ's human will, or the mission of the ministers empowered sacramentally. Such a permanent, universal effect could not be understood as depending simply on Christ's human will: it involves in every instance the exercise of divine power, not merely human. It is only as God, not as man, that Christ can make his historical human act effective here and now, anywhere, at any moment in time. Christ sanctifies principally as God, instrumentally as man. The Church's action in sanctifying is purely instrumental.

(4) *The Minister*.

It is only through the minister's action that any sacrament is performed. Concerning his intentional operations, from which the sacrament proceeds immediately, we must consider a number of questions.

(a) Power. The human symbolizer must be empowered to act as a minister. The necessary empowerment varies in the sacraments, as they are understood in the Church. One might object that no empowerment is required for the valid performance of baptism: any man or woman, baptized or unbaptized, believer or unbeliever, can be the minister of this sacrament. Yet it is only through the Church that this is known. In that sense, even in this extreme instance the administration of the sacrament is monitored by the Church. [8]

---

[8] To simplify the matter of language concerning the minister, I make clear once for all that in exceptional cases a woman can administer baptism, and that in

(b) The essential intentional operations. The minister must perform the prescribed essential symbolic actions, and intend to do what the Church does. This is enough to insert his action into the line of the divine-human action by which the sacrament is performed. Without this intention, the minister would not act instrumentally, his operation would be merely human, and the apparent sacrament an illusion. The sacrament has meaning for us, and is valid, only because we know by faith that if the minister has the power, has the required intention, and performs the prescribed symbolic act, his act is really an act of Christ and the Church.

(c) Additional levels of intentional actualization. Ideally the minister performs a rich personal act of worship. He himself comes to an enhancement of his own life in Christ, in Father, Son, and Holy Spirit. Moreover his own full personal action affects those who participate in the liturgical act. To understand both the minister's own full operation and its effect on the other participants in the full act of public worship, we must consider the relevance of the theory of human symbolizing which I set forth in the preceding chapter. In particular, we must consider the interplay which is involved in what I have called the intrapersonal and the interpersonal dialectics. [9]

In the minister's personal experience there is ideally a dialectic in which his own deepening insight into the mystery which he is performing stirs an emotional and volitional and motor response which in turn enhance his experiential knowledge of what he is doing. As a bishop or priest he should be growing steadily in his understanding of the Mystery which he is representing by his symbolic action. In moments of special grace and consolation, he should sense a joy and love and reverence which affect his whole manner of performing the act of public worship. He himself grows in faith and love as he performs his full ministerial act as well as he can. His external reverence is itself a powerful element in the total symbolism of his action. It both represents his interior devotion and stimulates in him a deeper devotion. By the personal elements in his

the sacrament of matrimony both of the contracting parties are the ministers. Apart from those cases, in the life of the Church today the minister of the sacrament is male. Respecting this fact, without going into the question here of whether that is a matter of divine law which could not be changed, I use masculine pronouns.

[9] See *Basics*, "The Dialectic of Charisms," pp. 198-212. In Chapter VI above, without using the term "dialectic," I have developed the conception of the interplay of intentional operations in the actualization of the symbolizer, and the interplay of persons in the interpersonal world.

total symbolic action he heightens the symbolic power of the total act of public worship. He contributes to imaging the Mystery which is represented.

The minister's own full act in turn contributes to an inter-personal dialectic, a mutual stimulus and response which enriches the personal lives of those who take part in the total act of the worshipping community. A devout celebrant stirs deeper devotion in all who sense his reverence and the mystery of his inner fulness. Moreover the enrichment is mutual. For the celebrant who is aware of the awesome mystery which he celebrates in Christ's person, the reverence of his fellow worshippers and the inner devotion which it symbolizes stimulates him in turn.

Here there is a mystery of the multiple efficacy of a beautiful celebration of the Eucharist and of the sacraments. The effect of the total act of public worship is richer than the grace which is at-tributed to the act itself. First, celebrant and fellow worshippers stimulate one another to greater devotion, contributing to enriching the disposition which is the measure of the grace which they receive through the sacrament. Further, in the mystery of the total interplay of members of the Body, they merit for one another a further increase of grace.

It is important here to note what I should call a transcendent human efficacy of the minister's act of worship. This has been overlooked at times in the concern to stress the dogmatic truth of the efficacy of the sacrament by virtue of the very act performed (*ex opere operato*), as contrasted with the meritorious act of the minister (*ex opere operantis*). By "transcendent human efficacy" I mean the efficacy of the minister's grace-borne human act, an act of worship which is far more perfect than the minimum act necessary for essential sacramental action. I should contrast this with what could be called the transcendent divine-human efficacy of the sacrament performed with the minimum essentials for validity. The rich per-sonal action of the minister, in which he reaches a greater actua-lization and relative fulness of life in Christ, complements the divine-human efficacy of the essential sacramental act. I say "com-plements." It is diverse from the efficacy which the sacrament has by virtue of the very act performed, an efficacy which is due to the power of God as the principal agent, and which is not exercised in the manner of an efficacious human act, stirring other worshippers to deeper devotion, and meriting for them. The minister's full personal worship is effective according to the structures of human interpersonal interplay. It is *transcendent* human efficacy, because it is borne and enriched by divine grace. Any valid sacrament, per-formed by any minister who has the necessary power and intention and performs the prescribed essential action, has equal efficacy as far as the sacrament itself is concerned: differences of grace received will be measured by the dispositions of the recipient. *This* act of sacramental worship, performed by *this* minister, a rich personal act of worship in which external worship and total bearing and tone are proportionate to internal dispositions, has a further powerful impact on *this* worshipping community. Both minister and fellow-worshippers affect one another in the interplay of persons in community.

(5) *The recipients and their personal worlds.*

Another factor contributing to the full act of worship and its effects is participation of the recipients. Here again one may distinguish what is essential to valid reception of a sacrament and the further riches of personal disposition which enhance the religious quality and the effect of the act in the worshipper. Any person who is capable of receiving a sacrament must have the intention of doing so: otherwise the apparent administration is illusory. Granted this, one must acknowledge the importance of the total personal world of the recipient. The sacramental symbol will have a meaning which has its unique personal factors in every recipient. Only a man or woman who approaches with faith can sense the meaning of what is done. The degree to which he or she has understood the Christian Mystery, and the unique personal resonance against the ground of every one's whole personal world, will determine the degree of enrichment by grace and the unique personal quality of the enriched life in the personal setting of every one.

Consequently, understanding of the mystery and of the structure of Christian experience, the quality of one's religious life, of firmness of belief and love and trust and fidelity, are extremely important. Here too, in a particular worshipping community, the minister may have had an effect by previous pastoral care which has mediated a high degree of belief and love, and thus has contributed to a heightening of the consciousness and of the total religious disposition of the recipient. This disposition will be the measure of the degree of grace received.

MULTIPLE INTENTIONALITY

As unique divine-human symbols, the Christian sacrifice and sacraments terminate the many intentional operations of God and of all of the human agents who participate. There is a fanning out of intentionalities as God's symbolic act is implemented by Christ and by members of his Body. It would be impossible to imagine and conceive fully what this involves. Similarly, we can only surmise the wealth of the effects of these divine-human acts as they reverberate in all of the men and women who share in the action and in the effects of the saving action as it continues to unfold throughout the Church.

First, every re-presentation of the Eucharist and every performance of a sacrament is a symbol which expresses God's eminent operation of intellect and will. Father, Son, and Holy Spirit represent in every sacramental symbol some special aspects of their saving action coming to another relative term in the symbol itself and in the men and women who share in the action and are affected by it. These symbols express divine truth and goodness. They at once manifest God's eternal plan and effect its realization in every instance in which men or women accept the divine gift which is offered.

Consequently, their meaning is both cognitive and volitional: they are revelations and commands, accomplishing what they reveal. The mystery of their unique efficacy, therefore, is somehow intelligible as long as we preserve the mystery, and do not attempt to work out a sort of "super-mechanism" of instrumental causality in a futile effort to explain it. The wonderful efficacy of the sacrifice and sacraments, by which they mediate grace, is as mysterious and as simple as one of the marvels by which Jesus pronounced a word which was both divine and human, and through which he cured the sick, or raised the dead, or forgave sin, acts which only God could perform, and which he could perform because he was both God and man. The Eucharistic sacrifice, Christ's one saving sacrifice repeatedly re-presented, and the sacraments are Christ's acts in and through his Church. They have his power and efficacy, divine and human.

When we turn to consider these symbols as acts of Jesus Christ, they involve his full human experience: perception, memory, imagination, feeling, insight, understanding, affirmation, love, and command. If, then, we ask what they mean to Jesus, we can only seek the answer by returning to contemplate him as the gospel reveals bits of his inner life. We grow in understanding him as we continue to grow in knowledge and love of him. And we can grow in our poor understanding of his action in the Church now in its full riches, praying that we, "... knowing the love of Christ, which is beyond all knowledge, ... [may be] filled with the utter fulness of God." (Eph 3.19: JB).

As I have suggested, the minister can come to a deeper understanding of the mind of Christ in his sacramental action, and to
a more personal sharing in the rich meaning of the action which he
performs in the person and by the power of Christ. He can come to
a deeper understanding of the Mystery, of the full ground against
which this act has its meaning. He can share what he senses what
must be Jesus' love and desires and intentions for those to whom he
mediates Christ. He can sense the mystery of the power and efficacy
of the act which he performs as a continuing act of Jesus Christ in
and through his Church, an act both human and divine. As human
participation extends to the minister's personal action, his own deep
love and devotion will add to the human meaning of the act of
pubic worship. Sharing Christ's love of his brothers and sisters, he
helps to symbolize, to unfold something of the rich meaning of the
essential sacramental act.

All of the participants in the Church's public worship can
contribute to unfolding the meaning and the full intentionality of
the act which they share in their own ways. All of the rites which
unfold the essential symbolism, all of the music, gesture, movement
can help to deepen our understanding and move our feelings and
our response of faith and love and hope.

A Unique Divine Efficacy

I have sought to bring out as clearly as possible the importance
of the full human participation in the act of public worship.
Without diminishing this it is necessary to recognize that the gift of
Christ's grace could not depend ultimately on the perfection of
fallible, and always somehow deficient, human ministers. No human
minister, by his grace-enriched interior and exterior worship, is an
adequate image of the transcendent reality, the Mystery, of which
he is the unworthy dispenser. Nor does he give of his own holiness.
The grace which he somehow transmits is a share in the divine life,
so precious and indispensable that its gift cannot depend on the
excellence of the minister. The efficacy of the sacraments must be
transcendent: depending uniquely on the power of God, the prime
symbolizer, acting through the agency of the human nature and
operation of Christ and of the Church and individual minister. We
never have absolute certitude of the gift of grace. But through his
Church and sacraments Christ gives us a moral certitude in which
we can rest. We know that if, as far as is humanly ascertainable, a
minister has been given the power, has the necessary intention of

doing what the Church does, and performs the prescribed essential sacramental action, the sacrament is valid, and is effective because Father, Son, and Holy Spirit are acting through the human nature and operation of Christ and of his Church and minister. Ultimately the decisive factor in the efficacy of the sacraments is the divine power and operation.

Our conviction of the efficacy of the sacraments by virtue of the very act performed (*ex opere operato*) is grounded in our firm belief that these are acts of God, of Christ in and through his Church. In turn they ground our firm hope in the gift of the grace of which they are the symbol.

Moreover, the mystery of the efficacy *ex opere operato* is a powerful reminder of the absolute gratuity of grace, of the consecration and sanctification which are pure gifts. They do not, and cannot, depend ultimately on any merely human holiness, either the minister's or ours.

SACRAMENT AND MYSTERY

There is an analogy of symbolizing and symbols: human on the one hand, and divine-human on the other. Recall the definition of the human symbol: a meaningful sensuous image which terminates a human intentional operation, represents the imaged reality, and may affect the human world with a manifold efficacy. [10] Similarities of human and divine-human symbols are apparent: the meaningful sensuous image, intentional operations of which the symbols are a proximate term, an imaged reality, and the symbol's affecting the human world with a multiple efficacy. It is important to reflect here on significant diversities of the two classes of symbols, lest we glide over a number of serious problems, and fail grasp some of the unique features of divine-human symbols.

To introduce the question I recall two similar observations in the thought of St. John Chrysostom and of St. Augustine. Chrysostom, elaborating the notion of *mystery*, distinguishes two elements in all mysteries, manifestations of the divine saving plan and action: the sensibly perceptible and the intelligible. His distinction is not philosophical, but theological. The *intelligible* element can be attained only by the Holy Spirit's gift of the power by which the believer believes, sees with spiritual eyes. "... God employs sensibly perceptible symbolic realities; all sacramentality, involving

---

[10] Above, chapter VI, p. 154.

sensibly perceptible symbols, remains imperfect as a manifestation of
the reality of the divine saving action and of its effects in men and
women: all of the manifestations themselves remain mysteries." [11]

Augustine, treating baptism and the Eucharist in several places,
distinguishes between what is seen and what is believed. In the
Eucharist we see what is on the altar, bread and cup, the appearances of bread and wine; we believe what it is, what it means,
what great thing it signifies, the body of Christ and the blood of
Christ, our mystery, the Body of Christ of which we are members,
our passage from death to life. In baptism we see the water of the
sacrament, baptism, water showing outwardly the sacrament of
grace. We believe what happens in the soul, faith, conversion, burial
with Christ, grace, remission of sins, new life, future resurrection. [12]

These observations by Chrysostom and Augustine suggest what
I should point out as the first diversity between the Eucharistic
sacrifice and Christian sacraments, as divine-human symbols, and
ordinary human symbols. It is what might be called the degree of
polarity of sensuous image and meaning, or the degree of inadequacy of the sensuous image to represent the imaged reality.

In all symbolizing and symbols the meaningful sensuous image
is an imperfect likeness of the imaged reality: it is not a presentation
of the full reality, but a representation. In other words, the full
intended meaning of all symbols is beyond the symbolizer's power
of expression and the perceiver's grasp. Symbols are inadequate,
and we may be frustrated continually by our inability to grasp and
express the full reality of what we know and how we react to the
world about us. Notwithstanding their inadequacy, however, symbols are human works, achievements grounded in the world in
which we are, and in the natural powers which we have. To the
extent to which we succeed in knowing something of the world
about us, and expressing what we know and how we respond by
emotion and will, we do so by exercising our human powers upon
the world which we encounter.

Divine-human symbols are incomparably more inadequate to
represent the imaged reality. They too are meaningful sensuous
images, but their meaning is inaccessible to our mere human powers.
By the power of human intellect we could never suspect, much less
grasp, the meaning. God is the prime symbolizer, and the meaning of
his symbols is his alone, hidden from eternity, only gradually revealed. We can know it only through revelation and the gift of faith.

---

[11] Above, chapter II, p. 10. Cf. p. 34.
[12] *Ibid.*, pp. 41-42.

In the Eucharistic sacrifice and the sacraments we have a polarity between sacrament and mystery, far greater than that between sensuous image and meaning in human symbols. Christ, Church, sacrifice and sacrament, and Christian life analogously are sacraments. They are divine-human symbols. Their meaning is God's: the Father, Son, Holy Spirit, and the unfolding of their Mystery of saving action. Without revelation and faith we could not know the meaning. We could not fashion the symbols, for no human knowledge or power could link the sensuous appearance and the divine cognitive and volitive meaning.

There is another diversity, consequent upon the remoteness of the meaning, accessible only through revelation and faith: only God can be the prime symbolizer: the meaning is his, and he alone can link it with the sensuous image. The Christian sacrifice and sacraments are not creations of any merely human symbolizer. Christ alone, the God-man, has given them. All further human roles in the development of the rites and the unfolding of the meaning are dependent, commanded by the basic meaning given by Christ. All authentic Christian public worship must be in harmony with that meaning: developed according to the analogy of the faith. Thus, only the Church is the sure guide of the development, as it is the sure guarantor of the revealed truth, of the meaning.

The third diversity is in the efficacy of the symbols. The Christian sacrifice and sacraments have a unique divine efficacy which goes far beyond the efficacy of merely human symbols in personal and interpersonal life. I say that it goes far beyond: not that it excludes the efficacy of an interplay which I have termed transcendent human. It is this latter efficacy which I have attributed to full human participation in worship, by grace-borne acts which are highly highly effective in a pattern of human interplay which is analogous with that of symbols in a world which would be purely natural.

I am concerned here with the unique relevance of Christ to all human religious experience, and of the Christian sacrifice and sacrifice as unique among all other forms of worship which seem similar and which may have been salutary means by which God has drawn men and women who have had no explicit belief in Christ or in the Christian Church and sacraments. Affirming the uniqueness of Christ and of Christian sacrifice and sacraments, I affirm also the mystery of the many ways by which God saves, implements his will to save all. [13]

---

[13] See *Telling*, II, pp. 60-75; III, pp. 263-313.

A Definition

I concluded my treatment of human symbolizing with a definition of the symbol: *a meaningful sensuous image which terminates a human intentional operation, represents the imaged reality, and may affect the human world with a manifold efficacy.* Having elaborated the analogy of divine-human symbolizing and symbols, I propose a definition of the Christian sacrament as a symbol.

The Christian sacrament is *an act of public worship by which Father, Son, and Holy Spirit, through the mediation of Christ as priest, the Church, the minister, and the essential symbolic action, represent the mystery of the divine saving action reaching this person, and by the actual performance of the rite consecrate and/or sanctify the person who is disposed to receive the divine gift.*

An act of public worship. The sensuous image is the sensibly perceptible aspect of an act of worship which is not private and purely personal, but public and corporate. It is the perceptible act of Christ in and through his Church, his Body, as an expression and implementation of the continuing saving action of Father, Son, and Holy Spirit. Only in the perceptible human actions regarding perceptible persons and things can the sacrament be somehow a sensuous image. Only as the symbolic words and actions are understood in the light of revelation and faith can the properly Christian imagery be perceived. Baptism is not any plunging into water, or sprinkling with water, or washing, with whatever meaning such an action might spontaneously suggest. Its meaning is not simply one of many which could be found in the interpretations of similar external actions observed or recorded in the wide variety of religious experience in human history. As its meaning is unfolded in the rich biblical teaching, and in the deepening insight of Christians illumined by the Spirit, baptism has all of the unique Christian meaning which I gathered in the opening chapter of this book. Analogously the other six sacraments which are the principal acts of Christian public, official worship, have uniquely Christian meaning, more or less clearly revealed in biblical witness, gradually more clearly discerned and differentiated in the experience of the Church guided by the Spirit.

It is an act of *worship*, an act of religion, not merely internal but also external and social, perceptible in a community of worshipers, honoring God and enriching the worshipers.

How, then, can it be an act principally of *Father, Son, and Holy Spirit*? How is it reasonable, intelligible, to consider the sacrament an act by which basically God honors himself? The questions seem to suppose a basic distinction between a descending, consecrating or sanctifying action of God, received by human persons, and an ascending act of worship by which men and women respond to the divine gift by honoring God. *Up* and *down* are hardly adequate concepts with which to elaborate a theological understanding.

I suggest turning the question, and asking how creation itself can be understood except as an act of God which is a sharing and manifestation of his "glory": the fulness of God's being, truth, and goodness. By this sharing and showing forth God is glorified. In all process of the universe, all human being and operation, God is acting in and through creatures. In the most perfect perceptible manifestation of worship and glorification of the Father, the whole human life of Jesus, his doing the will of his Father, his worship culminating in his sacrifice and the whole paschal mystery, his laying down his life and taking it up, his dying and being raised by God, in all of this "... God was in Christ, reconciling the world to himself...." (2 Cor 5.19).

If we do not know how to pray as we ought (cf. Rom 8.26), and "... when we cry 'Abba! Father!' it is the Spirit himself bearing witness with our spirit that we are children of God...."(Rom 8.15-16), and if it is only by the Holy Spirit that anyone can say "Jesus is Lord" (1 Cor 12.3) it will seem less strange that all of our worship of God is borne by God's grace.

Much less is it strange that the Christian sacrifice and sacraments, by which we are consecrated and sanctified, are principally acts of Father, Son, and Holy Spirit by which we are enriched and They are honored by our very consecration and sanctification. If we receive the divine gift, we are made holy, to the honor and glory of God. These acts of worship are not ordinary human acts, in which, as in the whole of creation, God is supporting his creation in being, and operating in and through the operations of all creatures. These are acts which show forth and effect what no mere human power can accomplish: the continuing divine saving action by which we are being brought to a relative fulness of our share in the divine life.

The roles of the three divine persons are clear in biblical witness concerning baptism. Analogously they are understood in all of the sacraments and in the whole of Christian life, in which the potential fulness symbolized by the sacraments should be gradually realized. A relatively adequate theology of the sacraments should be not merely christological, nor merely attentive to the roles of Christ and of the Spirit, but trinitarian, as all relatively full Christian life and theology should be.

Through the mediation of Christ as priest. Christian revelation
of both the Holy Trinity and the Incarnate Word are absolute
mysteries. They are truths which no human person could know
without divine revelation, and which no human person can comprehend even after revelation--nor indeed by the beatific vision. In
the roles of Christ in our salvation, both in his historic action
consummated in the paschal mystery, and in his continuing function
in giving us the fruits of his sacrifice through the ministry of the
Church, the mysteries fuse. The whole saving action is the work of
Father, Son, and Holy Spirit. As they are one eternally in union of
their unique fulness of being, so in their action in our regard they
are one. Yet we cannot overlook the distinct personal roles attributed by the New Testament to the three Persons. Nor can we
overlook the mystery of the God-man, Jesus Christ. As the eternal
Son, he is equal with the Father and the Spirit: as God he cannot be
subject, nor obedient. Having taken our nature into the oneness of
his being as Son, as man he is subject to the Father, obedient, and
honors the Father by the whole of his human life of fulfillment of
the Father's will, and especially by his supreme sacrifice.

It is no excessive subtlety which has brought theologians to
distinguish between what Christ could do by virtue of his human
power, enriched by the fulness of the Spirit, what he could do by his
divine power, equal to that of Father and Spirit, and what he could
do with his human power and operation as the unique instrument of
the divine power of the Three. Without this distinction, all would be
blurred. With it we can achieve some modest degree of understanding, the most to be hoped for.

As God, Jesus could not worship the Father, or be moved by
the Spirit: he is absolutely equal, differing only by the relations
following on his eternal generation as Son, and on the mutual
outpouring of love by which the Spirit proceeds from Father and
Son. As man, Jesus was subject, and he could and did worship and
obey. In him perfect human nature was enriched by the grace given
abundantly by the Spirit. By his human will, in an act of loving
obedience and worship, he could offer himself in sacrifice. By his
human will he could not perform what is within the divine power
alone. When he raised the dead, or forgave sins, or rose from the
dead, his human will and operation were instruments of the divine.

Glorified now, Jesus can continue to offer his worship as the
sole priest of the new covenant, and he presents forever to the
Father his one saving sacrifice. This he does by his human will
enriched by grace.

When, however, in his mortal life he willed that all of his actions should somehow show forth the presence and saving action of

Father, Son, and Spirit, that all that he did and suffered be effective for our salvation, and that his passion, death, and resurrection function in the grace which is given now to us, he was acting by his divine power principally. The role of his human nature and operation, and of all that he did and suffered, was instrumental. As high priest now, Christ acts through his Church, empowers human members of his Body, and applies the fruits of his one saving sacrifice to our consecration and sanctification. In these operations his human roles are instrumental. Thus he acts in every sacrament which is received by a man or woman disposed to receive his gift: principally as God, instrumentally as man.

The Church. Here again we must recognize the paradox of the Church as a prime sacrament in Christ. We believe that the whole Church is present and operating in every act of public worship. These acts are truly the acts of Christ through his Church. How? Again we face mystery, this time of the union of Christ and his Body, of Head and members. We face the mystery of both Christ and the universal Church, present, perceptible, and operating only in and through the perceptible human persons in whom their action is concentrated. Here too we face the mystery of the minister, as I shall set forth in what follows. Christ is in his Church, his Body. He has empowered his Church to act, to continue his saving action in the world today. Yet, except in rare cases of baptism and in matrimony, the power resides in his ordained ministers, sharing his priesthood, empowered to act in the name of the Church, by the divine-human power of Christ himself.

The minister. In the sacramental power and operation of the ordained priest we face again the mystery of Christ in his Church. No man or woman, by his or her human power, can consecrate bread and wine, so that really there is no longer bread and wine, but only the appearances, "beneath" which Christ, the glorified God-man, is truly present. We adore him present in the Eucharist because we believe that the marvelous conversion has occurred as Christ himself has acted in and through the words and actions of his ordained priest. The priest himself must marvel at the power given him to act in the name and power of Jesus Christ, God and man. We must marvel at the power. It too is an object of our belief. It would be folly to imagine the Eucharist without the action of a priest empowered to act in Christ's name and power. It would be folly or a blasphemous sacrilege to address an illusory act of adoration to bread and wine which remain bread and wine despite the human will of one or more persons who fancy that they

can perform the sacrifice and have the sacrament without the act of
an ordained priest.

In the perceptible words and actions of the humble person of
the ordained priest, enriched by a power to act in Christ's name and
power, the divine-human symbolizing action comes to its relative
term: the symbol is given. Here alone is the total divine-human
action perceptible and effective in the man or woman who is disposed to receive the divine gift.

The essential symbolic action. After all that I have written
above about the minister's full participation, full personal actuation,
and manifold efficacy in the whole act of public worship, it may
seem puzzling to some that I return to concentrate on the essential
symbolic action in formulating a definition of the Christian sacrament. Here again a distinction is necessary, without which we would
end in confusion.

The distinction is between the total act of public worship and
the essential symbolic action which is at its core. In the total act we
can embrace all that contributes to the full ceremony, the ritual
actions in their entirety, the personal worship of all participants,
and all that is done to spell out the symbolism of the sacrifice or
sacrament which is being performed, including music and dance and
any other sacred art. With regard to the minister, it is to this full
ceremony and all personal worship that his full personal actuation,
his full act of worship, pertains. All that is done reverently and
beautifully can and should contribute to expressing the meaning of
the sacrifice or sacrament. All of these elements of the total
ceremony can contribute to a manifold efficacy of the whole in the
interpersonal world of the worshiping community. Yet there remains what I have pointed out as the unique divine efficacy of the
sacrifice or sacrament.

At the core of the whole ceremony there is an essential symbolic action, varying in the elements which comprise it, without
which there is no sacrament. No degree of personal devotion, and
no cumulative symbolism of all else that is done, will supply for the
essential symbolic action. Nor will the lack of such devotion and
complementary symbolism nullify the sacrament.

This is not a matter of theologians' casuistry and speculation,
however that may seem to be the case in the manner in which it
has been treated at times. It is absolutely essential to be able to
know whether or not there has been a baptism, or confirmation, or
matrimony, or ordination, whatever the ugliness or awkwardness
of the minister's action. The essential symbolic action, the "matter
and form" of the sacrifice or sacrament in classic terminology, is

one of the elements which are indispensable for the validity of the action.

All else in the total ceremony should be such as to express more fully the meaning of the essential central symbolic action. It is most important that there indeed be a sacrament. Then the richer the full ceremony, the better.

The essential symbolic action *is* the sacrament, the symbol. Like any symbol, it is the relative term of an intentional operation, or complex of operations. In this case, the Christian sacrifice and sacrament are the relative terms of a multiple intentional operation. They proceed from the eminent divine operations, which we distinguish as operations of intellect and will.[14] Within the human frame, in which the divine operation is implemented, and the divine-human symbolizing occurs, the sacrifice/sacrament proceeds from the intentional operations of Christ and of the empowered ministers of his Church.

What are the modes of intentionality which are involved? They are cognitive and volitive. These divine-human symbols are both manifestations of the divine saving action, the Mystery, coming to term in this man or woman, and acts of the divine will by which the symbolized grace is given to those who will receive it. They are, then, both revelations and commands, and they bear divine truth and the power of divine will.

Hence the Christian sacrifice and sacraments *represent the mystery of the divine saving action reaching this person, and by the actual performance of the rite consecrate and/or sanctify the person who is disposed to receive the divine gift.*

What is the total reality which sacrifice and sacrament image, or represent? It is God, the eternal plan, the process of our redemption culminating in Christ and the paschal mystery, the saving action continuing and reaching this man or woman here and now, the consecration and/or sanctification effected now, and the thrust of the grace given and the commitment of the recipient to final fulfillment. The new creation is a process, and our consecration and sanctification involves us in a continual striving toward final relative fulfillment of God's plan for our personal enrichment, in our share in the life of Father, Son, and Spirit.

---

[14] For a consideration of these matters, see *Telling*, III, especially chapters IX, X, XIII.

Chapter VIII

IMPLICATIONS AND AGENDA

(1) *Multiple intentionality*.

In the broad sense, all of God's saving action in its many phases is sacramental, somehow sensibly perceptible, most of all in the mystery of the redemptive incarnation. All of God's saving grace is won and distributed somehow through the human nature and operation of Christ. Of all the modes of divine-human symbolizing, that which is involved in the Christian Eucharistic sacrifice and sacraments is unique. The incarnational principle is extended by analogy to human ministers, and God's consecrating and sanctifying action is enfleshed, not only in the human nature of Christ, but in the human action of the minister.

Consequently, when we think of the divine saving action as it is continued through the Christian sacrifice and sacraments, it is only by an abstraction that we can think of God's saving action as separate from the full human operations in which alone the Christ's one saving sacrifice is re-presented and sacraments are performed. The essential sacramental action occurs only as the full concrete action of the minister is realized. If then we consider the intentional operations from which these symbols proceed, and their unique efficacy, we must recognize a wonderful blend of divine and human.

The Christian sacrament is not a "thing," nor is it any sort of simple reality. It is a unique divine-human symbol, the proximate sensibly perceptible term of a multiple intentional operation. The operation, or action, which it terminates is part of a complex divine-human interpersonal event, an act of public worship of Christ in and through his Church. As I have used the expression, "proximate term" means that which results immediately from, or is the sensibly perceptible aspect of, intentional operation. It is proximate, not ultimate. The sacrament is performed, but it regards realities beyond the symbol. The realities themselves are multiple, or serial. First there is the knowledge communicated to the perceiver/receiver: some aspect of the Mystery. Second there is the emotional/volitional response which is evoked. Beyond these there are the further effects in the dialectic, intrapersonal and in-

terpersonal, which characterize Christian life, of persons living in
community, transcending the level of life and fulness of being
which they have attained at any stage of the process of the new
creation in them.

The multiplicity which I have just indicated regards first the
distinction of divine and human. God--Father, Son, and Holy
Spirit--is/are acting, and their eminent cognitive and volitional
operation is the source of their continuing saving action being
realized in this person here and now. Christ is acting through his
human nature, and the minister is acting with cognitive and
emotional/volitional intentionality.

The divine-human operation does not terminate in "mid-air."
It is meaningful, and can be realized, only as it regards the person
who is being consecrated/sanctified, and in whom the sacrament can
be validly and fruitfully performed only if the recipient acts to make
the whole event what it should be. Without the recipient's capacity
and, in an adult, intention to receive the sacrament, the sacrament is
not performed. Without the recipient's disposition to receive the
effects, the apparent sanctification does not occur. Consequently,
though the recipient does not perform the sacrament, his or her
action is indispensable for the realization of the full act of worship.

Clearly the Christian sacrament involves a multiple intentionality.

(2) *Multiple efficacy.*

As the sacrament proceeds from a multiple intentional operation, so too it has a corresponding multiple efficacy. Some of the
controversy over the defined truth that the sacraments have an
efficacy by virtue of the very act performed (*ex opere operato*) may
be due in part to a failure of Roman Catholic theologians and
controversialists to recognize and make clear that the full act of
worship, in which the essential act is set, has a multiple efficacy.
Some distinctions are needed here to enable us to reach a modest
understanding of this portion of the Christian Mystery.

First, I should distinguish between two classes of effects: consecration and sanctification. By consecration I mean a person's
being made sacred by becoming a member of Christ through baptism, or given a special place and function of witness through confirmation, or given a place and power through the sacrament of
orders, or united with a spouse through the sacrament of matrimony. In the case of baptism, confirmation, and orders, this effect is
the so-called sacramental character. It is given infallibly by a valid
sacrament, by the very act performed, whatever the personal holi-

ness or sinfulness of the recipient or of the minister of the sacrament. It does not admit degrees. It cannot be lost, whatever the subsequent sin of the recipient may be.

By sanctification I mean being made holy, enriched by the gift of a share in the divine life and a multiple heightening of one's powers by the virtues and gifts and actual graces, as they are understood in the Church and in classic theology. A valid sacrament confers such sanctification only if the recipient has the necessary disposition, varying according to the sacrament. Some degree of such sanctification may be understood to be the effect of the very act performed. The degree of grace or holiness varies according to the quality of the disposition of the recipient.

However that does not suffice to explain the effect of the total act of worship. In any given experience in an act of public worship of the Church, in the Eucharist or other sacraments, there are many other factors which may be efficacious for the sanctification of the worshipers. As I have maintained in treating the full role of the minister, his full actuation, and his transcendent interpersonal efficacy in the worshipping community, may have a powerful effect on other participants in the worship, giving them insight into the wonder of the mystery, and evoking a rich response which disposes them to be greatly enriched by their reception of the sacrament. Other members of the community may influence one another similarly. In the intrapersonal and interpersonal dialectic all may be enriched.

There is another factor involved: the possibility of members of the community meriting for one another, as they pray for one another and offer their participation for the enrichment of all.

All of these factors must be recognized in the effort to understand the multiple efficacy of participation in public worship, as well as in the whole of our living together in the Church, and in the larger communion of all men and women.

I have indicated in the preceding chapter that there is and must be a unique divine efficacy of the Christian sacrifice and sacraments. Belief in that efficacy, far from deserving accusations of a magical conception of the sacraments, is a recognition that God is the prime symbolizer, that sacrifice and sacrament represent divine power at work, as well as divine communication of the truth of the saving action which is continuing in a unique way in any act of public worship.

The unique efficacy of the sacrifice and sacraments by virtue of the very act performed is not a magical conception. Nor is it the only manner of efficacy of these acts of worship. We can and should acknowledge the wonder of such multiple efficacy. We cannot, and should not try to, discern by some sort of pseudo-introspection just what kind and degree of holiness can be traced to individual factors.

(3) *The real.*

In *Man the Symbolizer* and subsequent works I have stressed the reality of the being in intellect and will, and of our most important properly human achievements, works which we accomplish by operations commanded by intellect and will. Knowing is real. Loving is real. By works of intellect and will we create human worlds, societies, cultures. By works of intellect and will, knowledge and love we become better human persons, and we *are* more fully. We had our full human nature at our conception. Yet we were only at the beginning of our lives, in which we grow and achieve real greatness by human operations directed by intellect and will. We reach our relatively full human perfection by attaining knowledge and truth, and by loving the good, most of all by mutual human interpersonal knowledge and truth. In this we reach a fulness of being which we cannot attain alone. By our human powers we can come to be more fully, to transcend the degree of being which we have reached.

Symbolizing is properly human operation, and symbols the properly human works, by which we can be enhanced in our own being, and influence our many human worlds for better--or, sadly, for worse.

In God's plan for our share in his/their life and fulness of being, we are involved in a manifold divine-human symbolizing. The symbols which we have been considering are effective in heightening our powers of intellect and will, in communicating knowledge of the Mystery by faith, and in conferring on us the many divine gifts which constitute our consecration and sanctification. God's symbols, divine-human, are at once revelations and commands, accomplishing what they reveal. His saving action in and through them is enfleshed in the continuing wonder of the incarnation, somehow extended in the ministers of the sacraments. He acts only in and through the human share in divine-human symbolizing. His power is divine. The effects which he produces in the transcendent human worlds, personal and interpersonal are most real.

I entitled this series of reflections "Implications and Agenda." Here I suggest implications and agenda regarding some of the real effects which God produces in us through the sacraments, some of the classic themes of sacramental theology. I suggest them as implications and agenda: they regard further work of theological reflection which I shall not attempt here.

What are these implications and further tasks? They concern the nature of the sacramental character, the power of orders, grace, the marriage bond, and the Eucharistic conversion and the real presence of Christ "under" the appearances of bread and wine. In my judgment much remains to be done in the search for further understanding and more satisfying theological explanation of all of these effects. They challenge the utterly inadequate philosophical conceptions which hitherto have been adapted to the tasks of theological understanding of aspects of the Mystery. No theologian will ever comprehend these aspects of the Mystery--or any mystery. Yet I suggest that some progress can be made by passing beyond even the best of scholastic developments of natural philosophy and metaphysics. These effects are real in ways which are unique in the orders of transcendent personal and interpersonal worlds and in the mystery of the transcendent divine-human interpersonal world in which alone they can be somehow understood.

(4) *Instrumental causality of the sacraments.*

The instrumental causality of the sacraments is simply part of the mystery of divine-human symbolizing. God is acting in and through them.They really play a part, and the gifts which God gives through them are most real.

Regarding the efficacy of the Christian sacraments, two questions must be distinguished. One concerns the defined truth concerning the efficacy of the sacraments by virtue of the very act performed. That is what I have mentioned briefly in the preceding section. It concerns a matter of faith for Roman Catholics. The other concerns a theological explanation of such efficacy.

In the course of my rethinking of a philosophy of the human way of being and my study of symbolizing and symbols, and elaborating a theory principally in my work *Man the Symbolizer* and in the work which I now present, I have come to what seems to me a far simpler and more satisfying explanation of the instrumental causality of the human nature and operation of Christ, and of the sacraments.

If one accepts my theory of symbolizing and symbols, there is no problem in recognizing the multiple intentionality of human symbols, and their multiple potential efficacy in the human worlds, intrapersonal and interpersonal. Clearly by symbolizing we communicate knowledge and commands (within the limits of our authority and power), evoke emotional and volitional responses, and contribute to elaborating interpersonal worlds, real achievements, real effects in human society and in the many worlds of human creativity.

We cannot do what exceeds our human power. Within the range of efficacy of our intentional powers and operations we can and do increase or diminish our own real degree of being by knowledge and love, and collaborate in increasing or diminishing the fulness of being of other persons and of society.

When we seek to understand within a life of faith, we acknowledge the wonders of divine power, effecting results in human life, in persons and in community, which are in the transcendent realm of human participation in God's life. We acknowledge that God is at work in his universe, symbolizing in and through Christ in the mystery of the redemptive incarnation, and by analogy in and through men and women taken up into the Body of Christ.

The Eucharistic sacrifice and the sacraments are divine-human symbols, and they are effective in our consecration and sanctification. Call their efficacy instrumental causality, or whatever else seems a more apt term, their role seems intelligible within the Christian Mystery.

(5) *A theology of the spirituality of the priest.*

What I have proposed concerning the role of the priest in the divine-human symbolizing in the Eucharistic sacrifice and the sacraments suggests the possibility of a richer, more profound conception of the unique spiritual life to which the priest is called by virtue of his consecration and power of orders. The priest is called to a personal perfection which is proportioned to his unique role in the Body of Christ, and his relations to other members of the Body. The grace offered him is proportioned to his office and power and interpersonal relationships. For this perfection he should strive. In his unique life of union with Christ, he should find his relative fulfillment as a Christian. He lives his life in Christ as a mediator of the encounter of Christ and others called to be in Christ. With a sense of the mysteries which he ministers, he is called to attain a holiness which befits his place in the Body and the gifts which are his to receive. His way of love of Father, Son, and Spirit, and of all who are called to be in Them, is unique. The Spirit within him will offer the guidance by which he may find his own personal call within the mystery of his priesthood. He must be attentive to that guidance and docile, for no written treatise or code of conduct will spell out every detail of his personal way to full life in Christ, in Them.

(6) *Public worship and personal spiritual life.*

Finally I indicate some implications for all who share in the liturgy of the Eucharist and the other Christian sacraments. By the sacraments we are consecrated and sanctified. By our participation especially in the Eucharistic sacrifice we show forth with all the Church what we are all about. If we consider the dignity of the acts of public worship, we must recognize that in them we reach repeatedly relative highpoints in our lives. Yet in terms of the depth of our personal experience, we may have moments of prayer and experience of God which are far more intense. What is the relationship between our liturgical worship and our personal spiritual life?

First, evidently the two are not coextensive. Our personal spiritual life ranges far beyond the privileged moments of liturgical worship. It includes other actions by which we grow in experience of Father, Jesus, and Holy Spirit: prayerful private reading of the Bible, sharing our insights with others, private prayer which may become less and less verbal, as we tend toward a prayer of simple union, and many nonliturgical forms of worship which may foster a richer life of love.

Yet there is a unique interrelationship of the two. In a special way the sacraments by which we are consecrated--baptism, confirmation, orders, and in another way matrimony--demand a commitment to a way of life, to our participation in the new creation as process. All of the sacraments symbolize and confer some special graces, to be received not just at the moment of reception of the sacrament, but in our continuing lives, as they are needed. The Eucharist symbolizes our being taken up once more into the representation of the one saving sacrifice, of the pattern of the paschal mystery, of the union with Christ in his death and resurrection which defines us as Christians.

As we appropriate the meaning of the sacraments and of our participation in the Eucharist, they mean more to us. As we approach the moments of public worship, the faith and love and hope which have been nourished by all of the ways of personal spiritual life prepare us to receive more abundant grace, to be more greatly enriched by the sacraments.

So we should be involved in the intrapersonal dialectic of alternate enrichment by Eucharistic sacrifice and sacraments and by personal prayer and lives of love in which we live what we have symbolized in liturgy. And, living together in community, we are involved in the interpersonal dialectic by which we enrich one another. There is no chart, no one way. Sacraments and personal spiritual life figure in our unique personal way of holiness.

BIBLIOGRAPHY

Balthasar, H. U. von, "Le mystère d'Origène," *Recherches de science religieuse* 26 (1936) 513-562; 27 (1937) 38-64.

Baraúna, William, Editor, *The Liturgy of Vatican II*, A Symposium in Two Volumes. English Edition edited by Jovian Lang, S.F.M. Chicago: Franciscan Herald Press, 1966.

Beringarius, *De sacra Coena adversus Lanfrancum*. Edited by W. H. Beekenkamp. La Haye, 1941.

Bornkamm, G. "*mystērion*," in G. Kittel, *Theologisches Wörterbuch zum Neuen Testament* (Stuttgart, vol. IV, 1942) 820-823.

Brown, Raymond, S. S., *The Gospel according to John*. 2 vols. (*The Anchor Bible*, 29, 29a). New York: Doubleday, 1966.

———, "Mystery (in the Bible)," in *The New Catholic Encyclopedia* (New York: McGraw-Hill, 1967) vol. X, pp. 148-151.

Camelot, P.-Th., O.P., "Réalisme et Symbolisme dans la doctrine eucharistique de S. Augustin," RSPT., 31 (1947) 394-410.

———, "*Sacramentum fidei*," in *Augustinus Magister* (Congrès International Augustinien, Paris, 1954) vol. II, pp. 891-896.

Cerfaux, L., "Gnose," *Dictionnaire de la Bible, Supplément*, III (Paris, 1938) col. 659-701.

Chenu, M.-D., O.P., *Introduction a l'Étude de Saint Thomas d'Aquin*. Montréal: Institut d'Études Médiévales—Paris: Vrin, 1950; *Toward Understanding Saint Thomas*. Translated ... by A.-M. Landry, O.P. and D. Hughes, O.P. Chicago: Regnery, c. 1964.

Couturier, C., "*Sacramentum*" et "*Mysterium*" dans l'oeuvre de saint Augustin, in H. Rondet ..., *Études augustiniennes*. Paris, 1953, pp. 163-332.

Dalton, W. J., S.J., *Christ's Proclamation to the Spirits*. A Study of 1 Peter 3.18–4.6 (*Analecta Biblica*, 23). Rome: Pontifical Biblical Institute, 1965.

———, "Interpretation and Tradition: An Example from 1 Peter," *Gregorianum* 49 (1968) pp. 11-37.

Deden, D., "Le 'mystère' paulinien," ETL 13 (1936) 427-435.

De Backer, E., "Tertullien," in J. de Ghellinck, S.J., *Pour l'histoire du mot "sacramentum"*. Louvain, 1924.

De la Potterie, Ignace, S.J., "L'onction du chrétien par la foi," *Biblica* 40 (1959) 12-69, also published in S. Lyonnet and I. de la Potterie, *La vie selon l'Esprit*. Paris: Les Éditions du Cerf, 1965, pp. 107-167.

Dondaine, H.-F., O.P., "La définition des sacrements dans la *Somme théologique*," RSPT 31 (1947) 214-228.

Doronzo, E., *De Sacramentis in Genere*. Milwaukee: Bruce, 1946.

Féret, N.-M., O.P., "*Sacramentum, Res*, dans la langue théologique de S. Augustin," RSPT 29 (1940) 218-243.

Festugière, A.J., O.P., *L'idéal religieux des Grecs et l'Évangile*. Paris, 1932.

Finance, Joseph de, S.J., *Essai sur l'agir humain*. Rome: Gregorian University Press, 1962.

———, *Éthique générale*. Rome: Gregorian University Press, 1967.

Finkenzeller, Josef, *Die Lehre von den Sakramenten im allgemeinen*. (*Handbuch der Dogmengeschichte*, Band IV) Faszikel 1a: *Von der Schrift bis zur Scholastik*. Faszikel 1b: *Von der Reformation bis zur Gegenwart*. Freiburg: Herder, 1980, 1981).

Fittkau, G., *Der Begriff des Mysteriums bei Johannes Chysostomus*. Bonn, 1953.

Fries, Heinrich und Schwaiger, Georg, *Katholische Theologie Deutschlands im 19. Jahrhundert*, Band II. München: Kösel, 1975.

Frutsaert, E., S.J., "La définition du sacrement dans saint Thomas," NRT 55 (1928) 401-409.

Geiselmann, Rupert Josef, *Die katholische Tübinger Schule*, ihre theologische Eigenart. Freiburg-Basel-Wien: Herder, 1964.

———, *Lebendiger Glaube aus geheiligter Überlieferung*. Der Grundgedanke der Theologie Johann Adam Möhlers und der katholischen Tübinger Schule[2]. Freiburg-Basel-Wien: Herder, 1966.

———, *Die theologische Anthropologie Johann Adam Möhlers*. Ihr geschichtlicher Wandel. Freiburg: Herder, 1955.

Haring, N., S.A.C., "Berengar's Definitions of *Sacramentum* and Their Influence on Medieval Sacramentology," *Medieval Studies* 10 (1948) 109-106.

Hocedez, E., S.J., "La conception augustinienne de sacrement dans le *Tractatus 80 in Ioannem*," RechScRel 9 (1919) 1-29.

Kolping, A., *Sacramentum Tertullianum*. Regensburg-Münster, 1948.

Landgraf, A., "Die Definition der Taufe," in *Dogmengeschichte der Frühscholastik*, vol. III/2. Regensburg, 1955, pp. 7-46, also published in *Gregorianum* 27 (1946) 200-219; 353-383.

Lennerz, H., S.I., *De Sacramento Baptismi*[3]. Romae, 1955.

Lubac, Henri de, *Corpus Mysticum*. L'Eucharistie et l'Église au moyen age. Étude historique. Ed. 2. (*Théologie*, 3) Paris: Aubier, 1949.

———, *Méditation sur l'Église*[3] (*Théologie*, 27). Paris: Desclée de Brouwer, 1985.

———, *The Splendour of the Church*. Translated by Michael Mason. New York: Sheed and Ward, c. 1956 [based on second French edition, 1953].

Lugo, Ioannes De, S,I., *Disputationes Scholasticae*. Parisiis, 1869.

Lyonnet, S., S.J., "Hellénisme et Christianisme. A propos du Theologisches Wörterbuch," Biblica 26 (1945) 115-132.

Marsh, H.G., "The Use of *mystērion* in the Writings of Clement of Alexandria with Special Reference to his Sacramental Doctrine," *Journal of Theological Studies* 37 (1936) 64-80.

Martène, E., and Durand, U., *Thesaurus Novus Anecdotorum*, tomus IV. Lutetiae Parisiorum, 1717.

Michel, A., "Sacrements," DTC 14/1, col. 519-525.

Möhler, Johann Adam, *Die Einheit in der Kirche*, oder Das Prinzip des Katholizismus ... Mainz: Grünewald, 1925.

———, *Symbolik*. Regensburg: Manz, 1871.

———, *Symbolism*. Translated ... by James Burton Robertson, ed. 3. New York: The Catholic Publication House, no date [based on fifth German edition, 1838].

Mohrmann, C., "Sacramentum dans les plus anciens textes chrétiens," *Harvard Theological Review* 47 (1954) 141-152.

Pius XII, "Mediator Dei et hominum," AAS 39 (1947) 521-595.

———, "Mystici Corporis Christi," AAS 35 (1943) 193-248.

Pontet, M., *L'exégèse de S. Augustin prédicateur*. Paris, 1944.

Pourrat, P., *La théologie sacramentaire*. Paris, 1908.

Prümm, K., "Mystery Religions, Greco-Oriental," in *The New Catholic Encyclopedia*. New York: McGraw-Hill, 1967, vol. X, pp. 153-164.

Rahner, Karl, S.J., *De paenitentia tractatus historico-dogmaticus*. Innsbruck, 1955 (typescript multiplied).

———, "Die Gliedschaft in der Kirche nach der Lehre der Enzyklika Pius' XII, 'Mystici Corporis,' " in *Schriften zur Theologie*, Einsiedeln, 1955, Band II.

———, *Kirche und Sakramente* (*Quaestiones Disputatae*, 10). Freiburg: Herder, [1961]. *The Church and the Sacraments*. Translated by W. J. O'Hara. New York: Herder and Herder, 1963.

Savon, Hervé, *Johann Adam Möhler*. Paris: Fleurus, 1965.

Scheeben, Matthias Joseph, *The Mysteries of Christianity*, translated by Cyril Vollert, S.J. St. Louis: B. Herder, c. 1946.

Scheele, Paul-Werner, *Einheit und Glaube*. Johann Adam Möhlers Lehre von der Einheit der Kirche und ihre Bedeutung für die Glaubensbegründung. München-Paderborn-Wien: Schöningh, 1964.

Schillebeeckx, E., O.P., *Christus Sacrament van de Godsontmoeting*. Bilthoven: Nelissen, 1960. *Christ the Sacrament of Encounter with God*. [Translated by Paul Barrett, O.P. and N. D. Smith]. London-New York [different printings and pagination]: Sheed and Ward, 1963.

———, *De sacramentele heilseconomie*. Antwerpen 'T Groeit, 1951.

Semmelroth, Otto, S.J., *Die Kirche als Ursakrament*[2]. Frankfurt am Main: Knecht, 1955.

———, *Vom Sinn der Sakramente*. Frankfurt am Main: Knecht, 1960.

Suarez, Franciscus, *In Tertiam Partem D. Thomae* ..., (*Opera Omnia*, vol. XX). Parisiis, 1860.

Van Den Eynde, D., O.F.M., *Les définitions des sacrements pendant la première période de la théologie scolastique* (1050-1240). Rome-Louvain, 1950.

———, "The Theory of the Composition of the Sacraments in Early Scholasticism (1125-1240)" *Franciscan Studies* 11 (1951) 125.

Van den Meer, F., "*Sacramentum* chez saint Augustin," *La Maison-Dieu* 13 (1948) 50-64.

Van Roo, William A., *De Sacramentis in Genere*, Rome: Gregorian University Press, 1957, 1960 [slight revision], 1962 [reprint].

———, *The Mystery*. Rome: Gregorian University Press, 1971.

———, "Reflections on Karl Rahner's *Kirche und Sakramente* in *Gregorianum* 44 (1963) 465-500.

———, "Symbol According to Cassirer and Langer," *Gregorianum* 53 (1972) 487-534; 615-677.

———, "Symbol in Art and Sacrament," *Studia Anselmiana* 64 (1974) 159-171.

———, *Man the Symbolizer* (*Analecta Gregoriana*, 222). Rome: Gregorian University Press, 1981.

———, *Basics of a Roman Catholic Theology* (*Analecta Gregoriana*, 226). Rome: Gregorian University Press, 1982.

———, "Experience and Theology," in *Gregorianum* 66 (1985) 611-640.

———, *Telling About God*. Volume I, *Promise and Fulfillment*; volume II, *Experience*; volume III, *Understanding* (*Analecta Gregoriana*, 242, 244, 249). Rome: Gregorian University Press, 1986, 1987, 1987.

———, "Möhler's Earlier Symbolism," *Gregorianum* 72 (1991) 129-138.

[Vaticanum II] Sacrosanctum Oecumenicum Concilium Vaticanum II, *Constitutiones Decreta Declarationes*, cura et studio Secretariae Generalis Concilii Oecumenici Vaticani II. Typis Polyglottis Vaticanis, 1966.

———, *L'Église de Vatican II*. Tome I, *La Constitution dogmatique sur l'Église "Lumen Gentium."* Texte latin et traduction française par P.-Th. Camelot, O.P. ...[2] (*Unam Sanctam*, 51[a]). Paris: Les Éditions du Cerf, 1966. Tomes II, III, *Études autour de la Constitution conciliaire sur l'Église*. Guilherme Baraúna, O.F.M. [ed.], édition française dirigée par Y. M.-J. Congar, O.P. (*Unam Sanctam*, 51[b,c]). Paris: Les Éditions du Cerf, 1966.

Wagner, Harald, *Die eine Kirche und die vielen Kirchen*. Ekklesiologie und Symbolik beim jungen Möhler. München: Schöningh, 1977.

Weisweiler, H., S.J., *Die Wirksamkeit der Sakramente nach Hugo von St. Viktor*. Freiburg Br., 1932.

———, "Hugos von St. Viktor 'Dialogus de sacramentis legis naturalis et scriptae' als frühscholastisches Quellenwerk," in *Miscellanea G. Mercati*. Vatican City, 1946, vol. II, pp. 179-219.

Finito di stampare il 19 giugno 1992
Tipografia Poliglotta della Pontificia Università Gregoriana
Piazza della Pilotta, 4 – 00187 Roma